MW01120820

BECOMING CANADIAN
Memoirs of an Invisible Immigrant

Thousands of Western European immigrants streamed into Canada after the Second World War, seeking refuge from the economic devastation of their homelands. Many sought to assimilate as quickly as possible into the Canadian mainstream. Michiel Horn, in *Becoming Canadian: Memoirs of an Invisible Immigrant*, shares his reflections on the process of social integration. As a Dutch immigrant to British Columbia in 1952, Horn had to make sense of the cultural demands of two worlds. Over forty years later, a professor of Canadian history, he recounts his own personal history, relating it to broader issues. 'I have tried,' he writes, 'to describe the process of assimilation as I experienced it, and to make sense of the ambivalence immigrants feel towards their adopted country and their country of origin, the sense that they belong to both yet fully to neither.'

Horn's autobiography explores the story of his Dutch middle-class family and seeks to answer what it means to replace one nationality with another. He begins with his years in Holland during the Second World War, discusses his family's immigration to Canada, and explains how the family built a life for itself in Victoria. Several of the themes that run through the narrative relate to the often uneasy transfer of Dutch values to a Canadian context, the influence that Holland still has on Horn's life, and his own thoughts on multiculturalism as public policy in Canada. *Becoming Canadian* is a timely memoir, and Horn's consideration of the process of assimilation, and of his own position as an 'invisible immigrant,' is topical and revealing.

MICHIEL HORN is a professor of history at Glendon College, York University. He is the author and editor of several books on Canadian history, including *The League for Social Reconstruction* and *The Dirty Thirties*.

MICHIEL HORN

Becoming Canadian: Memoirs of an Invisible Immigrant

UNIVERSITY OF TORONTO PRESS
Toronto Buffalo London

© University of Toronto Press Incorporated 1997
Toronto Buffalo London
Printed in Canada

ISBN 0-8020-0855-0 (cloth)
ISBN 0-8020-7840-0 (paper)

Printed on acid-free paper

Canadian Cataloguing in Publication Data

Horn, Michiel, 1939–
    Becoming Canadian : memoirs of an invisible immigrant

    Includes index.
    ISBN 0-8020-0855-0 (bound) ISBN 0-8020-7840-0 (pbk.)

    1. Horn, Michiel, 1939–   . 2. Dutch – Canada – Biography.
    3. Immigrants – Canada – Biography. I. Title.

    FC106.D9H67 1997   971'.004393102   C96-931782-4
    F1035.D8H67 1997

Unless otherwise noted, the photos reproduced in this book are from the
author's family collection.

The passage from *First Intermissions,* by M. Owen Lee, is used by permission
of Oxford University Press, New York.
The passage from *Under the Ribs of Death,* by John Marlyn, is used by
permission of the Canadian Publishers, McClelland & Stewart, Toronto.

University of Toronto Press acknowledges the assistance to its publishing
program of the Canada Council and the Ontario Arts Council

For Daniel and Patrick

Contents

Introduction

The idea of writing this came to me on the evening of Friday, 26 September 1986, while my wife, Cornelia, and I were in Yorkminster Park Baptist Church to hear an organ recital. Among the pieces the young organist, Xaver Varnus, played was a movement taken from Widor's Fifth Symphony. This proved strongly evocative: the work was one of my father's favourites, and I was instantly reminded of him.

My mind already wandering, I began to speculate about the audience. I had heard quite a few of them speak in a language I did not recognize but which I took to be Hungarian (Varnus had recently immigrated from Hungary). Like my parents, these people had to make their way in an unfamiliar society, work in a foreign language – in a sense, remake themselves. What had it meant, did it mean, for them to try to replace one nationality with another, to become Canadian?

Well, what had it meant for me, twelve years old when *my* family came to Canada? As I pondered this, I suddenly decided that I had found something to write about.

Cornelia greeted my announcement that I was going to write a memoir with some scepticism: 'You're only forty-seven; isn't that a bit young?' I disagreed. 'Age and forgetfulness sweeten memory,' T.S. Eliot tells us in *Murder in the Cathedral*. The time to get things down is while they're still reasonably close and one's mind is clear. It was useful, too, to be able to quiz Father. Mother had died in 1985, but before Father's death in 1990 I checked a good many details with him. He didn't always remember things clearly, but he told me quite a few things that I would otherwise not have known. Some details, too, I have checked with one or another of my brothers.

Originally I had in mind a private memoir written for myself and close family members. As a consequence of this, my first draft contained a lot of personal information, only some of which remains. At some point, encouraged by Cornelia's generous reaction to what she was reading, I formed the opinion that what I was writing might be of interest to people beyond my immediate family. This opinion found reinforcement when I presented a short paper about our family's first years in Canada to the 1993 meeting of the Canadian Association for the Advancement of Netherlandic Studies (CAANS). Afterwards, several listeners said that my remarks had reminded them vividly of their own experiences.

My friend and colleague Roberto Perin, who is professionally interested in the history of immigrants and immigration, read the paper and urged me to try to get it published. My attempt to do so failed, but a friend at the University of Toronto Press suggested that I send the manuscript from which the address to CAANS was taken to the Multicultural History Society of Ontario. There Catherine Waite, Paul Robert Magocsi, the editorial board and two anonymous readers took pity on it; when the MHSO had to reconsider its publication program as a result of financial cut-backs, the University of Toronto Press took it over. This book is the result. I wish to thank all at the Press who helped to get it into print, notably Gerry Hallowell, Rob Ferguson, Karen Boersma, Darlene Zeleney, and my copy editor, Margaret Allen. David McQueen read my account of the troubles at York University in the fall of 1972 and offered his comments, for which I am grateful. Bennett McCardle made a number of helpful suggestions. Marina Sakuta guided several successive copies through the printer. Cornelia went painstakingly over everything I wrote and made many suggestions for improvement; much of whatever value this book has is due to her.

Authors are not reliable judges of the merit of their own work, and this is probably truest of autobiography. I hope, however, that this memoir may prove entertaining and useful to people interested in immigration, in ethnicity, and in Canada. I have tried to describe the process of assimilation as I experienced it, and to make sense of the ambivalence that immigrants feel towards their adopted country *and* their country of origin, the sense that they belong to both yet fully to neither. Other Canadians of recent vintage, especially from northwestern Europe, may recognize bits of their own experience in mine; those who were born here may find new insights into their 'home and native land.' My memoir may be of interest also to people interested in banking as it was practised in the 1950s, and in Canadian university life of the 1960s and since.

It was impossible to think about our early years in Canada without discussing why our parents had left the Netherlands. That in turn led me to think about our life there and about my childhood. The chapter I wrote about my childhood years may seem *de trop* in an account of an immigrant's experiences in Canada, but my life before migration has clearly influenced my life after it. And some people may judge that the chapter has intrinsic interest.

My brothers and I chose assimilation. I do not want to imply that the path we took was the best one or, indeed, that it was open to all immigrants. In Victoria, British Columbia, in the mid-1950s, assimilation was the sensible course of action for newcomers who faced no significant barriers to acceptance by the majority population, and had no good reason for adopting another course. Had our parents been Calvinists, I might on religious grounds have chosen not to become Canadian without some minor hyphenation. Had we come from southern or eastern Europe, from Africa, Asia, Latin America, or the Caribbean region, I would have faced obstacles of which I am well aware but have no personal experience. Had we been working class, I might have encountered hurdles that I, being a son of the middle class, cleared without knowing they were there.

It did not hurt that I was dark blond, blue-eyed, and even-featured, physically and mentally healthy, of better-than-average intelligence, and equipped with a surname that did not infallibly identify me as a foreigner. Within a short time I was able to 'pass for white.' Our parents moved down the social ladder as a result of leaving Holland, but mine is the tale of an immigrant who mostly had it easy.

Several explanatory comments seem necessary. One: the chapter titles, borrowed from books that I have read, are used with mild irony. They nevertheless seem apposite. Two: I have used the terms 'Holland' and 'the Netherlands' interchangeably. To be geographically and politically correct I ought to have used the former only to refer to the two western provinces, but I have usually observed North American usage instead. I apologize to any Netherlander who takes offence.

Three: although I use quotation marks around bits of conversation, I don't remember exactly what anyone, myself included, said twenty-five or more years ago. The reader will have to accept my assurance that the words capture the *sense* of what was said. Four: memory being fallible and the desire to put oneself in a favourable light strong, all memoirs must be read *cum grano salis*, with reservations. I have tried to be honest about myself and others, however, and hope that my training as a historian means I have given minimal occasion for using the salt-shaker.

Point five: this is *my* story. Each of my brothers still living can, if he wishes, tell his own tale, placing himself at the centre and pushing me to the periphery. Our parents loom larger than my brothers in this account because *they* made the decision to emigrate and therefore their reasons, and their reactions to their adoptive country, demand description and explanation. No doubt there are aspects of my assessment of their character, personality, motives, and behaviour with which they would have quarrelled. Moreover, my brothers may give a different account. One person's story is by its nature incomplete.

Finally: I have tried to fit my recollections into Canada's experience with immigration and multiculturalism. I don't think that what I have written will raise many eyebrows, but just in case anyone is offended: unless I am quoting someone else, the opinions expressed are mine alone.

Michiel Horn
Toronto, October 1996

Mother, aged two, with her younger brother, Kees, and their nanny,
Java, 1911

Father and Mother on their wedding day, 1936

Mother reads to Peter, Jack, and me (right to left), while Joe sleeps in his crib.

The house at Emmalaan 11a, Baarn. Built in 1938, it was where I and my four younger brothers were born.

Living-room of the house in Baarn

On the terrace, south side of the house, 1943. Peter is making a drawing of his pet rooster.

Peter, Jack, and I with soldiers of the 49th (W.R.) Division of the English army, May 1945. I am front left, Jack sits beside me, and Peter sits behind us.

My grade-four class with my favourite teacher, Juffrouw Muis, 1949. I am front, left; next to me sits Willem Hendrik de Beaufort and in front of me, Jan Escher. Jeannette Langenberg is in the middle of the picture; René Hooftgraafland sits next to her, one row over. Louise Hasseley Kirchner sits by the window, far right.

On the terrace of our house, 1951: (from left) Peter, myself, Jack, Joe, Steven, and Jan D.

The SS *Diemerdijk* has arrived at Ogden Point, Victoria, and we are
about to disembark. This photo appeared that day, 17 June 1952, in the
Victoria Daily Times. From left: Peter, myself, Jack, Joe, Steven, and Jan D.
(Courtesy of the Victoria *Times-Colonist*)

Peter, myself, Jan D., and Jack on the steps of the Parliament Building, Victoria, with Mother and Johanna Trapp, 1953

Kandersteg, Switzerland, 1962: Fred Schroeder, John Hill, myself, and friends. Margot Depiereux is to the left of John.

In the garden of our house at 523 Harbinger Avenue, Victoria, 1963: Father, Peter, Jack, Jan D., Joe, myself, and Steven

Relaxing in the quad, Massey College, spring 1964

Glendon College, 1969: the faculty soccer team. Left to right, front row: Roger LeBras, Gilbert Dussuyer, Lewis Rosen, Roger Gannon, Orest Kruhlak; back row: Rick Schultz, Dick Tursman, Brian Bixley, Nollaig MacKenzie, Terry Fowler, Pierre Fortier, myself, Irving Abella, Alain Baudot, Bob Brough

Father and Mother at Niagara Falls, 1971

Willem Cazant and Dora Cazant-van Oort, Baarn, 1972

Father and Mother in the living-room of their 'retirement shack,' Mill Bay, British Columbia, 1973

BECOMING CANADIAN

Prologue

Tuesday, 17 June 1952: the second front page of the *Victoria Daily Times* carries a photograph of six boys. Squinting into the sun, they sit in front of a ship's railing. One holds a fishing rod, the youngest clutches an ABC book. The photo is well-composed: the boys are seen from a forty-five-degree angle, and two of them squat somewhat behind the other four so that the six together make up a question mark. (Was this by design? Or did Jack and I, separated in age by only thirteen months and almost like twins, consciously or unconsciously set ourselves apart?)

'Shown above on arrival in Victoria today is the all-boy family of Mr Daniel Horn, architect, of Baarn, Holland ...' the photo caption states. 'The new immigrants arrived on the Holland-American liner *Diemerdyk* [*sic*] which docked here this morning. The boys are, left to right, Peter, Michael [*sic*], Jack, Joe, Steven and Jan.'

We were at the end of a five-week sea voyage that had begun in Rotterdam. As we sat there, waiting for the photographer to finish his work, another kind of journey was about to begin. Its goal was to become Canadian.

1
War and Peace

So long as people remember the twentieth century, one date they are unlikely to forget is Sunday, 3 September 1939. The British ultimatum demanding that Germany withdraw from Poland expired at 11:00 a.m. Greenwich mean time; the French ultimatum ran out later that day. After listening to the five o'clock news, Mother's sister, Phiet (Sophia), ran upstairs, where Mother was in labour. 'Frankrijk heeft oorlog verklaard' (France has declared war), my aunt reported. 'En ik heb een zoon erbij' (And I have another son), Mother replied.

So the story goes, as Mother used to tell it. When I once asked Tante Phiet about it, she said that she remembered the occasion but not the exchange with her sister. The time of birth, at least, is beyond dispute. 'Wel merkwaardig,' Father wrote in my *baby's boek*, a photo album and diary covering the first six years of my life, 'dat hij precies op het tijdstip geboren werd dat Frankrijk aan Duitschland de oorlog verklaarde' (Remarkable [is] that he was born on the precise point in time that France declared war on Germany).

It was not remarkable that I was born at home. In 1939 the great majority of Dutch children drew first breath there; even today hospital births are far from being the nearly absolute rule in Holland that they are in Canada. A midwife assisted in my delivery. My birth was uneventful on an otherwise eventful day.

My baby book states that I weighed 3.75 kg at birth and measured 54 cm, both somewhat above normal. Gaining weight rapidly, I earned the nickname *Motorschip Dikzak* (MS Fatso), then lost it as I lengthened and thinned out. (In early adulthood I would be 1.85 metres tall and weigh seventy kilos; I've tacked on eight kilos since then.) I had blue eyes and fair hair, but my hair darkened during my second year. Before I reached the age of thirty I would begin to turn grey.

My place of birth was Baarn, a prosperous but not otherwise especially noteworthy town of 20,000 souls that straddles the divide between the agreeably wooded Gooi region and the flat, low-lying Eemland. Six kilometres north is the IJsselmeer (IJssel Lake), formerly known as the Zuiderzee. Hilversum, home of the Dutch broadcasting industry, adjoins Baarn in the west. The old garrison town of Amersfoort lies eight kilometres to the southeast, the university city of Utrecht is twenty-five kilometres to the south.

Founded in the Middle Ages, Baarn enjoyed city rights but built no walls, its inhabitants taking refuge in Amersfoort when danger threatened. In the mid-nineteenth century the town benefited from the construction of the railway line that connected Amsterdam with the northeastern provinces. This attracted light industry, mainly publishing and food processing. Baarn also came to serve Amsterdam, forty kilometres to the northwest and half an hour by rail, as a bedroom suburb. Many commuters settled on the higher, sandy soils west and south of the town core, the rich building mansions and villas, the merely comfortable buying houses as large as their means permitted.

The woods that adjoin the best residential areas are mostly part of the *Koninklijk domein*, the Royal Domain. These are Baarn's pre-eminent glory: a vast park in which adults walk, children play, and both pick blueberries in midsummer and mushrooms in the fall. Soestdijk Palace, the home of Queen Juliana, is just inside the town limits. The baroque central portion was built as a hunting lodge for William III, later King of England; the regrettable wings were added in the nineteenth century.

The beeches along the old highway between Amsterdam and Amersfoort spread a magnificent canopy in summer. When the nuts ripened and fell we looked for them: three-sided, small, brown, plump, and tasty. The beeches end where the road has descended to the plain and a laneway leads to Groeneveld Castle. On its grounds we picked blackberries in August. Although of no great age – it was built in the eighteenth century – the castle, with its wide moat, looked impressive. The moat served skaters nicely when a cold spell lasted long enough. As I conjure up this memory in my mind's eye, I see also a round canvas by Hendrick Avercamp that hangs in London's National Gallery: a jolly winter scene, with skaters of all ages frolicking on a castle moat. Baarn was a good place for children.

Mother and Father were married on 21 April 1936. I have a few of their wedding photos. Mother, blonde and even-featured, smiles slightly; Father, bespectacled, already greying, looks a bit pugnacious, even fierce. They had first met three years earlier. Mother was teaching near Rossum in the Bommelerwaard, an area between the Maas and Waal rivers devoted to horticulture and mixed farming. The social amenities were few; she felt isolated and lonely. Father, an architect who normally resided in Laren, an artists' colony north of Hilversum, was living in the Bommelerwaard at the time while supervising the restoration of a church in the village of Ophemert. Taking pity on two exiles from civilization, as it were, a mutual acquaintance introduced them to each other.

Opposites are said to attract; they did so in this case. Even then Mother tended to brooding introspection and was subject to feelings of personal shortcoming and to depression. Father, on the other hand, seems to have been an unreflective extrovert, jovial with friends, abrupt with those who bored or irritated him. Her motto might have been 'the matter is serious but not hopeless'; his would more likely have been the reverse.

Before the year ended they were engaged, but they waited for Father's practice to get well off the ground before they married. As was the middle-class custom, Mother resigned her job when they did wed. They rented (from the then Princess Juliana) a row house facing Soestdijk Palace, but in 1937 they bought 0.15 hectares (roughly two-fifths of an acre) in Baarn's best residential area, and the next year they moved into a house that Father had designed. (The total cost was around 10,000 guilders, $4,000 Canadian at that time. In 1994 it was listed for sale at 875,000 guilders, approximately $700,000!) Detached residences, uncommon in Holland, were the standard in the neighbourhood. As a child I never realized just how privileged we were in being able to run around our house.

The house, whose address at Emmalaan 11A announced its johnny-come-lately status, was built of brick, then whitewashed. Its principal rooms faced south. The large L-shaped living-room focused on a huge fireplace into whose oak mantelpiece Father began to carve a motto that he never finished: TRY AND THEN TRVST (he told me the source once, but I have forgotten it). Also on the ground floor were a dining-room, a children's playroom, a guest room or study three steps up (usually occupied by a young woman who helped Mother with the household) called the *opkamer*, a hallway with vanity, and a kitchen. One entered the kitchen from the garage; stairs descended from the kitchen pantry into a cool cellar where fruit and vegetables were stored.

The second floor comprised three bedrooms, a bathroom, and a separate toilet. Father used one of the bedrooms as his studio; it also served as a guest room. We children occupied the largest bedroom, which with the passage of time came to resemble a boarding-school dormitory. When the fourth boy, Joe (Johannes Mijndert: Joop), was born, the house became a tight fit, at least upstairs. It would become tighter yet with the birth of two more boys. But we lived there until we emigrated in 1952.

I loved our house. It was *gezellig*, cosy, good fun to play in and around. I didn't realize its unconventionality. It presented a façade from which windows were virtually absent, whereas the customary Dutch model allowed passers-by to look in, as if to say, 'We have nothing to hide.' When I returned to Baarn in 1961 I learned that some people called our former home *het geheime huis*: the secret house. Father's comment when I told him this was that only an idiot would want to have a lot of windows facing north.

Father's parents, Hendrik Jacobus Horn, Jr, and Gesina Raisig, were married in 1886 and had nine children, eight of whom survived infancy. Father, the youngest, was born in Amsterdam on 26 April 1903 and christened Daniel.

Mother's parents, Steven Anne Reitsma and Maria Elisabeth Brutel de la Rivière, went to the Netherlands East Indies upon marrying in 1904. Two of their six children died in infancy; Mother was the second oldest of the survivors. Born in Madiun, Java, on 23 September 1909, she was christened Antje Elisabeth.

When I was young I thought that the sole interest in my family tree resided in the ancestors of my maternal grandmother. I learned about them in a genealogical publication, *Nederlands Patriciaat*, that I found on a bookshelf next to the fireplace (the book is now in my possession). One Gédéon Brutel, *conseiller du Roi et receveur général des gabelles de Languedoc*, and a Huguenot, fled Montpellier around 1685, taking refuge in Lausanne. His son, Jean, migrated to Rotterdam to become pastor to a Huguenot congregation. Jean's offspring prospered in Holland: my great-great-grandfather Jean Jacques was an adviser to King William I and personal secretary to his consort; his oldest son became a vice-admiral. So did one of *his* sons, my great-uncle. In addition to being clergymen, courtiers, and naval officers, the Brutels were merchants, lawyers, physicians, and university professors: solid members of the bourgeoisie.

My grandmother's family probably thought that she was marrying beneath herself, although the parents of her husband were almost certainly wealthier than her own. Her father, Carel Brutel de la Rivière, had embarked on a naval career but was forced to resign with the rank of lieutenant because his eyesight was failing. He turned to teaching mathematics at a secondary school in Assen. Although respectable, this work was less remunerative than the business of my great-grandfather Hendrik Reitsma, a jeweller and goldsmith with stores in Leeuwarden and Sneek. A century ago, even well-to-do shopkeepers were not top drawer socially, but by virtue of attending the Royal Military Academy in Breda my grandfather had become *salonfähig*, fit for polite company. He took a commission in the Netherlands East Indies Army; upon his honourable discharge he became an administrator with the East Indies Railways, working in several cities on Java until he retired at age fifty, each year in the tropics having counted double towards a pension.

Opa (Grandfather) Reitsma, as I remember him, was in his seventies: a prosperous-looking man with a fleshy face and a small *embonpoint*. He dressed carefully, always wearing a three-piece suit, a gold watch-chain across his waistcoat, and spats. In his buttonhole he had a decoration marking him as a knight of some order or other. At the time of my birth he was about to retire as editor of the magazine of the Netherlands Railways, a position he had assumed upon returning from the Indies in 1926. Having always written a good deal – a stint as acting *burgemeester* (mayor) of Bandung in the early 1920s, for example, inspired a book about that city – he became a travel writer in addition to his editorial duties.

My maternal grandmother was also a published author, with several children's books and a novel to her credit. She would have written more had she not died in 1929, aged forty-eight, her health undermined by two decades in the tropics. Mother felt this as a severe blow, one compounded when Opa remarried two years later. I don't remember my step-grandmother, who died during the war. I do know Mother and Father both disliked her.

I did not hear about my one indisputably famous (or notorious) relative until I was twenty-two. Tante Phiet told me the titillating truth: Opa was Mata Hari's cousin! (Upon returning to Canada I found that Mother regarded this as a shameful secret.) My cousin Tjitte Reitsma, who inherited some of Opa's letters upon his death in 1958, gave me most of the details. The mothers of Opa and Mata Hari, both named Antje van der Meulen, were first cousins. One married my great-grandfather, the other married a hatter named Adam Zelle. Their daughter Margaretha Geertruida was eleven months younger than Opa, who was born in September 1875. As children they played with each other; they also attended dancing class together. In time she married an army officer and accompanied him to the East Indies. After the marriage foundered she turned to exotic dancing under the name Mata Hari ('the eye of the dawn': the sun), and made Paris her new home. A pioneer of striptease, she was also a renowned courtesan whose lovers included the composer Jules Massenet and the Crown Prince of Germany.

Opa did not advertise his link to this scarlet woman. (Mores change: when I visited Leeuwarden in 1976, the centenary of his cousin's birth, postcards identified the city, in four languages, as the 'stad van Mata Hari.' More recently, a museum has been established in her memory!) But he went to his grave believing her to be innocent of the charge of spying for the Germans that led to her execution by a French firing squad in 1917. Probably he was justified in this belief. The historian Phillip Knightley has written that she was the victim of politics. France was weary of war; her trial offered a diversion. She was shot 'not because she was a dangerous spy, but because it was militarily and politically expedient to shoot her, and because of what she was.'*

An anecdote recounted to me by Tante Phiet tells of an exchange that purportedly took place in the 1920s between Opa and Georges Clemenceau, a prominent politician at the time of Mata Hari's death and soon after it France's prime minister. Taken to task for his country's execution of our relative, Clemenceau is supposed to have said: 'Quand il s'agit d'exécuter des espions, mieux vaut un de plus qu'un de moins' (Better to execute one spy too many than one too few). In the Great War's orgy of killing and destruction, Mata Hari's was just one more death.

Compared with Mother's family, Father's was thoroughly prosaic. The first Horn of whom I have any record, my great-great-great-grandfather Mijndert, was living in Amsterdam by 1807, but no evidence of his origin or occupation survives in the documents I have inherited. My great-grandfather Hendrik Jacobus was the oldest of five children left destitute when their father, a master carpenter, died of typhus in 1842 at the age of thirty-five. This forced the twelve-year-old Hendrik to leave school in order to support his mother and siblings. In time he became an ironmaster and gained a modestly comfortable place in life. Largely self-taught, he valued formal education and made sure his only child, my grandfather Hendrik Jacobus, Jr, enjoyed its benefits. Opa Horn

---

* Phillip Knightley, *The Second Oldest Profession: The Spy as Bureaucrat, Patriot, Fantasist and Whore* (London 1986), 49. An article by Russell Warren Howe in *Smithsonian* (May 1986) has the title: 'Mournful Fate of Mata Hari, the Spy Who Wasn't Guilty.'

taught art in Amsterdam's élite *Hogere Burger School* before retiring in 1925. Those of his paintings and drawings that have survived are conventional but technically good. One of his best pieces is a charcoal and pencil drawing of his father's mother, copied from a daguerrotype. The resemblance to my niece Kirstin is striking.

Opa Horn was a stubborn Lutheran, pacifist, and teetotaller. The last of these seems to have dominated Father's memories. He liked to tell a story from his twenties, when he lived with his parents in Amersfoort while apprenticing with a firm of architects in nearby Laren. Someone gave him a bottle of champagne for his birthday. Just after opening it he was called away to the telephone; when he returned he found that Opa had poured out the contents and filled the bottle with water!

Swallowing his chagrin, Father saved the bottle and was able to use it in taking sweet revenge. Some time afterwards there was a meeting of teetotallers in Amersfoort and a parade marking the event. Pleading old age, Opa did not join the procession but put a sign of support on his lawn. Then he stood by the window, expecting pleased smiles of recognition from the passers-by. Instead he got dirty looks. When he went out to pick up the sign he discovered the reason. Father, knowing that Opa couldn't see the sign from where he stood, had hung the empty champagne bottle from it!

Father remembered Opa as a stern paterfamilias; Mother recalled him as superficially austere but in essence warm and loving. This characterization is confirmed in two volumes of memoirs he wrote between 1925 and 1938. I found them after Father's death in 1990, and they are now in my possession. Opa writes simply but movingly about his life, his marriage, his work, and the death of two sons and a daughter in early adulthood.

His wife, Gesina Raisig, my paternal grandmother, was the daughter of a once-prosperous butcher who had fallen on hard times. She hailed from Hoorn, a small town north of Amsterdam. Father rarely talked about her, and I owe my sense of her personality and character very largely to my grandfather's memoirs. Describing her as fun-loving when young, and as a wife a good manager, he loved her deeply and long mourned her death in 1932,

aged sixty-eight. He remarried six years later. I have fond memories of my step-grandmother, who outlived Opa by a decade (Opa
died in August 1940 in his eighty-first year), but not of the lumpy
socks she knitted for us.

My third name, Daniel, comes from the Raisigs. My second,
Steven, I owe to the Reitsmas. My first name, Michiel, is a story in
itself. According to Father, one Michael Horn or Horne left Scotland as a mercenary soldier around 1710, during the War of the
Spanish Succession, eventually taking service under the Elector of
Saxony. He married a German woman; later they or one of their
sons migrated to Amsterdam.

The sole evidence for this tale is a candelabrum, cast in iron by
my great-grandfather, containing several Scottish symbols. Father
claimed to know our forebear's clan, Cameron of Erracht, but a
cousin who tried to trace the Horns in Scotland had no success.
That doesn't mean the story has no basis in fact, but the opinion of
Father's sister Gesien (Gesina) is at least as plausible. 'Je vader en
je nicht zijn allebei getikt: de Horns waren van oorsprong moffen'
(Your father and cousin are both daft: the Horns were originally
Krauts), she said to me in 1961. Father was irritated when I reported
this: 'Gesien is mesjokke; wat weet zij er van?' (Gesien is crazy;
what does she know about it?). He was even more annoyed to learn
that Rudolf Hess, Hitler's deputy, had assumed the name Alfred
Horn when he flew to Scotland in 1941: 'Waar kreeg hij het lef?'
(Where did he get the nerve?). In truth, Horn is a common name
throughout northwestern Europe.

Father wanted to give me the nickname 'Mike,' but this gave
way to *Motorschip Dikzak* and then to *Boeles*, coined by my older
brother, Peter (born in 1937), to mean *broertje*, little brother. Later
I became Chiel, the Dutch abbreviation for Michiel. In Canada I
was Mike until at the age of thirty I assumed my name at last,
spelling it in the Dutch manner but pronouncing it as Michael.

I cut my first tooth on 10 May 1940, the day Germany invaded
Holland. Baarn was located on the edge of the Grebbe defensive
line, so we had to be evacuated in Father's small DKW. (This car
was later confiscated by the Germans.) We were soon allowed to

return, however, the Dutch armed forces having surrendered on 14 May. 'Michiel trekt zich nergens iets van aan' (Nothing bothers Michiel), Mother wrote. 'Als hij zijn eten op tijd krijgt is hij tevreden' (Provided he gets fed on time he is content). I have always been a good eater.

My first memory of any kind is of Joe's birth on 9 April 1942, in part because of a tree in the garden that was cut down at this time, in part because of the private nurse, Ruth Cattaneo, Zuster Cattaneo as we called her, who stayed with us for a couple of weeks to look after Mother and Joe, and whom I liked a lot. (She was also there after Steven and Jan D. were born, and I later learned that she came to stay after every birth.) Joe was number four; number three, Jack (Hendrik Jacobus: Hein), had arrived on 3 October 1940. Mother loved infants and toddlers, and she was very good with us. I remember being in her bed, with Peter and Jack, listening to the stories she read to us. Before I turned five I had learned how to read; soon I occupied myself with Jan Pierewiet, Meneer Prikkebeen, Peter Rabbit, and that disconcerting German children's classic *Struwwelpeter*.

Life during the war wasn't easy, Father and Mother used to say, but it had its rewards. It forced people to focus on important matters and to make do with simple pleasures. After the 1938 Munich agreement, Father, convinced that war was near and that the practice of architecture would become difficult even though Holland was expected to remain neutral as in 1914–18, had taken a position as architect with the *Rijksgebouwendienst*, the Department of Public Works. As a result he had an income throughout the war. Although not large, it was sufficient to pay the mortgage and keep his family supplied with whatever food and clothing were available.

Father was involved in *het verzet*, the resistance, in some way. I became fully aware of this only in the 1980s, when his old friend Henri Gravemeyer applied for a pension on the basis of his resistance work and asked Father to be a reference. Father was unhelpful, claiming forgetfulness as his excuse. Perhaps he did not care to remember. He said he had once helped to kill an informer and still felt badly about it. He did often mention, however, being telephoned by the *Ortskommandant*, 'een goede Duitser' (a good

German) who warned him that 'visitors,' agents of the *Sicherheits-dienst* (security police), were coming to town. Father then warned two of his associates, who presumably warned others in turn. Whatever his role was in the resistance, it did not draw him to the attention of the police. That was just as well.

Baarn lacked military significance, so that we escaped bombing raids until very late in the war. Sometimes I woke up at night and heard a distant, reassuring drone: 'Tommies' on their way to bomb Germany or returning to England. I have vivid memories of dog-fights between German and Allied fighter aircraft. These were frequent by 1943 as the Allies sought to establish air dominance, a precondition for the invasion of western Europe. The screaming engines and rat-tat-tat of the guns frightened me. As with thunderstorms, I didn't quite believe Father's assurances that the airplanes constituted little or no threat to us.

Trains were favourite targets even though they included flatbed cars with anti-aircraft guns. We lived some 200 metres from the railway line connecting Amsterdam with Amersfoort and points east, and periodically it came under attack. Once I woke from an afternoon nap as a fighter plane passed low overhead; moments later I heard the rapid fire of its machine-guns. I was nearly witless with fright. Father later reported that a locomotive had been shot up and its engineer killed, less than half a kilometre away.

The villa immediately to our east was requisitioned at some point, and German officers lived there until the late winter or early spring of 1945. My memories include them, their horses, and their guard dogs, fearsome great German shepherds and Dobermanns. I also recall the rounds of machine-gun fire to which the horses were supposed to become accustomed. The poor animals found it just as hard as we did; we could hear them thundering through the backyard, neighing in fear. After a couple of days of this, the story goes, Mother (whose German was good) went next door to ask whether the guns might be silenced in the early afternoon, our nap time. The senior officer apologized to her, and the Germans complied with the request. Our parents used to say that the officers, although in principle unwelcome, were in practice always socially correct.

The summer of 1944 brought growing excitement, as our parents and their guests speculated about the landings in Normandy and the progress of the Allied campaign in France, about which Father and Mother heard on the radio they had kept illegally and hidden. Father paid someone to dig foxholes inside the fence along the Emmalaan. The Germans, preparing to defend themselves against attack, required this service, but I don't think they ever used the large holes. We were under strict instructions to stay out of them. At least once we disobeyed and got quite filthy, to Mother's great displeasure. Doing the laundry for a large family was difficult enough without gratuitous dirt stains on our clothes.

In September I entered kindergarten, which I liked. The school closed before Christmas, however, because fuel ran out. Grades one through six met in private homes on the understanding that parents would contribute fuel to keep a room warm. (This scheme resurfaced in the bitterly cold winter of 1946–7, when coal was still scarce.) My classes did not resume until mid-May.

The Dutch still talk of the *hongerwinter* of 1944–5. Food and fuel were ever more scarce in the densely populated west. The trains did not run because of a railway strike that began in September in order to assist the Allies during Operation 'Market Garden', the ill-fated attempt to capture the bridges across the great rivers. The 'bridge too far' at Arnhem remained in German hands, and in the aftermath of the battle the railway workers, fearing reprisals, remained off the job. The Germans would not move civilian supplies, however, and though some food came by water from the eastern provinces there was not enough and a January freeze-up interrupted even this supply. Worse still, the sole source of Dutch coal had been cut off when U.S. forces liberated south Limburg in October.

Official rations had been dropping for years, and serious deficiencies in protein and vitamins had developed. But nothing in their experience prepared people in the western provinces for famine. Rations became hopelessly inadequate, and thousands – the young, the old, and the poor – starved to death.

Supplying a large family with food and fuel was hard, Father said. Steven Anne (Stef) had been born in May 1944, adding the needs of an infant to those of three adults (our parents and Arda Groen, the mother's help they employed) and four children ranging in age from seven to two. We ate rye porridge in the mornings, consumed potatoes in their skins, and scraped pots for the last bits of food. It was almost unnecessary to wash the pots afterwards. By midwinter, official rations consisted of a bit of bread and some watery soup obtained from central kitchens. For a fee it was delivered to the door, which was how we got it until Father found the heel-plate from a shoe in his soup. A neighbour later told us the cart had overturned near our house. However, the delivery man had managed to ladle most of his precious load back into the kettle! Thereafter, we picked up our soup ourselves. I remember accompanying Mother to the central kitchen one time, waiting for what seemed like an eternity, weeping because my feet were so miserably cold.

We were lucky in living near a farming area, so that Father could go to trade for food. (Farmers were unwilling to accept the inflated paper money, preferring precious metals, china, textiles, and other intrinsically valuable goods.) From farmers in Eemnes and Hoogland we got milk, butter, wheat, and rye, ground into flour in our coffee mill, potatoes, sugar beets, and, delicacy of delicacies, the occasional calf's head. I didn't worry about the illegally slaughtered animal it came from: I merely savoured its tongue and brains. Once, late in the war, we ate tulip bulbs, but they made us sick.

To that winter I owe a reluctance to leave food on my plate (a virtual inability in the case of meat) and an almost visceral dislike of seeing food go to waste. Soon after the war I saw a slice of white bread floating in the pond near our house and was deeply shocked. White bread represented luxury: who would throw it away? The bread we ate in wartime was dark, mostly rye, with the exception of some white bread that, thanks to the Swedish Red Cross, came our way early in 1945. If I spread butter thinly on rye bread and scrape it off, eating the mixture of butter and crumbs brings back potent memories. So does watching Daniel and Patrick reject some part of their meal on the grounds that it is 'yucky.' When I was their age ... It's pointless telling them that, of course, though sometimes I find myself doing it all the same. Mother or Father could say, even years after the war: 'Je komt er nog eens aan te kort' (Some day you may not have enough), and those old enough to recall that last winter of the war would eat.

By the end of November all our indoor activities took place in Father's studio. Because it had been intended for use as a guest bedroom it had a sink, which was useful. Even better was that it had a fireplace: it served nicely for the stove we used for cooking and heating. (With five children under the age of ten in the room it must have been bedlam much of the time, unless malnutrition kept us quieter than we might otherwise have been.) The rest of the house was left unheated. At night this made no difference, for our sheets were warmed with hot-water bottles before we went to bed, but during the daytime we avoided the chilly rooms. Electric service had been cut off in late October, and we used oil lamps until Father decided to take advantage of the officers next door. Assisted by a neighbour, he tapped their electricity supply. Mother used the kitchen range from time to time, but this was risky because of its heavy consumption of electricity. We had light, however, and used the vacuum cleaner regularly. Because of the blackout no one could see from outside that we were cheating. And, able to listen to the BBC, our parents were better informed about the progress of the war than many people were that winter.

On *Sinterklaasavond* (St Nicholas's Eve), 5 December, we got a few simple presents, and on Christmas Eve we put up and decorated a small tree. Candles saved from the year before were lit for a few minutes each day; they survived to *Driekoningen*, Epiphany, as planned. Familiar routines largely prevailed until the last weeks of the war, when Father went into hiding. Before March he had freedom of movement, his age and employment exempting him from the forced labour on which German industry had come increasingly to rely. This freedom ended when he was called up to help guard the railway line against sabotage. He went into hiding instead. Henceforth, only Mother could go out.

It seemed strange to us that Father was around the house all the time; strange, too, were the instructions not to tell anyone he was home. Strangest of all were the efforts to ensure that we would not volunteer this information at night. More than once I was woken up and asked (by whom I can't recall) where Father was. Groggily I regurgitated the formula I had been taught: 'Vader is in Hilversum om centjes te verdienen' (Father is in Hilversum to earn pennies).

The Germans came to look for him in April, when it was already warm enough for us to be in the children's playroom. Soldiers clumped through the house; later on we saw them in the garden. They didn't find Father, who had a hiding place under the floor of the upstairs toilet – I didn't know of its existence until after the war – but they did confiscate his old typewriter.

Hostilities were drawing to a close. In March the Allies began an offensive in the Rhineland; after a few weeks, Canadian and English divisions swung into the eastern Netherlands and advanced towards the north and west. On 20 April, units of the First Canadian Division reached the defensive line that extended from the IJsselmeer to the Rhine. There they halted. There was no good reason for further advance. Civilian relief was more pressing.

We were in the line of fire at last. Several batteries of German field guns were scattered throughout Baarn: targets in the event of artillery bombardment. On the afternoon of 25 April, distant popping noises began, and Mother and Arda herded us into the cellar. Father had earlier reinforced its ceiling with posts, and Mother had stored bedding there. It was unexpectedly crowded, for joining us were Germaine Fischer, a French-born friend, and her children, Bert and Elsa. They had been visiting when the shelling began and dared not go home. (Their flat was damaged that night, and they ended up staying with us for 'trois semaines inoubliables!!' as Germaine wrote in Mother's guest book.) The shells fell for several hours, sounding like whistles that gained in loudness until they ended in an explosion, usually distant, sometimes nearby. The cellar stairs faced east towards the Canadian guns, and Father, who sat near the top of the stairs, later claimed to have lost several litres of sweat worrying about a direct hit. Not knowing how vulnerable we were in our refuge, I was more excited than afraid.

The shelling ended after I fell asleep. When dawn came, Father was able to determine that our house had escaped serious damage. A few windows were punctured by shell fragments, but the strips of paper that were glued to all windows in a criss-cross pattern had saved them from shattering. Some of our neighbours were not so lucky. The house west of ours had a large hole in its roof; the entrance of the house diagonally opposite had been badly damaged. But there were no casualties in our neighbourhood and not many in Baarn as a whole.

In the aftermath, we were not allowed into the garden until all shrapnel had been cleared out, and we slept in the cellar for more than a week lest there should be a renewal of artillery fire. It was annoying that the garden was out of bounds, and sleeping in the cellar soon lost its charms. We were glad to return to our own beds after the German surrender on 5 May.

The experience prompted a game, *granaatvuur* (shellfire), that Father later recalled for me. One of us would yell: 'Granaatvuur: vlug, de kelder in!' (Shellfire: quick, into the cellar!). We would scramble underneath the sofa and chairs; someone would then imitate the familiar shriek and bang. There would be a few moments of silence. Then chatter: 'Wat een klap! Waar kwam die terecht? Was dat een voltreffer?' (What a crash! Where did that one land? Was that a direct hit?). Father liked to mimic three-year-old Joe's lisping comment: 'Jawel, op het dak hiernaast, een gat groot genoeg voor een paard en wagen' (Yes, on the roof next door, a hole big enough for a horse and cart).

The houses were repaired in the course of 1945, but evidence of the shelling persisted. Years passed before our neighbour replaced the pickets of his fence that had been shattered by shrapnel. Some of the injuries to the oak trees along the Emmalaan were still visible when we left in 1952.

Liberation came to Baarn on Monday, 7 May 1945, the German forces in Holland having surrendered two days earlier. A cease-fire had come into effect in late April, the Germans agreeing to operations 'Faust' and 'Manna,' aimed at civilian relief. Food, medical supplies, and fuel for water-pumping stations and filtration plants came in by truck, barge, and, most spectacularly, airplane. Bombers, this time loaded with food parcels, flew over low on their way to the drop sites. But the biscuits and chocolate we ate were rich in fat and sugar to an altogether unaccustomed degree. We got quite ill.

We recovered well before 7 May, and on that bright spring morning we walked to the Oranjeboom, a crossroads about a kilometre south of our home. Having passed through Amersfoort and Soest, the column of vehicles approached us from the south; most turned left just beyond where we were standing, in order to take the road to Hilversum. We jumped up and down, waved little Dutch flags, and cheered as the long-awaited Tommies passed by in trucks, personnel carriers, and tanks that, their engines unmuffled, produced an almost overpowering din. The soldiers smiled broadly and waved back; happy civilians had draped themselves on many of the vehicles. The mood was one of joy – giddy, unrestrained, never-to-be-replicated joy. My memory of that glorious morning is unlikely to fade, even in my dotage.

That afternoon a small column parked along our street: a unit of the Duke of Wellington's Regiment of the 49th (West Riding) Division, which at the time was part of First Canadian Corps. (I later came to think that they must have been Canadians and that Father and Mother were mistaken in insisting they were English. In 1979, however, when I was in Ottawa to do research for the book *A Liberation Album: Canadians in the Netherlands 1944–1945*, I found that our parents were right.) We decorated the vehicles with flowers from our garden while the adults talked with the soldiers and smoked their cigarettes. I picked up an empty package and admired the image on it: a bearded sailor with a ship on the horizon. Years later I learned the brand name: Player's Navy Cut.

Mother seemed as happy as the rest of us. But she worried about her two brothers. The older, Aak (Isaäc) Reitsma, was a railway engineer who had been active in the resistance and was missing. Not long after the Liberation we learned that he had been killed in mid-April near Voorthuizen, a village between Apeldoorn and Amersfoort that had witnessed heavy fighting between Canadian and German forces. He left a widow and five children. There was news, too, about her brother Kees (Constant), the black sheep of the family. A member of the *NSB*, the Dutch Nazi party, he had joined the Netherlands Legion to fight on the Russian front, later serving in the *Waffen-SS*. He had lost an arm in action and was interned pending his trial for treason. One brother dead, another injured and in prison: Mother had cause to feel sad.

She was far from alone; but joy was dominant. After the deprivations and fears of wartime there was cause for exuberance, and the normally staid Netherlanders cut loose in spectacular fashion. The Canadians who marked time in Holland before their repatriation were the objects of nearly boundless gratitude and mendicancy. Cigarettes and other consumer goods, available to the soldiers but not to civilians, were in hot demand. So were the soldiers themselves. Moralists worried about their effect on Dutch womanhood; others joked about it. Should another war break out in twenty years or so it would not be necessary to send a Canadian army, some wag said: a few shiploads of uniforms would be enough! Like many young women, our Arda soon had a Canadian boyfriend; in due time she gave birth to a half-Canadian daughter. (After *A Liberation Album* appeared in 1981 in a Dutch translation, I got a few letters from people who wanted my assistance in locating their fathers. I was unable to do much.)

Baarn was a resting place for several Canadian units, among them the North Nova Scotia Highlanders. Bagpipe music is inextricably part of my liberation memories; so are jeeps racing madly along the highway. Father and Mother later recalled that the officers especially, most of them in their early twenties, were amply supplied with liquor and seemed hell-bent on having a good time. The parties they threw, from which civilians other than young women were usually excluded, in time became legendary for Dionysian excess. I imagine that they were in fact rather like fraternity parties without any neighbours to call the police. And, given that many of the men had recently faced death, they had a right to kick up their heels.

Officers occupied some of the larger properties in Baarn and seem to have kept house in a less than careful manner. When I did my research for *A Liberation Album*, I found an exchange of letters about a mansion that had belonged to the grandparents of a schoolfriend of mine, René Hooftgraafland. Its owners had been dismayed to discover that Canadian officers had done more damage to the house in a few months than the German officers who had preceded them had done in almost five years!

For me two events of that summer stand out. The first was the birthday of Queen Wilhelmina, back from exile in London. Netherlanders made the most of their first opportunity since 1939 to celebrate the day. The highlight was an evening when electricity (still rationed) was available until 9:00 or 10:00 for the illumination of the shopping district. In a state of high excitement, Peter, Jack, Joe, and I accompanied our parents into town to admire a fairytale wonderland: plywood triumphal arches decorated with flowering plants and bright light-bulbs. It did get late, however. Joe fell asleep in the wooden wagon that Father pulled along behind him. Peter and I walked; so did Jack until he got tired, climbed into the wagon, and began to whine. His complaint became a family joke: 'Ik heb altijd al gezegd dat kleine jongetjes om deze tijd in bed moeten zijn' (I have always said that small boys ought to be in bed by this time).

The second event was V-J Day, 15 August. This was the occasion for renewed celebration, because many Netherlanders had relatives and friends in the Indies. Having been born on Java, Mother was understandably concerned about the archipelago, which Japanese forces had overrun early in 1942. Father was even more worried: his brother Joop had been on the island of Borneo as a petroleum engineer, and there had been no news of him for years. (In time we learned that he had died in a Japanese internment camp.) I heard about the atom bombs dropped on Hiroshima and Nagasaki, bombs said to be far more powerful than anything used in Europe, but that meant little or nothing to me then. I could hardly have understood that a new chapter in human history had begun.

Japan formally surrendered on Sunday, 2 September. The next day was my sixth birthday and the first day of school. With two dozen other children I slid into a seat in the grade one classroom of the Nieuwe Baarnse School. *My* summer of liberation had come to an end.

The Nieuwe Baarnse School (NBS) had been founded early in the century by parents who didn't want their children to attend either a public or a confessional institution. Its academic reputation was excellent; the proportion of its matriculants admitted to the Baarnsch Lyceum, the only local secondary school to prepare for university entrance, was high. However, because it charged tuition fees to supplement its public grant – since 1917 *all* Dutch schools have received tax support – the NBS aroused resentment. The envious called it, with vulgar pronunciation, 'de zije zakdoeke school' (the silk-hanky school).

The NBS occupied a three-storey brick building on the Smutslaan. (Dutch public opinion during the South African War had favoured the Boers; roads carrying the names of Botha, Kruger, and Steijn were nearby.) It was perhaps fifteen minutes on foot from our home to the school; after the first day, Peter and I went by ourselves. The route was straightforward, and our parents did not think we needed to be protected from anyone or anything, whether human being, animal, or machine.

Many years passed before I realized how fortunate we were to have been children in a society in which few people owned cars. Even those who did own one used bicycles for local transportation; tradesmen still went about on horse-drawn carts. During my school days I admired extravagantly every car I rode in, from the small Hillman belonging to a friend's mother to the huge American *slee* (sleigh: a reference to the smooth drive of Buicks, Packards, and the like) driven by one of Father's business acquaintants. I envied those who owned automobiles: they seemed specially privileged beings. We did not have one. When we needed to go somewhere together, Father rented a limousine from a garage, and we all piled in (seat-belts did not exist yet). I liked its smooth ride and dreamed we might someday own something like it ourselves. In the meantime, the near-absence of cars meant that children used Baarn's roads in a safety scarcely imaginable today.

The paucity of automobiles was a real blessing, too, after we began to ride bicycles. Granted, we had to learn and obey the traffic laws; but into the early 1950s we had little need, while cycling in Baarn, to worry about anything much beyond pedestrians and other cyclists. And when we cycled to nearby towns, Hilversum, Laren, or Soest, bicycle paths along the highways were available for our safe use.

The shortest route to school took us along the Emmalaan, which was divided into parallel roadways by a long, narrow pond, the Wilhelminavijver. We skated on it when a cold spell lasted long enough, and raced around it on our bicycles in summer. Continuing on our way to school, we crossed the Wilhelminalaan and walked along the Nassaulaan, turned left into the Steijnlaan, and finally right into the Smutslaan. Sometimes we used a longer route through the *Maarschalkerbos*, better known to us as *het bosje van IJzendijk*, IJzendijk's Wood, a large park where within a fenced area peacocks displayed their plumage and deer roamed. I liked feeding the deer, their soft noses nuzzling my fingers as they took the bread.

We were in class six days a week; Wednesday and Saturday afternoons were free. The school year ran from the beginning of September into early July. The pace was steady but not slow, for we were working towards the *toelatingsexamen*, the exam governing entrance into the Baarnsch Lyceum. The hopes that middle-class Netherlanders nourished for their children included an élite secondary school, which was the passport into university, the professions, and the higher strata of the public service and the managerial world. For the intellectually weak and the easily distracted the NBS was a real grind. Some couldn't keep up and transferred to less demanding schools.

I was bright and generally tractable, took easily to rules, and got along with my teachers. Juffrouw (Miss) du Burck, a maternal woman, had the first grade. Corrie van der Baan, a cousin of Father's on the Raisig side of his family, supervised our passage from pencils to pen and ink. She was the first to notice that I needed glasses. Initially, these were a bother, but as my myopia grew worse I became reconciled to them. I liked best my teacher in grades three and four, Juffrouw Muis, a slender Eurasian who encouraged my growing interest in philately. Mevrouw (Mrs) Valkenburg was conscientious though a bit dull. Finally, Meneer (Mr) Oedekerk may have thought himself made for greater things than teaching us, but he took it seriously none the less.

I rather liked the art teacher, a dandyish man named van Ingen, but tried not to show it because he was widely regarded as a *zak*, a jerk. My cowardice was the more cruel because art was my favourite subject. When Father brought me my first box of *Caran d'ache* colouring pencils from Switzerland in 1946 I was in heaven. I liked to draw landscapes with trees, windmills, and church towers on the horizon, once winning a newspaper prize for such a drawing. I was also fascinated by war, soldiers, tanks, airplanes, and ruined buildings, and I threw myself enthusiastically into a project on Canada, colouring maple leaves, beavers, Indians, and tall structures that represented either the Peace Tower or grain elevators or both.

From the outset my report cards showed many eights and nines. I got my only tens ever (perfection!) in grade five history. History lessons were about heroes and dramatic events: the Christianizing of the Low Countries, the war of independence against Spain, the voyages of discovery, the Golden Age of the seventeenth century, the colonization of the Indies. It was uncritical stuff, but it captured my imagination.

At the end of grade three, academic success went completely to my head. To the annoyance of my brothers I did not stop crowing. But I got my well-deserved comeuppance when I went to Utrecht for a week to stay with Father's oldest sister and her small family. My cousin Geesje, well into her teens and preparing to enter medical school, was uninterested in me, so I set out to find playmates among the neighbourhood children. I introduced myself to two of them by saying: 'Ik heet Chiel Horn; ik heb acht negens op m'n rapport' (My name is Mike Horn; I have eight nines on my report card). The older, a girl, said coolly: 'Dat is een lange en erg rare naam' (That is a long and very strange name). Thoroughly mortified, I retreated to Geesje's childhood toys. When I re-emerged I did not mention my grades again.

Father left early for his office in The Hague and was rarely back for dinner, so we saw little of him during the week. Mother was in charge of us, our morals and manners. She stressed the former rather than the latter: I learned more about table manners in the course of visits to relatives than I did at home. Meals were noisy: Father called them 'het voederen van de kleine wilde beesten' (the feeding of the small wild animals), and he was not far wrong.

Father, nominally Lutheran, did not attend church. Mother was of liberal Reformed background, but while she rarely went to church she was not indifferent to religion. In order to inculcate morals she relied on biblical stories. Discipline consisted of scolding us or withholding privileges. When seriously provoked she might slap someone, but by and large she left corporal punishment to Father. He owned a piece of rattan with which he would deliver a few sharp blows on the behinds of whoever had offended. This would happen upon his return home, usually hours after the offence, and involved getting the miscreant out of bed. I disliked him as executioner; his lashing out in the flush of anger was easier to accept. Once, when I was cheeky during a Sunday lunch, he tossed half an Edam cheese at me. It hit me in the face, and my nose bled copiously. For days afterwards I minded my tongue.

His anger was sudden and sometimes, at least to a child, unpredictable. An incident when I was seven comes to mind. It had been cold for some time – the winter of 1946–7 was bitter – and a good deal of snow had already accumulated when yet another storm hit. I stood at one of the living-room windows, watching the snowflakes come twirling down, singing a song of my own composition about the beautiful snow. Happening by, Father boxed my ears and asked me in an irritated voice whether I, with my beautiful snow, could tell him where to buy more coal. A child's sense of injustice is strong, and I felt greatly aggrieved. How was I supposed to know that the coal dealer had nothing in stock?

I feared Father but also admired him. He was good with his hands, could make things and draw fine pictures, knew all sorts of songs and poems, enjoyed hearing a joke and telling one, and used picturesque figures of speech. To indicate that something was cheap, for example, he might say that it cost 'een hap snert en drie knikkers' (a mouthful of pea soup and three marbles). To indicate that something tasted especially good he might say: 'Het is alsof een engeltje op je tong piest' (It is as if a cherub is peeing on your tongue), or 'Het gaat er in als Gods woord bij een ouderling' (It goes down like God's word into an elder of the church). When someone spilled an alcoholic drink he would say: 'Er kan beter een politiebureau afbranden' (Better a police station should burn down). He habitually referred to us as 'het vee van Laban,' (Laban's cattle: see Genesis 30: 31-43) because we were alternately light and dark blond.

Another of his comments sticks in my memory. When he wanted to admonish a son who wasn't doing quite as well in school as he might, Father would say: 'Pas maar op, anders breng je het niet verder in 't leven dan putjesschepper' (Watch out, otherwise you'll have to settle for being a sewage worker). For me this conjured up the grimy workman who periodically turned up to do something about the open drain in the garage, just outside the kitchen door. For all I know he was a conscientious, hard-working, and God-fearing man, but at the time my only thought was: who wants to be like *that*?

I felt it as a privilege that I was allowed to do homework and work on my stamp collection in Father's studio, or examine there the latest samples – tiles, pieces of wood, and the like – that he had received from firms in the building industry. These carried the description 'monster zonder waarde' (sample without value), which appealed to my imagination, the Dutch word '*monster*' also meaning what it does in English. When Father was working in his studio himself, generally on Sundays only, he usually had the radio on while he drew, but at times he sang or, more often, whistled. I developed the same piercing whistle. Those dear to me do not much appreciate it.

On Sundays, the young woman who helped Mother had the day off, so Father took charge of the evening meal. Mother disliked cooking and showed little aptitude for it: her porridge was lumpy more often than not, and sometimes her meatballs could have done double duty in a game of lacrosse. Father's repertoire was limited, but he was competent. As he was particularly proud of the rice he cooked, its consistency always just so, he usually prepared a meal of rice with beef or chicken and fried eggs as well as vegetables, *kroepoek (shrimp chips), ketjap benteng manis* (sweet soya sauce), and a *sambal* (red pepper condiment) or two. Dessert was equally predictable and tasty: rice with butter and brown sugar. Sunday dinners were also special in that each child of school age got a few centilitres of beer in the silver beaker he had received at birth. I liked both the taste and the fizz.

Guests came often, over the weekend or for longer stays. Most were relatives and friends whose visits we took in our stride; at least one was memorable: the visit by the geographer Jan Broek and his family, our first Americans, in 1946. As a graduate student, Jan, who had been Mother's first love, had gone to the United States, where he had met and married Ruth. Returning to Holland with his bride in 1932, he had been unable to find an academic job and had taken one in Berkeley, California. The war interrupted contact, but in 1945 they restored it in spectacular fashion. Ruth Broek organized a network of families in the San Francisco Bay area, among them the Champions, the Finkbines, the Jolys, and the Sampsons, who sent parcels of food, clothing, and toys to us and to other Dutch families.

In August 1946, Jan having been appointed to the chair of geography at Utrecht, he, Ruth, their three children, and Jan's secretary arrived to stay with us for a few days – there were sleeping bags everywhere – before settling down in Utrecht. Jan Maarten was roughly my age; Janna and Trudy were a few years older. Both girls could draw horses, which greatly impressed me: I was quite unable to produce a satisfactory equine likeness. All three exuded an aura of wealth – in the clothes they wore, the toys they had, the way they behaved – that impressed me even more. An academic's family would not have been rich by American standards, but they were by mine. Holland was poor; America was the land of milk and honey. I was not surprised when they returned to the States after two years. Who would want to put up with the shortages and rationing of Holland when they could claim the riches of America?

There were always visitors on New Year's Eve. We were woken up just before midnight and sat in front of the large fireplace, gradually coming to, sipping a beaker of mulled wine, eating the deep-fried *oliebollen* and apple flaps, sprinkled with icing sugar, that were the only dishes Mother seemed to enjoy preparing. Just before midnight we got up on chairs, jumping off at the last stroke of twelve. Then we watched Father set off fireworks. At 12:30 we returned to bed, satisfied that the year had been well and truly brought in.

New Year's Eve was a major feast: the third within a month. We children received and, in time, exchanged gifts on St Nicholas's Eve; Christmas was an important religious and family festival. (Separating the two occasions has saved the Dutch Christmas from becoming the frantic potlatch and carnival it is in North America.) St Nicholas's Eve was great fun, not only because of the gifts but also because of the custom of giving elaborately wrapped non-gifts, lumps of coal and the like. Father got a lot of them. His reaction was superb: feigned surprise and mock distress. 'Daar hebben ze me weer!' (They've got me again!) he would exclaim as we collapsed in helpless laughter.

One custom associated with the festival is that children receive a chocolate letter, the first of their first names. Each letter had the same weight, so that my 'M' did not give me an advantage over Joe or Jan D.; but the convolutions of my letter encouraged a practice I might well have adopted in any case. Each day I bit off a small piece, slowly allowing the dark chocolate to melt in my mouth. In this way I managed to keep nibbling well into January. To my brothers, who rarely made their letters last a week, I sententiously quoted Father: 'Wie wat bewaart, die heeft wat' (He who saves, has). Neither this nor my frugality was endearing, but the practice probably reinforced my natural conservatism.

Each of us had a plot in the garden; mine contained a strawberry patch and some perennials in which I took great pride. The backyard sloped gently down, and on warm summer days we used the garden hose to start a creek that ran from the side of the house to a hole we had dug at the bottom of the garden, behind Mother's gooseberry and currant bushes. Our experiments in hydraulic engineering were marvellously muddy. Because we could not be seen from the road or from the neighbouring gardens we often shed our swimsuits. One Sunday Jack and I got annoyed with Joe and chased him past the side of the house into the Emmalaan. There he stood, naked and swearing, an affront to pious passers-by in language and appearance both.

Sheltered from the wind on two sides by brick walls, the sandbox was popular with the younger children. Behind one of those walls we held contests to see who could piss highest up the wall, or joined in *kruisjepiesen* (cross-pissing), the objective being to hit another stream of urine with one's own. These contests went undetected by adults who might have disapproved, for we could not be seen from the house. With lots of trees and shrubs, our garden was well suited to hide-and-seek, or cowboys and Indians. The front yard was good for kicking a soccer ball around, and several of the trees were fun to climb. Inspired by the 1948 Olympic Games, we tried to turn ourselves into track stars, wearing a path into the lawn in the process.

In winter, snow was always welcome. Holland gets more than its share of rain, however, and rain kept us inside. Until renovations eliminated it in 1951 we had a playroom off the dining-room, with a swing and benches and shelves for our toys. But we never liked to be confined to it, preferring to use the whole house for our games.

As we got older we played more board and card games: Parcheesi, Old Maid, Chinese checkers, Monopoly, canasta. None of us liked to lose, so games were apt to be disputatious. Opa Reitsma taught me chess. I was a keen pupil, and, finding my brothers to be no match for me, looked forward to visits from Opa or my cousin Tjitte, six years my senior. They almost always beat me, but there was no disgrace in that. Everyone's favourite game was *sjoelbakken*, a form of tabletop shuffleboard.

At school there was an annual cycle of games, among them marbles and *kastie*. I was good at the former, which made it a cheap way of enjoying myself. Once, however, I was almost cleaned out by an older girl. She set me up cleverly: at first she let me win. When she had me believing I was the better player her game steadily improved. By the time I withdrew in confusion she had most of my shooters.

Like marbles, *kastie* had simple rules and allowed any number of participants. Moreover, it was a game manufacturer's nightmare: literally dirt cheap, needing only a slit dug into the ground, a large stick, and a small one. A boulevard was space enough; there were no cars around to get in our way.

Kastie could be played as a two-team game or, more usually, as one in which each played against everybody else. In that case, one player was at bat, as it were, while all the others were in the field. In the first round, the batter placed the small stick over the slit, and used the larger stick to lift it out and as far away as possible. If one of the fielders caught the small stick, the batter was out. Failing that, one of the fielders tossed the small stick at the large one, which the batter had placed on the ground over the slit. Hit the large stick or get the small stick into the slit, and the batter was out. Assuming neither of these occurred, the batter got points according to how many times the large stick could be turned end over end in measuring the distance between the small stick after it had been thrown back and the nearest point along the slit.

The second round proceeded like the first, except that the batter held both sticks, tossed the small one in the air, and hit it with the large one. Failure to hit the small stick was an out. The third round was a bonus round because it was the most difficult. The batter leaned the small stick in the slit, using the large stick to hit the small one on the protruding end and then, when it was in the air, hit it again. The fielders could try to catch it, but if they did not, the batter was entitled to measure for points the entire distance between the slit and the spot at which the small stick came to rest. Then another batter took a turn according to a prearranged order. I spent many an enjoyable hour in this way.

In physical education we played outdoor games when the weather permitted: *slagbal* (a form of rounders), or *korfbal* (akin to basketball, it could be played indoors or outdoors). *Voetbal*, soccer, we played rarely at school because, unlike the other two, it was deemed to be unsuitable for girls. I was a mediocre athlete, just barely good enough to avoid the ignominy of being picked last or next-to-last when captains chose sides. My sole triumph was second place in the grade six high jump, the fruit of much practice in our backyard. But I enjoyed games.

Jack and I became cubs in 1949. The clubhouse of the Wilco Jiskoot scout group and cub pack was near our house, just across the Amsterdamse Straatweg, then the highway between Amsterdam and Amersfoort, on which I had almost been killed a few years before. (Peter and I had disobeyed a parental decree not to cross it without adult accompaniment. On the way back, I almost ran into the path of a car but stopped in the middle of the road. It missed me by a metre or two.) I liked the cub pack and the many games we played; I did not like the scout group I graduated into. A couple of the older boys were bullies, and the leader was remote and humourless, quite unlike the agreeable young women who had taken the roles of Akela, Bagheera, and Baloo. Before qualifying for initiation I quit.

Most of the cubs, like my playmates generally, were from the NBS. My first close friend was Joost Wolsak, who lived nearby with his younger brother, Diederik, their mother, and her parents. Their mansion on the corner of the Jacob van Lenneplaan and the Amsterdamse Straatweg was surrounded by an extensive garden, some of it wild and all of it superbly suited to games. One day we climbed a ladder to the second floor of a tool shed and found some novel toys. Joost's mother was appalled to find us playing with Sten guns and pistols (fortunately unloaded), complete with clips of ammunition. I imagine someone in the resistance had hidden them during or after the war and they had somehow been forgotten. We were greatly annoyed when she confiscated everything. What incredible spoilsports mothers can be!

Of the girls in my class, Louise Hasseley Kirchner was my early favourite. In grade four I forsook her for Jeannette Langenberg, however, who cemented our friendship by giving me stamps from Curaçao, a Dutch colony where her father was working. In grade five, peer pressure brought an end to playing with girls except at birthday parties. At mine, which I usually shared with Jack and Peter, Father showed films on a rented projector: comedies starring the likes of Harold Lloyd and Laurel and Hardy. We did not receive gifts from our guests, and they did not get 'loot bags.' In that more austere time it was apparently thought to be sufficient that everyone got a piece of birthday cake.

I remember also birthday parties at the homes of Louise, Willem Hendrik de Beaufort, René Hooftgraafland (after Joost, these two were my best friends), Karel Henny, and other children. Best of all were Jan Escher's parties in the house and garden of his home on the Van Heemstralaan. In fair weather or foul his father kept us engrossed. I knew that he had designed a postage stamp in 1949,

but neither I nor, I suppose, any of the other children who played
with his son knew the tall man with the tidy beard and penetrating
eyes as the renowned graphic artist M.C. Escher.

Illness, not my own but Peter's and Mother's, affected me markedly. I had a robust constitution, and my ailments were limited to
colds and children's diseases such as measles and mumps. I was
in hospital only once, to have my tonsils removed. (The anaesthetic
was inadequate and the surgeon still at work when I came to.
Perhaps my good health since then has a psychosomatic origin: a
fear of operations!) Peter suffered from asthma, however, and in
1946 he was sent to Switzerland, where the air was better for someone with respiratory problems. He returned little improved and
departed again in 1947, this time for a year. Later he stayed for
some months at an institution on the North Sea coast.

In his absence, I became the oldest child, a role I was loath to
surrender when he returned. With Jack as my ally, I fought to retain
it. Mother wrote in my baby's book at some point that he and I
were thick as thieves while neither of us got on well with Peter.
That pattern continued, to my advantage.

We were habitually put to bed early, to free the mother's help
and allow our parents to dine without being disturbed by children.
In bed before I was ready for sleep, I became a storyteller, entertaining my brothers with tales of my own invention about Piet
Sjarrink the detective, Tuschinsky the bicycle racer, Popeye the
sailor, and the families we would have when we grew up. When
Peter came home he tried to take over. I opined that his stories,
which tended to the fantastic, were inferior to mine. (To this day I
have little use for fantasy or science fiction, with rare exceptions
such as Walter Miller's A Canticle for Leibowitz.) Jack and Joe backed
me; Peter was reduced to a resentful silence. He justifiably resented
also that in his absence we had largely demolished his Meccano
set. In turn we resented him because our dog, Brummel, had to go:
it was feared that Peter might be allergic to him. Had a vote been
taken ...

It would have required skill on our parents' part to maintain
Peter as an effective oldest son, not least because he wasn't strong

enough to beat me in a fight. But they were too preoccupied with Mother's health to give him the help he needed. After Steven's birth, Mother's physician had advised her against having another child. Eager for a daughter, she had rejected his advice. Our youngest brother, Jan Daniel (Jan D.), was born in April 1947. Immediately afterwards Mother got phlebitis, and for the rest of her life her health was more or less impaired.

Father's reaction was symptomatic of a less than harmonious marriage: he partially blamed her for her illness. Indeed, he rarely gave her much support, tending to find fault instead. However, Mother gave as good (or bad) as she got. Having hoped for a secure middle-class marriage, she found that money was not infrequently in short supply. She blamed Father's indifference to wealth and position, his unwillingness to cosy up to influential people or entertain for professional advantage, his disagreeable frankness when he thought that someone, even a client, was wasting his time. Mother sometimes claimed we could not afford this attitude; he said we could, were it not for her extravagance. They yelled at each other a good deal. Both had tempers that flared up suddenly, but while he restricted himself to words she sometimes kicked or hit him. Once she took off her shoe and whacked him on the head with the heel, cutting his scalp; on another occasion she pelted him with porridge. If nothing else, this had the force of novelty.

In defence of Mother: there were two adults and six children to be fed and clothed, a mother's help, a twice-weekly charwoman, and an occasional gardener to be paid, mortgage payments, light, heat, and maintenance, medical expenses, school fees, and so on and so forth. In defence of Father: in order to augment his income he spent most of his spare time designing houses for private clients. (He also won the competition to design Baarn's war memorial. It faces the railway station, a gently curved wall adorned by a cross and the dates 1940 and 1945.)* But when I overheard our parents, I didn't worry about right and wrong; I wanted them to stop fighting. Years later, when I read D.H. Lawrence's short story 'The

---

* Wim Ramaker and Ben van Bohemen, *Sta een ogenblik stil ... Monumentenboek 1940–45* (Kampen 1980), 45, 144.

Rocking Horse Winner,' I could identify with its young protagonist.

Aware that money was often tight, I thought of us as poor or close to it, the more so because some of our neighbours had cars, tennis courts, and swimming pools. I knew we weren't *really* poor, but the condition of the genuinely deprived did not shape my standards of wealth and poverty. After all, I had no way of knowing how those people lived. Indeed, except in so far as they provided services, I had no contact with the working-class poor, in school or outside it. They lived in *het rode dorp*, red village, so called either because all the roofs were red-tiled or because its inhabitants voted Labour or Communist.

One woman who lived there kept our house clean for a while, until Mother dismissed her after a flaming row that I witnessed because it was summer and we were home from school. One of this woman's remarks made a big impression on me. When the revolution came, she warned Mother, we would be kicked out of our nice, big house, and she and her family would move in, while we could try living in their *krot*, their slum hovel. I felt a bit threatened but even more surprised: if she thought *our* house was big, how would she describe the homes of some of my friends – Louise's, for example, or Willem Hendrik's, or René's?

After Jan D.'s birth, Mother was hospitalized periodically. Even when at home she had to rest a good deal. She continued to read to us, do needlepoint, and knit sweaters (she was able to knit while reading), but she had less energy than before. We suffered some neglect as a result. No mother's help or housekeeper could be a fully effective mother surrogate to six boys, and Father was unable to pay much attention to us. However, that neglect enabled me to act in many ways as though I were the oldest son.

As a result of Mother's poor health, too, I spent a certain amount of time away from home after April 1947. Jack and I together were easier to accommodate than either of us alone, for we kept each other busy. Usually, then, he and I went together. Soon after Jan D.'s birth, we stayed with Father's favourite sister, Toos (Catharina), a cheerful, matter-of-fact woman whose two daughters had already left home. Her husband, Oom Hans, was mayor (in Hol-

land an appointed official) of Neede, a town in Gelderland near
the German border, but we were less impressed by his eminence
than by the fresh eggs we got at breakfast. Eggs were still rationed:
at home we saw them only on Sundays. But Tante Toos or, perhaps
more accurately, one of the servants kept chickens in a corner of
her large garden.

An attempt to place Jack and me with two of Mother's maternal
aunts was less successful. Three of these great-aunts of ours lived
in nearby Bussum. The oldest, Tante Wenda (Wendelina), was in
her seventies. Whether her husband, a Reformed clergyman, was
still alive I don't know; I do remember that she lived in a large
house with a large garden. Her sisters shared a more modest home.
Tante Phie (Sophia) was the widow of a Lutheran professor of
divinity; Tante Loes (Louise), the youngest, had never married and
worked in Bussum's public library. We stayed with Tantes Phie
and Loes for several days in the summer of 1947 or 1948. I recall a
plethora of Indonesian *objets d'art*, none of which we were allowed
to touch except under close supervision, and a garden where we
had to be careful not to stray off the path. Our aunts were sweet,
but they had trouble coping with two boys. From our point of view
the restrictions were too many. We were happy when Father
turned up to take us home.

At least twice I visited Opa Reitsma in Utrecht, going by myself
because I could play with my cousin Hans (Steven Otto), who was
a year older than I, while his mother, Tante Tück (Ruth), would
make sure that I was fed and bathed. Opa lived on the ground
floor of a stately three-storey row house on the Stadhouderslaan.
Oom Kees, Tante Tück, Hans, and his older sister, Marlies, occupied the rest.

As I collected stamps and played chess, pastimes Opa also enjoyed, I got on famously with him. Most of the time I spent with
Hans, however. Usually we played well together, but once, while
marching some toy soldiers around the floor of his bedroom, we
got into a fight that began when I insulted Germans. Hans objected:
his mother was German. I indignantly demanded to know whether
he was a *landverrader*, a traitor. This cut very close to the bone, as
his father had fought in the *Waffen-SS* during the war and had been

deprived of his Dutch nationality as a result. (Although my parents suspected my uncle of still holding his Nazi views, in dealing with me he was always sweet-tempered and very kind. Agreeable people can have execrable morals or opinions – I'm now thinking also of a neo-conservative friend – while people who are good may well be quite disagreeable.) Hans yelled at me; I yelled back.

Drawn to the commotion, Tante Tück, upon hearing what the quarrel was about, told her son to button up. He did, but for the remainder of my visit he was cool. He carried no long-term grudge, however: the next time I came to Utrecht he invited me to a First Division soccer match. I also climbed Utrecht's Dom tower with him. The central part of the great cathedral's nave had collapsed during a storm in the seventeenth century; since then the tower, at over 100 metres the tallest in the country, stood by itself. When I reached the top I was thrilled to see the city and much of the province at my feet. I even fancied I could see Baarn.

My preferred destination was the house of Mother's widowed sister-in-law, Tante Pieta (Pieternella). She, her companion, whom I remember only as Oom Fer, and her brood of five lived in Doorwerth, a village near Oosterbeek, west of Arnhem. The house was on the Italiaanseweg, a narrow brick road said to have been built by Napoleon's engineers, which wound its way from the wooded heights above the Rhine down into the plain. It passed by Doorwerth Castle, a favourite place because it housed mementoes of Operation 'Market Garden' in the fall of 1944 (the English bridgehead had been nearby).

Military equipment, including a damaged German tank and several field guns, decorated the grounds. These were impressive; but more deeply engraved in my memory are two photos that I first saw there. They were of a German staff car with two bodies hanging half in, half out, blood oozing from each. (Years later I read in Cornelius Ryan's book *A Bridge Too Far*, which contains one of the photos, that the men were a Major-General Kussin and his driver, who had been ambushed by an English patrol.) Somehow this made the war more real than anything I actually remembered of it. One moment these two men had been alive, alert, on urgent business; the next moment they were dead. I was still at a stage where I tended to think that the only good German was a dead one, but these photos took me aback.

Tante Pieta's house had been damaged during the battle, and restoring it was a time-consuming family project in which Jack and I were encouraged to join. During our stays in Doorwerth we chipped mortar off dozens of bricks, at one cent each. But there was lots of time for play, to which the park-like surroundings were superbly suited.

Our cousin Tjitte, good at soccer and chess, was our hero; his younger brother, Henk, was less accomplished but played a mean game of table tennis. Both allowed us to take an occasional drag from the cigarettes they smoked; this made me feel grown-up, even though I didn't like the taste. Maja, a sober-minded girl, *nuchter* as the Dutch say, was a few days older than I; some said we were a lot like each other. Thera, more whimsical than her older sister, was a month or so Jack's junior. They were the next best thing to having sisters of our own. Ineke, born in 1944, was of little interest.

In August 1948 Jack and I stayed with wartime neighbours who had moved to The Hague, the Gevers Deynoot family (Meneer Gevers Deynoot had helped Father tap the German electricity supply in 1944). Here we were introduced to mixed nude bathing. At first we were reluctant to remove our underpants in the presence of Elisabeth, who was Joe's age, but her mother insisted. Whether she was trying to save hot water or time I don't know. Whatever the case, we soon lost our inhibitions.

Though on the young side, Elisabeth was an agreeable companion, and there were lots of other children in the neighbourhood to play with, but for me the greatest attraction was the North Sea at nearby Scheveningen. I can't recall whether I was on a beach before that year. I do remember that I loved both the salt water and the sandy beach.

When Father announced in 1949 that we would spend two weeks in Wijk aan Zee, for him the scene of fond childhood memories, I was thrilled. Few other holidays do I remember with so much pleasure: frisking in the breaking waves, catching shrimp with small nets attached to sticks, building sand castles and watching them erode at floodtide, walking along the *strand* to the IJmuiden breakwater where we watched ships enter and leave the canal to Amsterdam, admiring the view from the dunes behind our *pension*, exploring concrete bunkers that had been part of the German defence line (for adults grim reminders of war; for us, exciting aids to play), eating ice-cream wafers and *patates frites*, falling asleep to the rhythmic grinding of the village water pump (we gave it the onomatopoeic name *tetjeroem*), and above all celebrating my tenth birthday in glorious sunshine on the beach. Nobody worried about ultraviolet rays or the ozone layer, and only the occasional stinging jellyfish reminded us that nature is less than perfect. *Où sont les plages d'antan?*

The next year we rented a house in Katwijk aan Zee for all of August. That was too long. It rained a lot, and when the weather kept us indoors, away from the beach, we got cranky. The best time was when Maja and Thera came to visit. In 1951 we returned to Wijk aan Zee, this time having luck with the weather. I wanted to keep going there forever.

Outside of the provinces of Utrecht, Gelderland, and the two Hollands I saw little of my country of birth. I went on two school trips into the south, the most interesting to Valkenburg and Vaals in Limburg. Near Vaals was the highest point in the Netherlands, the 330-metres-high Drielandenpunt. Here one could, by walking around a post, pass through both Belgium and Germany. It was the only time before our emigration that I 'left' my native country. I returned home full of the hilly country I had hiked through, only to be squashed by Peter. *He* had seen real mountains in Switzerland; what I had seen were little more than pimples in comparison. I did not thank him for the correction.

Father liked taking us to the city of his birth. I thought Amsterdam was splendid, although when I first heard that all its buildings were supported by wooden piles, some 14,000 for the palace on the Dam alone, I worried a bit. A children's song came to mind: 'Amsterdam, die grote stad, / die is gebouwd op palen; / Als die stad eens ommeviel, / wie zou dat betalen?' (Amsterdam, that great city, is built on piles; if that city should collapse, who would pay for that?). (This financial query was perhaps typical: like the

Scots, the Dutch are proverbially *zuinig*, frugal.) I liked the hustle and bustle of the Damrak, Rokin, and the narrow Kalverstraat; I loved the picturesque canals in the older part of the city. (The splendour of the seventeenth-century 'big three,' the Prinsengracht, Keizersgracht, and Herengracht, was largely lost on me until I saw them again in 1961.) Along one of these old canals Mother's sister, Tante Phiet, lived with her husband, the University of Amsterdam political scientist Jef Suijs, and, after May 1949, their daughter, Flora. Nearby was the Oriental quarter, where scores of restaurants served Indonesian and Chinese food. Everywhere, sidewalk stalls sold pickled herring: I liked mine filleted and chopped into pieces, then dipped in diced raw onion. But herring tasted almost insipid compared with *paling*, eel, smoked or poached. Infinitely rich in taste and texture, eel was a Lucullan delight.

The city held many marvels. In the Rijksmuseum, one Rembrandt painting, *De Staalmeesters* (The Syndics of the Cloth Guild), made an impression on me: the tablecloth looked so real! But I preferred Artis, the zoo with its exotic animals. Then there was the Bijenkorf, the big department store on the Dam. The first time I got on one of its escalators was a magic moment.

Hilversum, easily reached by bicycle, I got to know almost as well as my home town. My usual destination was a stamp dealer near the railway station, where I added to my collection of Dutch and colonial stamps. After I had almost exhausted my money, I would cycle farther into town, buying an ice-cream wafer or Mars bar before returning home. A market day offered diversion, but not as much as the occasional *kermis* (fair) with its rides and games.

Baarn was adjacent to the Eemland, where dairying was the economic mainstay. I did not like farms. Cows frightened me, manure stank, and, misunderstanding an anecdote Father told about the early days of the automobile, I had got the idea that farmers were unintelligent. Some of them had taken to feeding their chickens in the road, Father said, using a Klaxon to signal mealtime. When a motorcar happened along, its driver warning of his approach with his horn, chickens rushed to meet it. Close behind were their owners. Failing utterly to grasp the point of the story – the shrewd farmers must have exacted a handsome price for any fowl run over – I concluded that they were not much brighter than their stupid chickens.

Early in 1946 a Lutheran clergyman who had been a friend of Opa Horn reminded Father that so far only Peter had been baptized, and urged him to correct the oversight. On 21 April, our parents' tenth wedding anniversary, Jack, Joe, and Steven joined me at the baptismal font in the Evangelical Lutheran Church in Hilversum. Two years later we were enrolled in the Lutheran Sunday school in Baarn. The teacher was an old friend of Father's, Dora Cazant-van Oort, with whom we got on famously. In 1949, Jack and I began to spend weekends with her and her husband, Willem Cazant.

The Cazants were in their forties and childless. She was tall and generously proportioned, with a beaming smile behind thick spectacles. He was short and almost spare, and his somewhat dour expression, Jack and I thought, gave his face a slight resemblance to that of the goat he kept at the back of the garden. She was even-tempered; he was prickly, with a waspish sense of humour. She liked to talk; he said little. But we liked both. They lived on the Kettingweg, near the railway station, in a large house more crowded than one might have inferred from its size. It was not only a residence but also a place of business, for the Cazants owned and ran a small firm that made support hose and therapeutic foundation garments. It must have been reasonably prosperous: they owned a car at a time when few people did, and they holidayed annually in Switzerland.

On a typical weekend we arrived in time for Saturday dinner, with Meneer's mother, whom we called Mevrouw Oma, usually there as well. After washing up we played games until the radio was turned on for a variety show, *Negen heit de klok* (The Clock Tolls Nine). At 10:00 Jack and I went to bed. The next morning we accompanied Mevrouw Cazant to Sunday school or church (Meneer Cazant never went). After lunch the four of us hiked into the woods of the Royal Domain unless the weather was foul. From the Cazants I learned an abiding disapproval of litterbugs. We did our bit to keep the woods clean, using sharpened sticks to spear rubbish and depositing the harvest in refuse bins. By 4:00 we were back at the Cazant home, drinking tea; then Jack and I cycled home.

The Cazants acted as though sensible behaviour could be expected from us; I think we obliged. We probably sensed that, if we were difficult, the weekends would end. (Children behave worst with their parents, partly because they know these are stuck with them. Others can always send them home.) The Cazants were genuinely good people, and she was lovable. She lived according to the dictates of her faith but didn't burden others with it. She simply made them its beneficiaries. At the time I loved no one more, not even Mother.

Astonishingly, given my current interests, music did not form a large part of my life. No one insisted I take lessons, and I didn't volunteer. My hobbies were philately, drawing, and reading. I became steadily better informed about stamps, and by the time I was eleven I was buying First Day covers. By that time, too, I had moved beyond Harlekijntje, Bolke de Beer, and Nils Holgersson to novels by Karl May and Jules Verne, savouring the adventures of Old Shatterhand and Winnetou, Captain Nemo and Phileas Fogg. I was also starting to read adult fiction: Anne de Vries's *Bartje* trilogy and the historical novels of Marjorie Bowen. I read Tante Phiet's book on Greek mythology, written for use in secondary schools. Its style was conversational and its illustrations racy: the men wore little or nothing, the women had shapely breasts, splendid hips, and, in the case of Aphrodite, shown rising from the sea, an enticing thatch of pubic hair. (Later editions were more demurely illustrated in order to secure a wider market.) This volume supplemented my perusal of van de Velde's *Encyclopedie der sexuele wetenschappen* (Encyclopaedia of Sexual Knowledge) a book not on the open shelves but accessible. Mother and Father probably wanted us to read it because it saved them having to explain the facts of life to us. Neither ever did.

Radio was an important source of entertainment. I listened to children's drama, music shows, and sports. American pop hits were popular: I recall songs by Nat 'King' Cole, Doris Day, and

Teresa Brewer. U.S. cultural influences were strong in other ways. Walt Disney comic books were available in translation; the films we watched were mostly American: *Pinocchio, Bambi, Alice in Wonderland, Lassie Come Home,* and various westerns. Television, of course, was not part of my life: it did not reach Holland until late 1951 or early 1952. I was part of the last generation to reach adolescence without TV, and in this respect as in many others I count myself as blessed.

We subscribed to a Hilversum daily and a Baarn bi-weekly. At first I read only the comic strips: *Panda, Tom Poes, Olle Kapoen, Kapitein Rob.* But I followed the 1948 London Olympic Games because a Dutch sprinter, Fanny Blankers-Koen, won four gold medals. By 1948, too, I was beginning to read news stories: about Czechoslovakia, the Berlin airlift, and the end of the Dutch empire in the East. The communist victory in China troubled me; in 1950 I followed the course of the Korean War almost as closely as I did the Tour de France.

I had no doubt about the nature of the war: the Soviets were seeking to subjugate Korea as a step towards conquering all of Asia. This analysis I owed mainly to Father and Mother. Neither was notably well-informed, but both were opinionated. Supporters of the right-wing VVD,* successor to the pre-war Liberal party, they feared and hated what Father called 'het rode tuig' (red scum). Fervently wanting to see the East Indies retained for Holland, for example, they saw little but communism behind the movement for Indonesian independence.

Mother's interest, of course, was due to her birth on Java. Father, who actually took the harder line, expressed the view that if only the government had shot the nationalist leader, Sukarno, in the 1930s, there would have been no talk of an independent Indonesia ten years later. At the time I believed this; later I would realize it was nonsense. The drive for independence in 1949 was a foregone conclusion. Whether it has served most Indonesians well is another matter, and the peoples of West Irian and East Timor have had

---

* Vereniging voor Vrijheid en Demokratie.

cause to regret the replacement of Dutch and Portuguese by Indonesian imperialism.

In the spring of 1951 I joined scores of other children in the gymnasium of the Baarnsch Lyceum to compete for a place in first year. We wrote papers in Dutch language and literature and in mathematics; there may have been one in French as well. Unable to imagine that I could fail, I didn't worry about the outcome. Some time later, the headmaster, Meneer van Dijk, entered our classroom and read the names of those who had been admitted. Only six had fallen short, among them, unhappily, my friend René Hooftgraafland. The failure of a few classmates didn't dampen the general mood of joy, however. Indeed, for some it may have intensified it: 'There but for the grace of God ...' After six years in the NBS we were ready for something new.

The Baarnsch Lyceum, which I entered in September, was a private, non-sectarian institution reputed to be among the best secondary schools in the country. It drew its students not only from Baarn but from several nearby communities; among them were Crown Princess Beatrix and, in due time, her younger sisters and her children. Most students came by bicycle. The school being located in the Villa Waldheim on the Stationsweg near the railway station, a few arrived by bus or train.

The Lyceum boasted some very good teachers. I liked most of my courses, especially English, geography, classics (ancient history and mythology: the study of Latin and Greek would have begun in second year had I chosen the humanities option), mathematics, music appreciation, art, and physical education. I enjoyed Dutch language and literature, even though the teacher didn't bathe often enough and stank of rancid sweat. Science, on the other hand, was boring, and French I hated because the teacher was a bully who seemed to have it in for me. Ever since, I have thought of him as a model of what a teacher should *not* be.

We were in class Mondays through Fridays from 8:00 a.m. to 2:00 p.m., Saturdays from 8:00 to 12:00. A twenty-minute break at noon was just long enough to allow us to eat a sandwich. After school I usually cycled home, where a snack and a mug of cold tea would be waiting. Homework, up to three hours of it, followed, but if I wanted to play I generally managed to find time for it.

The school imposed a tougher grind than the NBS, but in the autumn term I easily held my own. In January I got a serious respiratory infection, however. I was quarantined and had to sleep in Father's studio; only a series of penicillin shots kept me out of hospital. I missed five weeks of school. Having made an effort to do some work only in the subjects I liked most, classical studies, English, and geography, I was still struggling to catch up to my peers when I learned in late March that further effort would be unnecessary. We were leaving for Canada in May.

2

The Great Migration

When did our parents begin to think about emigration? I don't know, although it must have been sometime in 1951. Nor do I know with complete certainty why they decided to leave. Father used to say that Mother wanted to go, that he had been sceptical but had given in. Having come to the view that emigration had been a mistake – 'de grootste stommiteit van m'n leven' (the biggest blunder of my life), he said to me once – it may have suited him to hold her responsible. The only benefit of going to Canada, he added, was that he had ended up in a place whose scenery and climate were superior to Holland's. Professionally and financially he lost ground that he never regained. In Holland he had connections, in Canada none. He had to qualify himself anew at an age when architects have either attained some eminence or are close to it. And Canadians were much less likely than Netherlanders to ask an architect to design a house for them. But he didn't dwell much on such matters. It helped that, although he liked to do good work, he was not otherwise especially ambitious.

Mother never admitted – not to me, in any case – that emigration had been a mistake. Holland had been in danger of falling prey to communism, she said, and had offered us no future. She had found it easier to leave than Father, I think, because she was less rooted in the Netherlands. Born in the tropics, living in the highlands of Java for her first fifteen years, she was unimpressed by Holland's dank climate and its flat terrain. (It was meant as great praise for southern Vancouver Island when she said that it reminded her of the area around Bandung.) And in an important way she found life in Victoria easier than in Baarn. Father's income was lower, and without domestic help she had to work harder. But there was no one in Victoria she felt the need to impress.

In Baarn she did feel that need. A telling incident comes to mind. At the start of the 1951–2 school year, Queen Juliana and Prince Bernhard transferred two of their daughters to the NBS. Princess Margriet joined Steven in a regular grade three class; Princess Irene, who had lost a year, was placed in a special grade six class. The half-dozen or so children joining her were mostly Jack's classmates, but he was not among the elect. Jack didn't mind, nor did Father, for he was not notably *oranjegezind*, monarchy-minded. Mother, however, lobbied hard to have Jack included: in vain. Soon afterwards, she and I cycled to Hilversum together. Her conversation with me on the way there and back made it abundantly clear that she felt the implied slight to her social status as a humiliation.

Far more important than this incident was that late in 1951 she and Father faced a difficult decision: should he stay with the government or set out on his own? Since the war he had resumed a private practice in his spare time. The anti-modernist houses he designed were very much to his clients' taste, and his income from this source grew steadily. Then he designed an entire subdivision of row houses, the *Schildersbuurt* – its streets were named after Dutch painters – on the northeastern outskirts of Baarn. This was too much for his superiors to ignore, and they ordered him to cease moonlighting or resign.

This put him in a quandary. His salary alone was inadequate for his needs, yet private practice was risky. He had been able to rely on a single source of income in the 1930s, but since then he had acquired a large family. He doubted that he could earn enough, alone or in partnership, to compensate for the loss of his civil service income. In spite of the Marshall Plan, the economy was recovering only slowly and the future seemed unclear. What to do?

Emigration seemed to offer a way out of his dilemma: an avoidance-avoidance conflict, as years later I learned to call it in a psychology course. Instead of having to decide between his job and private practice, he could escape. Had he been faced with the choice two or three years later he would probably have chosen private practice and might well have prospered. He might have chosen it in 1952 had Mother wished to stay. But she wanted to go, and he fell in with her. Giving their sons a better future became the justification for their choice.

A better future for the children: this motive served many Netherlanders as reason for leaving during the immediate postwar years. In 1947 farm and factory workers began to emigrate; by 1951 interest had spread to the middle classes. Thousands of people saw overseas as more promising than Holland, still struggling to recover from the war. Young adults and parents of large families were particularly apt to form this view. The Gaasenbeeks, neighbours with five or six children, were planning to leave. (They settled in Hamilton, Ontario.) This helped our parents reach their own decision.

Canada was not their first choice. They would have preferred California because they knew people there. Mother, her English better than Father's, wrote to Neil and Evelyn Sampson, acquaintances in Berkeley, to inquire what the opportunities for an architect might be. California was a magnet for Americans, Neil replied; it would be hard for a foreigner to make his way. The United States had a quota system for immigrants, moreover, so we would face a long wait. Why not try Canada? It lagged behind the States economically but was eager for immigrants.

When Father made inquiries at the Canadian embassy he learned that Canada had no compulsory military service, a key point to a man with six sons (Holland had conscription). He also learned that a job offer eased the process of applying for immigration and set out to obtain one. A friend knew someone who knew someone; soon Father had an offer from a Victoria firm of architects for a job as a draughtsman at $300 per month until he should have qualified himself as an architect in British Columbia. This translated into 1200 guilders, not a lot but acceptable. And Victoria, described by their friend as the 'Riviera of Canada,' sounded charming. By now committed to the emigration project, our parents did not ask whether costs of living were comparable, whether Father could soon expect to qualify, and what his prospects might then be.

One day we went to The Hague in the familiar rented limousine to be vetted by the Canadian immigration authorities. We hung about in a large room while Father and Mother talked to an official. The room was packed with young adults and children, many of them speaking what we had learned to consider a vulgarly accented Dutch. I was glad when we were free to leave. On the way home our parents sounded pleased: our admission to Canada was a certainty.

The house went up for sale. Currency-export restrictions were still in effect to protect Dutch foreign-exchange reserves, and emigrants could legally take with them only $100 per adult and $25 per child. Our parents therefore sought a purchaser with unblocked foreign currency: U.S. dollars or Swiss francs. People with the necessary resources soon turned up. The Schoute family had an account with a Swiss bank and transferred some thousands of francs to our credit with the Royal Bank of Canada.

Even after paying off the mortgage, a few thousand guilders, Father and Mother had a lot of money left over from the roughly 40,000 guilders ($10,000 at the then prevailing exchange rates) they had received. Not wishing to leave any of this in Holland, they spent some of it on clothes for all of us and some on a second honeymoon in Paris. The bulk went to pay for the passage to Victoria. The Holland-America Line had freighters on the Northwest Pacific run that accommodated passengers. The fare was not low, but that was not an issue. Indeed, we took our furniture, antiques, and most of our books. An embassy official had counselled against taking furniture, which he said was cheap in Canada and of high quality. But it made no sense to our parents to spend hard dollars on furniture in Canada when they could use guilders to take along their familiar possessions. This decision, at least, was wise.

At school I was a momentary centre of interest: the first (not the last) in my class to emigrate. My feelings were mixed. Emigration meant leaving behind classmates I had known for most of my life, and that I did *not* like. But it also meant not having to catch up, and being able to say farewell to my hateful French teacher. And after several years of reading Verne and May I was ready for some adventure of my own. On the whole, I looked forward to the change of scene. It must have been more difficult for our parents to say farewell to friends, relatives, and the house they had built for themselves. He would see it again, she would not.

In the late afternoon of Monday, 12 May 1952, we boarded the local train to Utrecht. It was pleasant spring weather, and many people had come to see us off. We changed trains in Utrecht, where Opa Reitsma and his companion, Mevrouw den Ouden, joined us for the second leg of the journey, the express to Rotterdam. After breakfast the next day we were on our way to the docks, noting that much war damage remained unrepaired. The SS *Diemerdijk*, one year old and 11,000 tons, looked glossily inviting. We said farewell to Opa, Mevrouw den Ouden, and a few others who had come to say their farewells; then the gangplank was taken away and the lines cast loose. The ship slowly left the quay while we waved and threw streamers to those staying behind.

A little over half of the forty-nine passengers embarked in Rotterdam; the remainder joined us in Tilbury, downstream from London, the next day. Some of them must have felt a twinge of apprehension as they read the passenger list and saw the names of *six* Masters Horn. We were the only children on board.

It took a good twenty-four hours to take on cargo in Tilbury, and the Holland-America Line laid on a bus trip (the first and last of its kind during the entire journey) so that those who had boarded in Rotterdam might while away the time. We went to Windsor Castle, where the Royal Chapel greatly impressed me. I was fascinated, too, by the Eton schoolboys, or, more accurately, by the top hats many of them wore. Lunch was served at a Windsor restaurant. I don't recall what the meal consisted of, but I do remember several of the Dutch passengers complaining that they hadn't eaten this badly since the early postwar period.

The passengers were of half a dozen or so nationalities, with American, Dutch, and British predominating. Almost all were middle-aged or older, the sole exception being a German woman in her twenties who was joining her physician husband in Vancouver. All were well-to-do; the most exalted, though probably not richest, passenger was a Bourbon princess of the Naples and Two Sicilies branch. I particularly liked Ella Rice, a fiftyish, chain-smoking widow from Seattle. She tried to improve our English, and as she rewarded progress with American coin I became a keen pupil. We had much to learn. Jack and I once visited her on the lower deck, where the cabins were smaller and the bathrooms had a shower stall instead of a tub. (Steven and Jan D. were quartered with Father and Mother in a stateroom under the bridge; the rest of us were in a large cabin farther back on the upper deck.) 'You have a douche,' I noted. She looked confused until I added that *we* had a bathtub. 'Don't call this a douche or people will think you rude,' she instructed us: 'It's called a shower.' Mother couldn't explain why 'douche' was rude. Our cabin attendant was more helpful.

Of the crew, I remember clearly only this attendant, Lucas Pama, and Captain L.M. Scriwanek, an avuncular man with a full head of grey hair and a kindly smile. Although he looked like St Nicholas, I vividly remember how he dressed down a passenger who, in defiance of the clearly posted regulations, had flicked a cigarette butt overboard. Did he not understand that this might cause a fire if the butt blew into an open porthole? and would he in future please use the brain God had given him? the captain said. The offender looked like a schoolboy caught cheating on a test.

On 19 May, Steven's eighth birthday, we passed through the Azores. By this time we had found our sea legs, and life had settled into a routine of eating, drinking, sports and games, and reading. The meals were good: there was ample choice, and the quality of the food was high. Those who got hungry between meals consoled themselves with snacks in mid-morning, at tea time, and late in the evening. I rarely got bored, for I liked reading, drawing, and playing games. There were a few chess players on board, but I quickly found that none presented a challenge. An English couple taught me cribbage, and I often joined them in the evening. The main sports were shuffleboard, table tennis, and quoits. There was no swimming-pool, but a small salt-water pool was set up on the cargo deck once we entered the Caribbean, and we spent a good deal of time in it.

Some evenings featured recorded dance music, but this was not a dancing crowd. Gambling was a different matter. The number of nautical miles covered during each twenty-four-hour period was the subject of a daily wager, and at least two evenings a week there were horse races, with the purser making book and the first officer throwing the dice that determined which wooden horse would win. I saved my own money, preferring to cheer on Mother's horse or that of Mrs Rice.

We reached the eastern entrance of the Panama Canal late one afternoon, passing through the canal the following day. A cold lunch was served on deck so no one would miss anything as we travelled through Gatun Lake, ringed by lush foliage, the steep-walled Gaillard Cut, and the locks. We exited in the afternoon, and set out on the large body of water ahead of us, the fabled Pacific Ocean. For the next few days we steamed up the west coast of Central America, looking at fishing villages and resort towns through Father's binoculars, marvelling at waterspouts, taking delight in the dolphins that sometimes swam alongside. Our first North American landfall was San Pedro, south of Los Angeles. In honour of the passengers who were disembarking, Captain Scriwanek hosted a gala dinner the evening before – the baked Alaska we had for dessert greatly impressed me. Many passengers collected signatures on menus. One woman wrote on each of ours: 'And may you become a good Canadian.'

Sunbaked and dusty, San Pedro did not impress. I didn't expect the quays or streets of America to be paved with gold, but these looked downright shabby. Only the palm trees and oil derricks kept the port from being commonplace. One day we took a streetcar into Los Angeles. I noted with amazement the large numbers of black people, the many large cars, and the ubiquitous television antennas. When we got to downtown L.A., Father rented a chauffeur-driven limousine, and we set out on a guided tour. Beverly Hills was everything I had imagined the United States to be: large houses and even larger gardens, complete with orange trees. Hollywood, on the other hand, was disappointing. We had been unable to get tickets for a studio tour, and fabled Sunset Boulevard looked run-down.

After Los Angeles we stopped at San Francisco, where we met the families who had sent the parcels of clothing and food that had brightened the early postwar years. They outdid each other in entertaining us, taking us to Golden Gate Park, the Muir Woods, Chinatown, and the University of California campus. Most memorable was the view from the Sampsons' home on Berkeley's Grizzly Peak Boulevard, 300 metres above San Francisco Bay: a panorama that included San Francisco as well as the Golden Gate and Bay bridges. There was nothing like this in Holland!

My memories of Seattle date from later visits; of Tacoma I remember next to nothing. On 17 June we berthed at Ogden Point, Victoria's outer harbour. After breakfast we finished packing and waited for an immigration officer to clear us. Father's employer, an ebullient Englishman named Patrick Birley, arrived with a newspaper photographer in tow. My brothers and I posed for the photograph referred to in the prologue. It appeared in the afternoon newspaper: six boys squinting into the morning sun.

We got into two cars and were driven along the waterfront. The views were superb: the Strait of Juan de Fuca, gentle hills to the west, snow-capped mountains to the south and east. This, too, was utterly unlike Holland! After fifteen minutes we stopped at a large white house. Here, at 1512 Beach Drive, Birley had arranged for us to stay until we found a place of our own. The Stenner family, whose home this was, were staying at their cottage at Patricia Bay, but Mrs Stenner was at the front door to welcome us and show Mother around the place. Although I liked the house, I was more impressed by the bay across the road. Soon we were playing along the rocky shore, Mt Baker dormant in the distance.

Located at the southeastern extremity of Vancouver Island, Victoria was founded by the Hudson's Bay Company as a trading post in 1843. It grew rapidly during the gold rush that began on the mainland in the late 1850s, and in 1871 it became the capital of the province of British Columbia. Eight decades later, the four municipalities of Victoria, Oak Bay, Esquimalt, and Saanich had a combined population of 120,000, with the provincial government, the naval base, the tourist industry, and retired people as the pillars of the local economy.

The city is among the most beautiful in North America. Wooded and hilly, no part of it is far from salt water and much of it is in view of mountains. The climate matches the scenery. Summer highs are in the low twenties, winter highs rarely much below ten degrees. Whereas the temperatures are typical of the West Coast marine climate, however, the rainfall pattern is Mediterranean. Most of the annual precipitation falls from October through March. Autumn lingers into December, frost and snow are rare even in January, and in February spring arrives. Trees and plants that grow almost nowhere on the Canadian mainland thrive in Victoria and its environs. Among them are the Garry oak, the California redwood, the rhododendron, and, most distinctively, the arbutus, a broad-leafed evergreen with an orange-brown trunk.

Beginning to explore our new home town, Jack and I made friends with Simon Wade, a boy Jack's age who lived on Beach Drive a few houses north of the Stenners. He was an architect's son who didn't seem to mind that our English was primitive. I did mind. It was frustrating not to understand or be understood. Early on, I bought an unwanted bottle of Coca-Cola in a store near Windsor Park because I was unable to explain that I really wanted ginger ale. I had asked for Canada Dry, which was what we had called ginger ale on the ship. The proprietor may have asked what kind of Canada Dry soft drink I wanted, but I did not grasp what he was saying. Unwilling to admit this, I chose a Coke instead.

We went to the main branch of the Royal Bank, a handsome building on Government Street (now occupied by Munro's Bookstore), where the dollars purchased with our Swiss francs were waiting for us. A few blocks down the street we admired the Inner Harbour, flanked by the Empress Hotel and the Parliament Building. We discovered that the latter was outlined by light-bulbs at night. Now, this strikes me as garish and wasteful; at the time I thought it was marvellous beyond words. Not only the effect impressed me but also the careless disregard for the cost of electricity. Such extravagance, unthinkable in Holland in the early postwar years, seemed proof positive of the wealth of our new country!

We visited our immigration officer, Hilda Parkinson, in her office near the Inner Harbour. She was a charming and refined woman of English background whom we were soon calling Aunt

Hilda. During the next few years she regularly dined with us; when we celebrated St Nicholas's Eve in 1952 she was an appreciative guest. (In 1953 or 1954 we began to exchange gifts at Christmas.) In turn she invited us to her cottage on Shawnigan Lake.

Father bought a McLaughlin-Buick limousine of late 1930s vintage that was large enough to carry us all in some comfort, and we began to explore the island. We drove along the west coast to Sooke and beyond – the tearoom at Point No Point became a favourite destination – and along the east coast north to Qualicum Beach and Parksville. The Malahat Drive was impressive, a real mountain road with splendid views south along Finlayson Arm to the Olympics, east to the Cascades and Mt Baker, and north to Saltspring Island. Driving into the Saanich peninsula, where farms were dotted between bits of forest, we saw our first North American Indians. A reserve near Patricia Bay was home to some hundreds of them. To me they seemed unimpressive compared to the Indians of film and fiction. Those were splendidly garbed in buckskins and feather headdresses; these looked scruffy and dispirited. It didn't occur to me at the time that much of our new country had been stolen from them.

During the next years, Indians remained remote from my mind. They didn't seem to be 'real' Canadians; in seeking to become Canadian, I did not see them as a model. In 1953 Mungo Martin created a replica of a Kwakiutl house in Thunderbird Park near the Empress Hotel. We watched him at work, carving and teaching his craft to an apprentice. Although picturesque, his labours seemed irrelevant. In fact, his activity may have reinforced my impression that Indians belonged to the past, not the future.

Our parents had hoped to buy a house, but the first time Mother went shopping she realized that Father's salary was much less ample than she had assumed it would be. The money that had been earmarked for a down payment would be needed for living expenses. We rented a white stucco bungalow on St Charles Street, two short blocks north of Ross Bay Cemetery. The large refrigerator was imposing, for at the time few people in Holland owned refrigerators, but we were less impressed by the house. The best that one could say for this rectangular box with its asphalt shingle roof was that it looked no worse than its neighbours.

Victoria's natural environment was magnificent; much of the man-made environment was not. The strips of motels, eateries, car dealerships, and other service industries that stretched along the two highways leading into the city were particularly ugly. They were also a waste of land, of course, but that aspect struck me less forcefully, if at all. If Victoria was typical, Canada had an endless supply of it. (This delusion many Canadians still labour under.) I thought it rather fine that even people living in less than prosperous neighbourhoods occupied detached houses with their own gardens. On the other hand, many houses looked ticky-tacky, while almost everywhere wires hung untidily overhead from wooden poles. (In Baarn, utility wires had been buried well before the war.) When a storm hit, some of the wires would come down, leaving entire streets without electricity. This inconvenience was tolerated because the cost of burying the wires was thought to be too high. The aesthetic benefits of putting them underground seemed to interest few people.

Juan de Fuca Strait was within easy walking distance of our house, and we soon became familiar with the shore from Beacon Hill Park to the Chinese cemetery at Harling Point. The ever-present tang of salt in the air was exhilarating. No one swam off Dallas Road, however, for the water was polluted. Raw sewage entered it south of Clover Point, Victorians being unwilling to invest in a treatment plant. (They still are.) The water in the other bays was said to be clean, but it was also cold. We preferred Crystal Gardens, a large indoor pool behind the Empress Hotel. Rumours occasionally linked the Gardens to outbreaks of polio, an ever-present menace before the development of the Salk vaccine in 1955, but we had to swim *somewhere*.

A woman who lived up the street came to inquire whether one or more of us would cut her lawn. She offered three dollars, and although her lawn was very large we gladly took her on. This led to work in other gardens in the St Charles–Richardson area. One method of making money was unavailable, however: there was no market for the scrap paper or metal we had collected for sale back home. Canada was rich enough to discard commodities that still had value in Holland.

A short, smiling clergyman, Canon Tomalin, dropped by to welcome us to the neighbourhood and, should it please us, to his church. His timing was excellent. Mother's interest in religion was increasing, but the aura of the Lutheran Church in Victoria was unacceptably German. I don't know whether there was already a Christian (Dutch) Reformed Church, but had there been one Father would have vetoed it even if Mother had wanted to attend, which seems unlikely. To say that he disliked Calvinism is an understatement. The Anglican Church was, like the Lutheran church, episcopal; it was also Canadian and highly respectable. It would do very nicely, Mother thought, and we became parishioners at St Matthias' Church.

Even more important than church was school. Mother scouted the system to find out where we would enter it and didn't like what she heard: we were to drop down a grade or two until we had mastered English. This struck her as pedagogically unsound. She read some curricular material and came to the conclusion that British Columbia schools lagged behind the Dutch in most subjects. Armed with our report cards, she went to see Dr J.F.K. English, the district superintendent of schools, to plead our case.

Years later, when he was deputy minister of education and I had a summer job in his department, English told me that Mother had been 'like a tigress protecting her cubs.' It helped that she had herself once been a teacher. She convinced him that, surrounded by English-speakers, we would soon learn the language; he decreed that we could enter the grades indicated by our ages. All except me, that is. Mother, her opinion of my ability being high, argued that I should be allowed to skip a year, and English probably found it easier to agree than disagree. She did my social development no favour, but I continue to be grateful to her all the same. Had I been placed in a lower grade I would have been bored to distraction. Skipping a grade made this a less likely fate. About to turn thirteen, I would enter grade nine.

Central Junior High School occupied several buildings on Fort

Street at Moss, about two kilometres east of the downtown core. The newest dated from 1901, but they served until they were razed in 1953 to make room for the bland structure that now occupies the site.

My home-room teacher, who taught our division English and French, was Sybil Reay, a woman with a beautiful smile. She had no time to go out of her way to help me with my English, but she did make allowances for me. She didn't need to do so in French. I had begun it in grade four, while my classmates were neophytes. Algebra seemed to be new to them as well, and my mathematics teacher told me to work on my English instead. I also took science, Canadian geography, physical education, and something called Effective Living, a course that was supposed to prepare us for the adult world. Possibly because students referred to it as 'effective loving,' the name was soon afterwards changed to 'Health and Personal Development.' I quickly recognized it as a waste of time.

Finally, I had two periods a week of typing and one of study. The latter I used to work on my English and to learn the imperial weights and measures. Sixteen ounces in a pound, four quarts in a gallon, heaven knew how many feet in a mile: who had devised this tangle? How much easier and more elegant was the metric system, with its multiples of ten. Still, mastering the imperial mess was clearly part of becoming Canadian. (I felt vindicated when, years later, the federal government undertook to metrify weights and measures. There was much opposition to this, and in the mid-1980s Ottawa adopted a perhaps characteristically Canadian compromise: *both* systems could be used. As might have been anticipated, this produced confusion, but it appeased traditionalists and slow learners, together probably more than half the adult population.)

The only one in my class not to have been born in Canada, I floundered at first. When my classmates laughed I chimed in so as not to be seen to have missed the point, but much of the time I had no idea why I was laughing. During the early months I frequently felt at sea as I struggled to understand what was going on around me. There were many exhilarating moments as I began to catch on, however. The idioms and slang expressions were hardest, but they were also most fun. 'Hit the road,' 'out in left field,' 'you're all wet,' 'shake a leg,' 'get lost': I imagined returning to Baarn and dazzling my old friends with these and other pithy phrases.

I got into the habit of asking for an explanation of anything that sounded unusual, once discomfiting my math teacher by asking him for the meaning of 'stunned Arab' (pronounced ay-rab). This was a common term of abuse at the time, but I was more usually called 'Dutchie' or 'DP.' I didn't mind the former, but when I learned what the latter meant I was outraged. We were *not* displaced persons! It didn't occur to me to ask: 'What of it if we are?' The charge was too potent and hurtful: it had to be denied.

Central Junior High and Victoria High schools, like their larger community, harboured a lot of more or less casual racism. I recall little evidence of anti-Semitism, other than the unthinking use of the expression 'to jew' for to bargain sharply, or of anti-black feeling. But few Jews lived in Victoria and virtually no blacks. Native Indians, on the other hand, were a recognizable and generally despised presence: the noun 'Indian' was usually preceded by the adjective 'drunken.' Reflecting virulent decades-old prejudices, Canadians of Chinese origin were still routinely called Chinamen or even chinks, and Sikhs, at least those wearing turbans, were commonly known as ragheads. Mandarin oranges were referred to as jap oranges. Anti-Asiatic prejudice was gradually waning, however, and in 1957 Howard Lim, who later became a friend of mine, was elected student council president of Victoria High. This would have been unthinkable before the war.

If ethnic prejudices seemed stronger than in Baarn (they did exist there, as anyone of Indonesian stock could testify), class prejudice was weaker. Victoria was by no means a classless society, but it lacked the hostility between social classes that I had known in Baarn. The sort of quasi-warfare that had occasionally broken out in IJzendijk's Wood between middle- and working-class children seemed unimaginable in Victoria. Wealthy and well-to-do people lived in the municipality of Oak Bay, in parts of Saanich such as Ten Mile Point, and in the city of Victoria along Rockland Avenue and several streets adjoining it. But poorer people did not, I think, feel that they were trespassing when they ventured into these areas.

I did not get a strong sense of class in Canada until I went to Toronto in 1963.

Probably because I looked no different from my classmates, I felt no discrimination. It helped, too, that Joe Haegert befriended me and undertook to coach me in English. Highly intelligent, he was also the school's best athlete and all in all one of the kindest people I have ever known. In the fall, once a week after school, I accompanied him to his home where, our books spread on the kitchen table, he tried to make things clear to me. Other than Joe, most of my grade nine classmates are now little more than faces in the class photo.

Victoria was not really the 'little bit of Olde England' of tourist propaganda, but few of its inhabitants doubted the superiority of British institutions. When Queen Elizabeth II was crowned in June, Miss Reay expressed the hope that hers might be the last coronation we would witness, for that would mean her reign would be long. I thought this unfair, given that she was older than we were, but none of my classmates seemed to think the sentiment strange. That fall, at Victoria High, we watched the film of the coronation with rapt attention. By this time I had adapted to the prevailing sentiment, singing 'God Save the Queen' and 'O Canada' with gusto.

Although we had more material goods than in Holland – a car, for example, and a refrigerator – we were relatively worse off. For the first three years we lived on the edge of poverty. Father's income was insufficient for our needs, and soon Mother started thinking of ways in which her sons could pitch in. At a meeting of the Central Junior High Parent-Teacher Association she met parents whose sons delivered the morning newspaper, the *Daily Colonist*, or the afternoon *Victoria Daily Times*. (The two are now one; the result is less than the sum of its parts.) In Holland, this kind of child labour would have been unthinkable for middle-class children and may, indeed, have been prohibited by law for children of *any* social class, but she probably thought: 'When in Rome ...' Father, who tended to follow Mother's lead in matters such as these, did not argue. In February 1953 Peter and I became *Times* delivery boys; Jack soon joined us.

My first two routes centred on hilly Rockland Avenue, but in the summer of 1953 I got one in South Fairfield, less prosperous but, happily, almost flat, which I tended carefully for two years. Among my customers was Lester Patrick, the famous Silver Fox of hockey, who lived on Linden Avenue at Chapman. I soon learned to schedule my collection calls from the fall into the spring for the time, between 7:15 and 7:30, when I knew he would be watching the last period of *Hockey Night in Canada*. Usually he invited me to watch to the end of the game, then paid me my $1.50 and sent me on my way. I liked the Montreal Canadiens; he favoured the New York Rangers, whom he had helped lead to the Stanley Cup as general manager as recently as 1940. At Christmas he gave me two tickets for a Victoria Cougars' game in Memorial Arena, worth three dollars, the most generous tip I got from any of my customers.

My first district manager, Bob Wright – we always called him *Mister* Wright – was an energetic man in his mid-twenties who wore a pork-pie hat and, except in summer, a woollen overcoat with upturned collar. A cigarette usually dangled from his lower lip, and he spoke the way I imagined Mickey Spillane's Mike Hammer might. He probably thought that in dealing with teenagers he needed to look and sound older and tougher than he was. Actually, he was a bit of a softy and much more likable than his successor, whom I remember only as 'Mudguts' Wellburn.

In April, Wright announced that everyone selling twenty subscriptions during the next six weeks would win a free weekend in Seattle. To Victoria schoolboys in the 1950s Seattle was the 'Big Smoke,' the place that everyone wanted to visit (I did not see Vancouver until 1957). I set out to qualify with a will. My accent did more for me than the product I was selling, I suspect. Judiciously bending the truth also helped. The fib I used was that I needed three more subscriptions to win. This seemed to be the psychologically correct number. One I might easily get somewhere else; more than three might suggest that the prize was beyond reach. If I needed only three, however, the new subscriber would be giving me a significant boost. Of course I knew this line, which I continued to use even after I had secured twenty subscribers, was dishonest, but I decided the end hallowed the means. And did any salesman ever get very far without taking liberties with the truth?

If nothing else, I learned to think on my feet. One young man told me he and his wife had just moved from Vancouver and preferred to take the *Sun*. We were from Holland, I responded, but *we* didn't subscribe to a Dutch newspaper to the exclusion of a local one. Bill West, then an art teacher at Central Junior High, later at Oak Bay High and the University of Victoria – I would buy one of his woodcut prints in 1958 – told me many years afterwards that he had signed up because he liked my rejoinder.

I secured some thirty new subscribers and was one of perhaps thirty-five boys to qualify. We went by chartered plane on a Saturday morning: my first airplane flight ever. Seattle is known as the Emerald City because it gets a lot of rain during the summer and stays green (it has adopted the lowly slug as mascot). It didn't rain that weekend, fortunately. I spent Saturday afternoon shopping for clothes, which were cheaper than in Victoria. After dinner we saw a thoroughly charmless movie, *I, the Jury.* On Sunday morning we got a guided tour; during the return flight that afternoon our DC-3 circled over Victoria: a spectacular climax to the weekend. I won the Seattle trip again in 1954, as did Jack and Joe. That year we travelled by bus and ferry, however, which was less exciting than the flight had been.

Folding and delivering the papers took no more than ninety minutes at most, and normally I was home soon after five. The most irksome part of being a carrier was collecting the subscription fees. Some people didn't have $1.50 when I called towards the end of the month, and at least once my imperfect English complicated matters. A woman, having asked me to come back in two days when her husband would have been paid, told me when I returned that he hadn't yet got his wages. In what I thought was a sympathetic manner I said: 'Isn't it odd that people say they will pay you and then don't?' I meant the 'you' to refer to her and her husband; she understandably took my remark as criticism. The next day Bob Wright came to query me about my 'cheek.' Soon recognizing the problem as one of language, he said I wasn't to blame but should apologize all the same. Seething with resentment I did so, then waited until Hallowe'en for my revenge. In Victoria, young children go trick-or-treating; older children set off fireworks. Under cover of darkness I lobbed a four-inch bomb onto the woman's front porch. It exploded with a satisfyingly loud bang. Take that!

The commissions, twenty-eight cents per subscriber per month, went to Mother. This helped her with household expenses, especially after Joe and Steven joined Jack and me as carriers. (Peter had been excused because of his poor health.) We kept the tips, although at Christmas they became part of the family gift fund. I kept the money I earned by mowing lawns, baby-sitting, and feeding the hopper of an aged neighbour's sawdust furnace. (These were common at the time; our house on Moss Street also had one.) As a result, I had enough for soft drinks, ice-cream cones, and the occasional comic book (*MAD* was a favourite). However, I regretted not being able to participate in after-school activities.

Although Mother in her letters to Holland pretended that all was well, the truth was impossible to hide from friends in Victoria. Some of them were in Fairfield United Church, which we began to attend in 1954 chiefly because it was within easy walking distance (Mother didn't drive). Just before Christmas that year some young people from the church turned up with a big hamper. Mother accepted the largesse with visible pleasure, but after the donors had left, Peter, Jack, and I urged that the gifts be returned or given to someone else. Surely we were not so poor that we were appropriate objects of charity? 'Geen van jullie heeft enig begrip hoe arm we wel zijn' (None of you has any notion how poor we are), Mother said. Father settled the dispute. The turkey might spoil before someone else got it, he said, so we might as well eat it. The other things we would pass on.

To have to ask for hand-outs is demeaning; to find one's need is so obvious that it is unnecessary to ask is more humiliating still. Among my memories the incident rates as an absolute low point. Thereafter, matters improved somewhat. One reason was that Peter graduated in 1955 and joined an engineering firm as an apprentice draughtsman. The $80 he paid to Mother each month made a real difference. Later that year, Father left the employ of

Patrick Birley to work for the B.C. Forest Service. It paid no more, I think, but the health and pension benefits were better.

There were few people of Dutch extraction in Victoria in 1952, but this soon changed. At some point Father designed a simple church on Douglas Street, a building that did double duty as a school, for the growing Christian Reformed community, all from Holland. Around 1956 the Schaddelee family opened the Dutch Bakery and Coffeeshop on Fort Street near Douglas, and at much the same time a store that sold Dutch comestibles opened on Quadra Street. In our first few years in Victoria, Mother had bought from a travelling salesman such products as *speculaas* (windmill cookies), *zoute drop* (salty licorice), *pepermunt* (peppermint rolls), chocolate letters (for St Nicholas gifts), and Indonesian condiments and spices.

Beyond sharing familiar confections with friends, I saw no need to draw attention to our background. I don't recall other Dutch children in school and would probably have avoided them had there been any. Being identified as Dutch was no real disadvantage – at the time of the disastrous floods in Holland in early 1953 Miss Reay pronounced the Dutch to be 'plucky,' which was clearly good – but it offered no advantage either. Part of our image struck me as negative, as in expressions like 'Dutch treat,' or cloyingly cute: the girl on containers of Dutch Cleanser, for example, or Hans Brinker and his unlikely silver skates. I came to dislike being asked whether I had worn wooden shoes (yes, but only while working in the garden), eaten tulip bulbs (once, during the war), or stuck my finger in any dikes (never!). Laboriously, I tried to explain that inserting a finger in a leaking dike would do no good, but no one cared to know, not even after the floods of 1953.

I was not ashamed of our background or of our parents – embarrassed at times, yes, but do not all teenagers occasionally regard their parents with embarrassment? – but I did very much want to be Canadian. Within months we boys were speaking English among ourselves, using Dutch only with our parents. They didn't object: far from it. They, too, wanted us to be Canadian, to fit in.

For themselves they had no such expectation. They were too old to try to remake themselves and didn't want to make the effort.

They remained expatriates, fish out of water, for the rest of their lives. Unlike us, then, they looked for other Netherlanders. But not just anyone would do. Although Father was fairly flexible, Mother felt fully at ease only with people of her own social milieu. Those from a lower class in Holland were kept at a distance, their status in Canada being largely irrelevant. 'Goede mensen, maar wel wat ordinair,' Mother would say: Good people, but a bit common. She worked with one or two of them on Dutch flood relief in February 1953. They did not become close friends. (Interestingly, social background seemed to be almost meaningless to her where her Canadian friends were concerned.)

One who did become a friend was Philip van der Goes, the son of a Dutch diplomat. (Father later designed a house for him and his wife, Joan, which they built with adobe bricks that they made themselves.)* And Mother was clearly delighted when friends from Baarn, Karel and Hansje van Voorstvader, arrived in 1954. Four or five years later another family from Baarn turned up, Bas and Willy de Groot. Bas and Father, I later learned, had worked together in the resistance in some way, but the de Groots' Roman Catholicism and their comparative youth had been barriers to close association. In Canada they became good friends, however. Even Mother's new-found Protestant fundamentalism could not negate the attraction of the new arrivals, coming as they did from the same neighbourhood and social class. The estate that they bought in Metchosin, perhaps fifteen kilometres west of Victoria, Deerleap, with its huge house and its twenty acres complete with swimming-hole and view of the strait and the Olympics, became a favourite weekend destination.

Other friends included Bob Beerstecher, a diffident architect who had lived in South Africa for a time, and Lodo Aymes, a charming adventurer who in time built a large yacht for himself and left Victoria with his second wife and step-daughter to sail the world.

Although their closest friends were Dutch, our parents did not become part of the Dutch-Canadian community that took shape in Victoria. Mother's somewhat snobbish attitude may have partly

* See *Harrowsmith* (July–August 1988).

accounted for this. More important, however, was that we were not *gereformeerd*, orthodox reformed. Moreover, Father scarcely bothered to conceal his hostility to Calvinism. This may explain why, when the Christian Reformed congregation built a proper church, they turned to a Canadian-born architect, even though Father had designed their first building and had also been responsible for the new St Matthias' Anglican Church. Mother was annoyed, not just because she sensed a slight but because we could have used the money. Father seemed not to mind, however. 'Grotendeels zijn 't hufters' (Mostly they're clodhoppers), he dismissed his Calvinist countrymen.

In the spring of 1953 the last mother's help we had in Baarn, Johanna Trapp, joined us in Victoria. She was twenty-one and eager to leave Holland; Patrick Birley sponsored her and lent her the money for the passage. Mother welcomed the help with the younger children and the cooking. I, for one, appreciated the latter: though not an imaginative cook, Johanna was better than Mother. Besides, she was a cheerful and agreeable young woman.

To accommodate her we moved to a larger house, on Moss Street near Dallas Road. The arrangement didn't work, however. Johanna quickly sensed, I imagine, that our social status was significantly lower than it had been in Baarn. In Victoria we were quite simply not the sort of people who employed domestic help. As well, she soon learned that she could earn far more than Father and Mother could afford to pay her. As soon as she could, she moved out and went her own way. We lost track of her almost immediately.

While we lived on Moss Street we chummed around with a group of other boys who lived in the neighbourhood, playing roller hockey, touch football, softball, and often, on summer evenings, release. This was a stirring game of hunters and hunted for which we used the wooded southeastern part of Beacon Hill Park known popularly as Lovers' Lane. No lover was safe there while we were rushing around in the underbrush.

The preferred winter game was roller hockey. Point Street, a cul-de-sac that adjoined our house, was perfect for this. The rumour was that Lester Patrick had once persuaded the city to pave the street with a very fine asphalt so that his sons, Lynn and Muzz, could skate on it. If this was true – I think I once asked him, but can't recall his answer – we boys owed him a debt, for the surface really was smooth. Few if any cars were parked in the street during the daytime, moreover, and from October well into the spring we sped along it on our skates, pretending to be Doug Harvey, Gordie Howe, and Maurice 'Rocket' Richard.

In April or May we switched to baseball. This sport, I now realize, greatly assisted my assimilation into North American life. It is played in Holland, where it is known as *honkbal*, but was unknown to me until school began in 1952. Sides formed spontaneously at lunch time and after classes ended, I noticed, and in late September several boys carried radios on which they listened during the lunch hour as two clubs from the New York area contested a match they were pleased to call the World Series. (In those days, series games began at 1:30 p.m., 10:30 a.m. on the West Coast.) I quickly became interested and by 1953 was rooting for the Dodgers, probably because Brooklyn had been named after a Dutch town, Breukelen. Forgotten were the soccer players I had so recently idolized, Piet Kraak, Abe Lenstra, Faas Wilkes, and the rest. My new heroes were Pee Wee Reese, Jackie Robinson, Duke Snider, and the other 'boys of summer' later immortalized by Roger Kahn.

That fall I agonized as the Dodgers lost in six games to the New York Yankees. Sweet revenge came two years later when Johnny Podres, aided by Sandy Amoros's spectacular catch of a Yogi Berra line drive, beat the Yankees 2–0 in the seventh and deciding game. It was the only time that Brooklyn won the series; before the 1958 season the owner moved the team to Los Angeles. The transplanted Dodgers triumphed in 1959, but this time my joy was muted. Perhaps there was something in a name after all.

I was not content to listen to the radio and read about baseball in the *Times*. Victoria had a team in the class-A Northwestern League, and I learned to keep a box score in Royal Athletic Park as the Tyees played clubs from places like Spokane, Wenatchee, and Yakima. With three poker dice I made up my own baseball game, keeping careful track of the batting and earned-run averages of my fictional players. And, of course, I played the game. I had no power at the plate, and I was an ineffectual pitcher, but I could field a ball and throw it with some pace and accuracy. As a result I usually got to play second base/shortstop, the most interesting position. (We did not have enough players to permit the luxury of four infielders.)

The diamond we staked out for ourselves was near Clover Point, between Dallas Road and the beach. It sloped down gently, the outfield ending abruptly at the rocks and logs fringing Juan de Fuca Strait. Mindful of the danger of losing a ball, we mostly played softball. Only Joe's friend Ray Harris was strong enough sometimes to reach the beach on the fly; ground balls died in the long grass before they could go over the edge.

My first glove was the result of a stroke of good luck. Mother listened to a radio quiz show, *Six for One*, and during the 1953 summer holidays I often subbed for her. One day the telephone rang. It was the program host: did I have answers to the day's questions? Knowing I was allowed only one wrong answer out of five, I nervously gave the ones I had jotted down. Four were correct: I had won $425! Mother was as excited as I: the sum equalled almost six weeks of Father's salary. Most of the money went for household expenses, but she used some of it to buy baseball gloves for Jack, Joe, and me. (Peter didn't play; Steven was supposed to use one of ours.)

I tend to agree with the Indian in W.P. Kinsella's *The Iowa Baseball Confederacy*: baseball is the only thing the white man got right. Four decades have passed since I stood at the plate in full view of the strait and the Olympics, seeing neither because I was looking for my pitch: straight down the middle and not too fast. I still love the game: its arithmetic, its geometry, its freedom from limits set by time. I stopped playing about the time I turned fifty, but I continue to watch the Blue Jays.

Today, my idea of a perfect day away from teaching or writing would include winning a close squash match in the morning. In the evening, after an early dinner, Cornelia and I would attend a performance of one of opera's great romantic comedies: *Le Nozze di Figaro, Falstaff, Der Rosenkavalier*, even *Die Meistersinger* (a long day, that!). In the afternoon, however, I would be at the Dome with

Daniel, Patrick, and Daniel's godfather, Ian Alexander. Ideally (this is a fantasy, after all), both pitchers would take no-hitters into the ninth, with the Jays winning by a run in their half: Otis Nixon walking, and, with two outs, Joe Carter doubling him home from first. A man can dream!

In September 1953 I registered in Victoria High School. With a thousand students it was the largest high school on the island; academically it was among the three or four top schools in the province. Located on Grant Street at Fernwood, Vic High comprised two buildings. The larger was a handsome four-storey brick structure dating from 1914. Separated from it by a playing field and cinder track was the newer, low-slung F.T. Fairey Technical Building, where boys in the General Programme took courses in metal working, carpentry, and auto mechanics. We in the University Programme felt superior to them; they did not feel inferior to us. Some of them owned cars and this gave them self-confidence. 'You guys got brains,' a tech boy said to me once, 'but us guys got wheels.'

Inspired by my home-room teacher, an enthusiastic amateur actor named Tommy Mayne, I shone in the subject he taught, the history of Europe. I also did well in mathematics, English, French, and commerce, but struggled to maintain a good grade in science. When my counsellor told me that I need not bother with the subject after grade ten, I took the hint and dropped it. This has become a source of some regret.

Although I had always liked physical education, in grade ten I came to hate it. The youngest in my class and slow to mature physically, I was, moreover, unique in being uncircumcised. I became a target for harassment in the showers. Some boys flicked wet towels at my private parts; a couple of them liked to grab me from behind. I dared not complain to the teacher or my parents, however, fearing a retaliation that would have been certain and unpleasant. No one liked a rat. (I have no trouble understanding why many women are reluctant to report sexual harassment. The consequences of doing so can easily seem worse than the objectionable words or acts.) Fortunately, I didn't have to take phys. ed.

in grade eleven, and in grade twelve, having matured, I escaped further bullying.

George 'Porky' Andrews, our physical education instructor and coach of the school basketball team, the Totems, was a muscular man with an expressionless face who usually made us do push-ups, sit-ups, or squat-jumps, or sent us out to circle the track no matter what the weather. Tough as he seemed, however, I once managed to discomfit him. A book we were reading in Effective Living stated that taverns were associated with 'soliciting for pros-titution.' I asked him what this meant. Visibly ill at ease (in a boys-only class!), he suggested that I see him at the end of the period and he would explain. This proved to be unnecessary: several of my classmates quickly enlightened me in simple, unadorned Eng-lish.

Noting my facility with numbers, my grade nine mathematics teacher had urged me to consider chartered accountancy as a ca-reer. That seemed to point to a bookkeeping major, for which a course in business basics was a prerequisite. Having enjoyed this course, I secured a letter of introduction from Patrick Birley and in the spring of 1954 looked for a summer job in a C.A.'s office. At one of the firms the man who interviewed me said they had nothing for me but took time to quiz me about myself. Chartered account-ancy was a good career, Lloyd Jermain said, but that was years away. It was more immediately important for me to master Eng-lish. He recommended that I read works by acknowledged masters of prose such as Winston Churchill.

Storing this advice up for future use, I presented myself at Gun-derson, Stokes, Walton and Cockburn, in the Royal Trust Building on View Street. Here I succeeded. I earned $50 for the month of July, working from nine to three, adding columns of figures, bring-ing loose-leaf books of taxation-law information up to date, and beginning to learn the basics of bookkeeping. Odd though it may sound, I liked the sober atmosphere. It made me feel like an adult. So did meeting Father for dessert in a coffee-shop on Broad Street, where I got a piece of pie and a coffee for a quarter.

My clerical job ended when July did, and in August I had a lot of spare time on my hands. I decided to devote some of it to caddying at the Victoria Golf Club, where Joe had begun to earn a bit of extra cash. No experience was necessary, and if you got a job it meant a minimum of three dollars for a round lasting perhaps four hours. The bags were not heavy, and the work was pleasant. Few club members paid more than the minimum – I dare say their membership fees were high enough – but that was not true of the business and professional men who arrived from all over the Pacific Northwest in late August to play in the annual Seniors' Tournament. I was lucky to get a dentist from Tacoma who had a high handicap and did not blame me if he played badly. He paid me four dollars for each round, and tipped me five dollars when he exited in the quarter-finals. I felt sorry for him and for myself: had he won the finals of his flight, I thought, my tip might have been *really* big!

Aside from the week of the Seniors' Tournament, I did not get a job every day, but even twelve dollars a week was nothing to sneeze at. The work was healthy, moreover, and it gave me an appreciation for the game. When I watch golf on TV, as I occasionally do, I know enough to admire the skill of the men and women who mostly make it look so easy, and to feel for them when a shot does go astray.

In grade eleven I registered in six subjects: history, English, French, mathematics, law, and my favourite that year, bookkeeping. The idea that for every debit (asset or expense) there should be a credit (income or liability) was a fifteenth-century North Italian innovation that enabled people to keep track of complicated business enterprises and became the basis of modern commercial life. Its essential tidiness appealed to me. The subject was unquestionably the most 'useful' I ever took: over the years I have been treasurer of many groups and organizations, from the Glendon College Senior Common Room to the Ontario Confederation of University Faculty Associations. My bookkeeping skills also proved valuable when in the late 1970s I put in three years as associate principal (finance) of Glendon College.

I learned a few things besides making double entries. One boy owned a pack of pornographic photos. Eye-popping as his glossy close-ups of fellatio were, however, they paled alongside the short stories one of the girls was writing. She once allowed me to read a vividly realized account of a girl's self-defloration, carried out so that no man should 'take her cherry.' I was deeply embarrassed but tried not to show it.

I had a daily study period, which I spent in the library. Heeding Lloyd Jermain's advice, I tackled Churchill's history of the Second World War. This proved heavy going, and I abandoned it for historical fiction, Dumas, Scott, Forester, Sabatini, and the Baroness Orczy. All this reading helped me in my courses. By Easter of 1955 I had As in every subject, including English. High grades did not rank with conspicuous athletic accomplishment as a claim to recognition, but they were the best I could do.

In addition to reading, I enjoyed listening to the radio, often doing the two simultaneously. The adventures of Sir Percy Blakeney, the Scarlet Pimpernel, thrilled me, and I listened avidly to the radio show by that name: 'They seek him here, they seek him there; / Those Frenchies seek him everywhere. / Is he in heaven or in hell, / That damned elusive Pimpernel?' Other shows I liked were *Our Miss Brooks, I Was a Communist for the FBI*, the hit parade on Saturday evening, and occasional sports events. Not until years later did I actually *see* 'the Catch,' Willie Mays's grab of Vic Wertz's drive to deep centre field in the first game of the 1954 World Series. It looked as it had sounded: almost impossible. Then there was the smashing triumph that the Penticton Vees scored over the Soviets in the 1955 ice hockey world championships. Canadians regarded hockey as their peculiar property, and dismay had greeted a Russian victory the year before. When the Vees won, 5–0, in March 1955, Canadian relief was real. Foster Hewitt did the play-by-play; I recall him exclaiming happily, after the Vees scored their fourth or fifth goal: 'They're playing rings around the Russians!' Subsequent championships unhappily made clear that not the Soviet triumph of 1954 but the Canadian victory of 1955 had been the anomaly.

Television played little part in my life. Our parents did not own a set until the late 1960s, but once in a while I saw TV at a friend's place: *Ozzie and Harriet, The Life of Riley*, Groucho Marx's quirky

You Bet Your Life, and, in summer, the NBC game of the week. Professional theatre did not exist in Victoria, though at some point I watched a visiting company perform *Charley's Aunt* – but there were eight movie houses. I was especially fond of historical romances, war movies, and westerns: *Scaramouche, Young Bess* – Stewart Granger was the height of suavity – *The Desert Fox, High Noon*. I also liked comedies such as *Roman Holiday* and *Sabrina*, Audrey Hepburn being a favourite because she was half Dutch and seemed so classy. I had less taste for melodrama, musicals (although I liked *Guys and Dolls*), or science fiction, and none at all for horror.

In July 1955 I quit my paper route, hoping to find a summer job, knowing I could always caddy at the Victoria Golf Club. An ad in the *Times* brought one response: a farmer in Saanich wanted help with the slaughter of a batch of chickens at a dollar an hour. The money was too good to refuse. My job was to grab the birds by the legs and shove them head first into a funnel. The rubber coat, gloves, and boots I wore were indispensable, for in a last futile protest each fowl defecated on me. On the bus home other passengers sniffed the air with distaste; those who took a seat near me soon moved. It took two baths before I ceased to reek of chicken shit. The farmer wanted me again the following week but I declined: carrying bags of clubs around the Victoria Golf Club might pay less, but it smelled a whole lot better!

In August I got a call from Bob Wright, who was by then circulation manager of the *Times*. He needed a station manager and offered me the job. I took it. 'G' station, located in a garage on Collinson Street near St Joseph's Hospital, was used by eleven or twelve carrier boys. My job was to ride herd on them six days a week as they folded their papers and on Monday evenings when they were supposed to be canvassing. I reported first to the despised 'Mudguts' Wellburn and later to Dave Dreaper, a young man not quite out of his teens. Trying to gain respect, he came on very strong. This was a mistake: the boys mimicked his mannerisms and called him Dave De Raper. I tried half-heartedly to stop them, but in fact my opinion of him was not much higher than theirs. Of the adults I dealt with at the *Times* I really respected only Wright.

Sometimes I had to deliver a route when a boy got sick and no substitute turned up; once I did a month's collection. This opened my eyes to one of Victoria's seamier sides. The route included the southern half of the downtown core; in and around it were tenements and decrepit hotels used mainly by poor pensioners. Victoria was a haven for retired people, some of them well-to-do, others not. Federal old-age pensions were $40 monthly, with a further $20 available from the British Columbia government to those who could prove need. But even $60 was a pittance, and many pensioners lived in want. Some nevertheless took a newspaper. As I collected the $1.50, I saw and smelled real poverty. Compared to *these* people we were well off.

That winter I paid $20 monthly to Mother, but because of bonuses I soon earned over $30, and I usually had a few dollars in my pocket. With Peter now out of school and contributing significantly to family income, Mother also had more money than she was used to. Some of it she used to buy suits for Jack and me. We chose them: charcoal grey with small white flecks. With mine I wore a pink shirt, mauve necktie, and pink socks, a bit garish but 'with it.' To school I wore V-neck sweaters or open-necked shirts over white T-shirts, gently draped pants (nothing zooty!), and thick-soled shoes. Teenagers tend to believe that they are what they wear, and at last I was wearing the right things.

In that last year of high school I was in Division 4. Supervised by the diminutive but forceful Jessie Roberts, it was academically the strongest division in grade twelve. I was separated from my best friend in grade eleven, a tall, witty, future Anglican clergyman named John Lancaster, but was reunited with my friend Joe Haegert, who had in the spring been elected student council president. Other grade twelve classmates included Robin Farquhar, like Joe an athlete and 'brain,' and the accomplished John Gilliland, cross-country runner, actor, and amateur magician.

I joined the swimming team and won the inter-house junior breast-stroke; a second-place finish in the inter-high school meet followed. This earned me a modest amount of recognition, some of it in the form of lewd remarks that gave me considerable secret pleasure. My domination of the chess club also attracted some minor attention, the annual *Camosun* voting me 'most likely to beat Reshevsky.' My chances of ever beating the U.S. grand master were just slightly better than my chances of winning the Miss Canada pageant, but I enjoyed the flattery.

My renewed interest in chess I owed in large part to Ted Harvey – or Edward Burns-Harvey, as he liked to style himself. A future sociologist who was marking time as a clerk in the provincial civil service before going to college, he had, I believe, been one of Peter's classmates. He approached me in the fall of 1955. Peter had told him that I played a good game of chess: would I teach him? He proved to be an apt pupil who within a couple of months was beating me more often than I him. This led him to suggest that we join the Victoria City Chess Club in order that we might improve our game.

The club used the rooms of the British Empire Club, on the penthouse floor of the Royal Trust Building at Government and View – I recall going out on the roof one evening to get a better look at *Sputnik I* or *II*. A preponderance of the members were in their forties or older, and I felt intimidated at first. This did not last long: from the outset I won more often than I lost. (In the summer of 1956 I won the club's ladder championship.) Encouraged by my success in playing with adults, I joined John Gilliland early in 1956 in founding a chess club at Vic High.

More important than swimming or chess was that in my final year of high school I got a social life. When Jack entered grade ten I got to know more of his classmates. Two of them, Harold Ridgway and Wendy Love, I already knew because they lived on Point Street; I now met others as well.

Harold was for a couple of years one of my closest friends. I delivered his *Colonist* route when he went on holidays; he introduced me to the intellectual delights of *Pogo* and the physical rigours of boxing. I preferred Walt Kelly's creation.

Wendy was quite literally the girl next door. An artistic girl – she and Jack designed the cover for the 1955 Central Junior High annual – she was one of 'the Gang,' five girls, all from South Fairfield, who palled around together. The other four were Patsy Horne, Barbara McMaster, Alayne Waller, and Jean Warren; around them circled a larger group of young people, among them Harold, his good friend Ed Pomeroy, the wise-cracking Eric Robinson, and David Skillings, a somewhat self-important son of a local politician. Jack and I latched on to this group by hosting a party in the early fall, having been encouraged by Wendy to do so and having bribed our brothers to stay out of sight. Our plan worked: henceforth we were regulars at Gang parties.

This made me feel that we belonged at last. At the same time, I got a sense that being foreign was not altogether the handicap I had thought it was. When our parents came home, around 11:00, Wendy asked Father for a dance. He was a good dancer; the Gang were impressed. 'Your dad is such a smooth dancer,' I heard afterwards, and also, admiringly: 'He is so *continental*.' Father reinforced his image by tipping his hat whenever he met one of the girls in the street (he rarely ventured into public without a hat). Some of the girls, moreover, liked our furniture and antiques. Our elegant mahogany sofa and chairs, for example, were compared favourably with the overstuffed Chesterfields and Davenports that were ubiquitous in Victoria at the time.

I took to rock 'n' roll with gusto. Wendy taught me the basic jive steps, and for years afterwards she was my favourite dancing partner. But I went well beyond what she taught me. 'Surprisingly enough, Div. 4's math genius can really cut the rug,' the *Camosun* noted. This was the nicest thing anyone had said about me since my arrival in Victoria, and I wasn't thinking about the math. That was in any case untrue: the real math genius was John Gilliland. But *he* couldn't jive worth a dime.

Bill Haley's 'Rock Around the Clock' was great jiving music; so were Fats Domino's 'I'm Walking' and Buddy Knox's 'Party Doll.' But my favourite was Jim Lowe's 'Green Door.' I can still sing much of it. The refrain asked, insistently: 'Green door, what's that secret you're keeping?'

The secret was sex, the unmysterious mystery we were circling, oh so cautiously. There was little or no overt hanky-panky in our group: some more or less surreptitious necking was probably as far as anyone went that year. No one had a car and few of us drove, so that opportunities for even the next step – petting, as we called it – were limited. The door widened, of course, as people started driving. But in that era before the pill, when condoms were kept under the pharmacy counter and abortions were both criminal and dangerous, the fear of pregnancy kept many students virgins though not chaste. I still recall the *frisson* I felt in 1958 upon learning that two friends were dropping out of college in first year because 'they had to get married.'

Safer than actual sex was romance, which entered my life that fall in the person of Vivien, a petite blonde fifteen years of age. She was in grade ten and caught my eye in the hallway; a mutual friend arranged a first meeting. Although shy, she seemed to like me. I certainly liked her and asked her to a Gang party, then to a movie, and to yet another party. It was puppy love, and it felt good. I tried to hide from others what I felt, however, and this got me into trouble.

During the Christmas holidays there was a Gang outing to see *Picnic*, a melodrama starring William Holden and Kim Novak. I had not invited Vivien because I was short of money, but when someone asked me why she wasn't there I muttered something which implied, quite groundlessly, that she was not my sole interest. This got back to her, and although I managed to explain the remark away, or so I thought, she may have felt a need to get even.

In February there was a Sadie Hawkins dance to which girls invited boys – name and concept were derived from Al Capp's comic strip *Li'l Abner*. I expected Vivien to invite me, but instead she asked a friend of mine, Winston Roberts. I learned of this when he inquired whether I minded. Minded? Of course I did! But I wasn't about to admit that, to him or anyone else. It was okay by me, I told Winston with all the casualness I could fake. Wendy, dear Wendy, spared me the ignominy of not going to the dance. And I stopped asking Vivien out.

During a Gang party not long afterwards a couple of girls urged me to listen to a popular music request show around ten o'clock.

The reason soon became clear: Vivien had dedicated a sentimental ballad to me. She was at the party, and it would have been boorish not to ask her out for the following weekend. I did so, but reluctantly.

The evening was an unqualified flop. We went bowling, but somehow I ripped my pants. The film we then went to was *I'll Cry Tomorrow*, a tear-jerker neither of us liked. Worse awaited us: when we emerged from the theatre it was raining hard, but we had no umbrellas and no money for a taxi. We knew that the bus would be slow in coming, so we walked the fifteen minutes to Vivien's house and got sopping wet. We didn't date again.

This caused me no vast regret. Romance had proved to be more trouble than it seemed worth. Besides, the object of the exercise, I later came to believe, had not been love but something else. I had demonstrated, to myself and anybody else who cared, that I was able to engage the affections of an attractive Canadian girl. That mission accomplished, I decided to put romance on hold. Several years would pass before I again fell in love.

During grade twelve I began to think about university. To that point I thought I knew what I would do upon graduation: qualify myself for the practice of chartered accountancy by articling with a local firm. There was another, more expensive route, however (today it is the only one): a degree in Arts or Commerce followed by articles. A good many of my classmates were headed for Victoria College; should I not join them?

I was angling for a summer job, as bookkeeper in a cannery at Namu on Fitzhugh Sound, that would have paid enough to cover my fees, books, and most of my incidental expenses, when Mother lowered the boom. She and Father wanted to buy a house and needed my contribution to household income for a year or two. After that I could go to college if I still wanted to.

Although I accepted this decree with ill grace, I had no real choice. Peter had been required to work for two years, and it would have been unfair to him had I gone on without stopping. The episode was a crushing comment on our parents' decision to emigrate, however. They must have realized that they would not benefit from emigration, but they had believed their sons would. Yet in order to secure a thin margin of comfort they had to interrupt our educations.

I still hoped to attend college. For that reason I rejected articles in chartered accountancy. The low wages – $80 to $90 per month was standard – would not have allowed me to save. A Bank of Montreal advertisement inviting applications caught my eye. Soon I was writing an aptitude test in the branch at Douglas and Yates streets. A personnel officer told me that bank salaries were not high, but that there were good opportunities for bright young men. And, if you were loyal to the bank, it would look after you: 'Not a single officer lost his job during the Great Depression!' It was the first reference I can recall to an event that has occupied me for a large part of my academic career.

A few days later I got a telephone call. I had been judged to be promising banker material; would I please report to the branch at 1200 Government Street right after Dominion Day? My starting salary would be $1,750 a year. This was hardly riches beyond the dreams of Croesus, but it would suffice.

With Mother setting my contribution to the household budget at $80 per month, she and Father now felt able to service the mortgage on a large house at 523 Harbinger Avenue, just north of Fairfield Road, bought for $11,000. Clad in whitewashed cedar shakes, it had two storeys and a full basement. Better yet: the room assigned to Jack and me had a balcony facing west. We moved in late June.

This was some days after my graduation from Vic High. Although I had never felt fully part of my grade, that evening I came close. The ceremony was boring but the dance was not. Rock 'n' roll was allowed, for once, and I taught two of my classmates, Joanne Dawson and Barbara Wallace, how to jive. Afterwards there was a party at Barbara's home, where we danced and played parlour games into the small hours. With a few others I then went to another party, in South Fairfield. Here some of my classmates were drinking liquor, and two or three were obviously drunk. This bothered me. The United Church frowned on the use of alcohol, and it was in any case illegal for teenagers to drink. Feeling censorious, I walked home in the early morning coolness.

Educationally, my high school years were disappointing. This was not the fault of my teachers, most of whom were conscientious and able. Their employment was no sinecure, moreover. I doubt that many people who criticize high school teachers would last a week in front of a roomful of adolescents. (This is probably true even of critics who earn vastly more than teachers do.) The fault, rather, lay with an undemanding system. We went through courses at a leisurely pace that wasted the time of the talented, and not only theirs. It didn't help that little homework was required, perhaps because of an awareness that many students had jobs after school. Rarely at Victoria High did I spend as much time doing homework as I had in Baarn by grade six.

British Columbia children in the 1950s spent fewer hours in school than I had been used to, and they studied fewer subjects. In my first year at the Baarnsch Lyceum I was taking seven academic subjects as well as art, music appreciation, physical education, and one period a week of biblical knowledge from a scholarly perspective. In grade nine I took five academic subjects, Effective Living (a non-subject if ever there was one), two periods of typing, and two of physical education. During my three years at Vic High I never took more than six academic subjects a year. The result was a comparatively impoverished education, intellectually as well as culturally. (Canadians who praise the high quality of public education three or four decades ago are probably spinning nostalgic fantasies. Hilda Neatby's *So Little for the Mind*, a devastating critique of that education, appeared in 1953. Within months of its publication someone gave Mother a copy – it is now in my possession – but I didn't read it until I was in college. I found much to agree with.)

For immigrant children, however, school is even more important as a socializing than as an educational agency. I had become fluent in English, made friends, learned my cues. Except for a slight accent, I had become indistinguishable from people who had been born in Canada. My assimilation was not complicated by my appearance – dark blond hair and blue eyes did not stand out – or my name. Mike Horn *sounded* right. I entered school in 1952 a Dutch boy and four years later emerged, for all practical purposes, a Canadian teenager. Now I would have a go at becoming a Canadian banker.

3

Chartered Banking in Canada

On 3 July 1956, two months shy of my seventeenth birthday, I reported for duty at the Government Street branch of the Bank of Montreal. It stood at the foot of View Street, where it enjoyed a pleasing prominence. Constructed in 1896 to be the main office of the bank in Victoria, the building had been designed in the château style by Francis Mawson Rattenbury, a Yorkshireman who had arrived on the coast in 1892 to become one of the most popular architects in the British Columbia of his time.

The courthouses in Nanaimo, Nelson, and Vancouver (now the art gallery), and the CPR hotels at Banff and Lake Louise attest to Rattenbury's eclectic talent. He left his mark on Victoria more than anywhere else, however, for three of his buildings flank the Inner Harbour: the Parliament Building, the Empress Hotel, and the sometime CPR steamship terminal. One of his designs that no longer survives is the old Cary Castle. Known as Government House, it dominated Fairfield from its site on Rockland Avenue. One morning in 1957, as I looked out the bathroom window, I was startled to see it in flames. The building was a total loss. The Government Street branch survives to this day, no longer as a bank branch but as an upscale clothing store.

I joined a staff of twenty or so. Most were women: a receptionist, a stenographer, half a dozen tellers, four or five clerks. The six officers were all men. The manager, H.B. Twiss, a heavy-set man around forty-five years of age, was transferred in 1957; I can recall neither the face nor the name of his successor. The accountant was perhaps twenty-five years old, able, eager, and on the way up; so was *his* successor. The assistant accountant, soft-spoken and kindly, was in his forties, his career stalled. Next in line was a cheerful young Irishman who answered to the name of Wally. He soon left to become second officer of a small branch in the Vancouver area, not before he had tried without success to teach me how to play golf, said to be a useful game for officers. Joining the branch when I did was John Gray, a graduate of Mount View High who was transferred to Kamloops after a year. That I, too, wasn't transferred I owed to my youth: a personnel officer thought me too young to be living away from home. I was happy to stay.

My first job was as a teller in the savings department. For a day or two I observed one of the veterans; then it was 'learn by doing, and if you don't know, ask.' What marked a good teller was accuracy, scrupulous care in handling cash, cheques, and bond coupons, and in recording them. Courtesy came a close second. Mere speed counted for little, although slowpokes were unpopular. Fortunately, my bookkeeping courses had drilled me in recording transactions neatly and exactly. I never had trouble balancing my blotter (worksheet) at the end of the day, or reconciling my cash. I was also never victimized by a hoary banking practical joke in which a junior is sent to another branch 'to borrow the scales for balancing the ledgers.' This monthly task involved adding up all the accounts in a ledger (savings, current account, or loans) in order to ensure that it balanced with the amount carried on the branch books: dull work but indispensable.

We were not very far into the machine age. Some of our adding machines were electric; at least one was not. The cash book and loan ledgers were done entirely by hand. Savings and current-account ledger entries were posted with the help of a kind of adding machine that printed; a few years earlier they, too, had been posted by hand. The purchase in 1957 of a Marchant calculator (at $800, more than a third of my annual salary at the time!) was a big advance. To that point we calculated interest with the aid of a book of interest tables; now the machine did the work. The savings in time were considerable, especially after I figured out how to calculate mortgage interest in a single operation (mortgagees were entitled to interest credits on the monthly payments they made, which made for lots of finicky work before we got the Marchant).

Large and costly as it was, the calculator was unsophisticated by present-day standards. The cheapest of today's pocket calculators indicates with an 'E' that it cannot divide by zero; the mechanical monster lacked this insight. Sometimes, to amuse ourselves when things got slow, we made it try to do so, forcing it to run noisily through all its columns before admitting defeat.

For several weeks I worked on cash book, a comprehensive record of the day's operations in all departments. At first I worked under the assistant accountant's vigilant eye, then on my own. This was straightforward bookkeeping: no big deal for someone who had taken a high school commerce major. Problems arose only when someone had erred in recording a transaction. Detecting such errors could last into the next day, though usually I was in balance by 5:00 p.m.

Next I served as a current-account teller and also put in two weeks as head teller, the conduit of cash to and from the other tellers. The trick was to have enough cash on hand but not too much. I didn't want to have to go to the vault all the time, but it would not have looked good had a robber relieved me of fifty or sixty thousand dollars when much of that should have been in the vault. Not that we worried about robbers: the last bank robbery in the Victoria area (in Oak Bay, of all places) had occurred in 1953.

Three or four .38 Smith and Wesson revolvers were distributed around the branch during the day, but we were under strict instructions never to use them. Their sole purpose was to enable the bank to collect insurance should a robbery take place. I was licensed to carry a handgun and did so a few times when the branch needed banknotes and there was no time to use the armoured-car service. My jacket pocket bulging with a gun I had not been taught to use, I felt oddly vulnerable as I set out for the main branch.

By and large, my fellow workers were competent, and some were very good indeed. Among the latter was Ruth Williams, the clerk in charge of the loans and mortgage department. She was in her late twenties, a young woman with a nose and hairstyle that reminded me irresistibly of Lucy in the comic strip *Peanuts*. She was fun to be around. Her sense of humour could be either subtle or raucous, and she was the only one in the branch who dared to twit the manager on occasion. She got away with it because both Twiss and his successor had a high opinion of her abilities, an opinion she richly merited. I learned far more about banking from her than from anyone else I worked with.

It is clear to me now, and may have been clear to me then, that she was the ablest person in the branch. She was not an officer, however: in the 1950s the bank admitted few if any women to that class. That I nevertheless chose her to be my mentor suggests that I didn't care enough about the realities of power in the branch or the bank to adapt myself to them. In this I was my father's son, and it established a pattern that has governed my life ever since. Without exception I have chosen my friends and associates not for what they can do to advance my career but for what they can do to enlighten and amuse me, or to confirm my prejudices. And at 1200 Government Street no one was more enlightening and amusing than Ruth.

She was good to work with for another reason. She was the only one of my fellow-workers to be interested in literature, music, or the visual arts. These also increasingly interested me. I got to know her and her husband, Rod, a customer's man with A.E. Ames and Co., quite well. Not only were they good cooks, as I discovered when Ruth invited me for dinner, but their furniture was attractive and the prints on their walls had merit. To me, a scruffy teenager, they seemed to be exciting, well-informed adults, the sort of person I was hoping to become.

I worked as Ruth's assistant for most of my second year with the bank. My stint under her tutelage was instructive not only because of her skills as a teacher but also because loans, then as now, are at the core of banking. Our loans, payable on demand, were mostly made to businesses, with a few made to individuals against collateral in the form of marketable securities. One of my tasks was to do a weekly update of clients' portfolios to ensure that they continued to be worth at least twice the amount of the loans they secured. This gave me an interest in the stock market. I graphed market indices and tracked the performance of several common stocks that I had selected for hypothetical purchase. The year 1957 was unkind to stocks, and my fictitious portfolio lost in value. I learned a useful lesson cheaply: stocks can go down as well as up.

My own money I put in Canada Savings Bonds. Was this a typically Canadian choice, preferring the safety and, at 3 per cent, low return of government-guaranteed securities to the greater risks (and rewards) of common stocks? If it was, it is not clear whether my choice was purely personal – I have never liked risk much – or was culturally conditioned. I have invested modest amounts in common stocks from time to time since then, with mixed results.

My interest in stocks was part of an increased interest in riches that lasted for about a year. Several of our clients were very wealthy. They had savings balances in five figures and were constantly in receipt of cheques for dividends and bond interest. One older man routinely kept between eighty and a hundred thousand dollars in his account, comparable to perhaps a million today! I liked the thought of that, and fantasized about becoming wealthy myself. In my dreams I made great speculative coups and distributed large dividends to the shareholders of MSDH Ltd.: myself, my parents and my brothers. I even brought home cheque-books for the purpose, but remained sufficiently rooted in reality not to circulate any of the cheques I wrote, and kept my fantasies and my game a secret from my family.

Dreams were for my spare time. On the job I continued to learn the ins and outs of banking. Demand loans carried interest rates that ranged between 5 and 6 per cent; similar rates applied to mortgages and home improvement loans guaranteed by the Central Mortgage and Housing Corporation. As the Bank Act limited interest to 6 per cent, banks were not interested in consumer loans: the return on them did not justify the risk. Still, we carried thirty or forty chattel mortgages, usually secured by automobiles. These loans were subject to a hefty service charge. This confused me: a chattel mortgage was no more work than a demand loan, so why the extra cost? Ruth set me straight: the charge enabled us to exceed the 6 per cent ceiling without breaking the law. Was this really honest? I asked. She gave me the pitying half-smile that she reserved for those occasions when I betrayed my greenness. The bank didn't concern itself with that, she said: the practice was legal, and *that* was all that mattered.

We also discounted promissory notes assigned to us. These were among our toughest accounts. The company that gave us most of this business was in the fields of paving and roofing. Some of the people that it dealt with would never have qualified for bank credit in their own right; others, dissatisfied with the way work had been done, became reluctant to continue making payments. Ultimately, the company was on the hook, but as it was in constant financial hot water we tried hard to collect from the signatories. When I wondered why we bothered to keep this account at all, Ruth said that, on balance, it was more than remunerative enough to justify the trouble.

The adage that you could borrow from a bank only if you could show you didn't need to was close to the truth. Before the intro-duction of bank credit cards, about twenty-five years ago, many people obtained credit directly from merchants. Oil companies and department stores issued cards; other firms were less formal. When I bought a jacket I paid the clothier ten dollars down and five every two weeks until my debt was paid. People who needed a loan but lacked security used finance companies. 'Never borrow money needlessly, but when you must ... ' began a well-known advertising jingle of the time; the company using it was Household Finance. We regarded its customers as just a step above the clientele of pawnbrokers.

My work in the loans department consisted mainly of making monthly charges to accounts and taking payments at the counter. I also calculated interest, made a few fully secured loans, balanced ledgers, and looked after whatever other business presented itself: selling money orders, drafts, and travellers' cheques and, in season, Canada Savings Bonds, or authorizing the payment of cheques drawn for cash on other branches. The normal practice was to register a hold by telephone, deducting the cost of a long-distance call from the face value of the cheque. Clients tended to resent this, so we sized them up on the basis of demeanour, clothing, and home address. If these seemed good we might forego the call. This had risks: a dishonoured cheque came out of the cautionary fund, $100 to $150 annually, of the person who had authorized it. I must have been a shrewd judge of financial worth, for no cheque came back to haunt me.

I took part in several inspections. Bank inspectors held their positions full time, but their teams were assembled from branches other than the one to be inspected. We burst into a branch unannounced at closing time, 3:00 p.m., and worked until all counts of cash and securities were complete and all ledgers had been balanced. This normally took several hours.

Of the inspections I took part in, all but one were uneventful. The exception occurred in the branch in Nanaimo, about a hundred kilometres north of Victoria and the second-largest town on the island. My first task was to count the head teller's cash: some seventy thousand dollars in all. When I finished she turned out to be an even thousand short. I must have made a mistake, she said. Someone else got the same result, however, and the teller set out anxiously to check the day's transactions.

Around 5:30 I was beavering away at an adding machine, trying to balance a ledger, when the inspector interrupted me. He seemed ill at ease. The teller was saying that I must have taken the money: would I be willing to undergo a body search? Indignantly I said that I would, but under protest. He did not insist and walked off unhappily.

For another half-hour the increasingly distraught woman pored over her blotter, trying to puzzle out what had happened. The mystery dissolved at six when someone phoned: did the head teller realize that she had given him a bundle of tens without getting anything in return? He had been at her wicket when the inspection team entered, and she had been so unsettled that she had forgotten to get his cheque!

I liked banking: it was varied, interesting, and increasingly remunerative. In two years my salary went from $1,750 to $2,800 (the Consumer Price Index rose by less than 5 per cent in that time). Christmas bonuses added 10 per cent to my salary in 1956 and eight in 1957. The hours were good – I arrived at 9:00 and usually left before 5:00 – and my evenings and weekends were almost always free.

And yet: a career in banking did not appeal. The unwelcome

transfers that would come my way bothered me as I thought about them, but not as much as my growing conviction that I was not cut out to be a banker. When I read *Babbitt* I recognized the type: he was omnipresent at the bank. Government Street staff shared in a perk enjoyed by Victoria main branch employees: a free cafeteria lunch. Listening to the other officers as I ate my roast beef or fried chicken, I became aware that none seemed to have interests beyond spectator sports, television, movies, hunting, fishing, golf, gardening, and, for those still moving up, The Job. (Some were merely marking time, for the main branch was home to at least half a dozen men who had proved wanting in some way and were waiting to qualify for their pensions. Their tenure was at least as secure as any professor's: in those days, the bank fired officers only for dishonesty, immorality, or gross neglect of duty. That has changed since then.)

I didn't like gardening, didn't regard fishing as an adult activity, and had no taste for hunting. (Once I accompanied Joe on a deer hunt in the Sooke Hills and realized what the Western front must have been like on a slow day: long spells of tedium punctuated by brief bursts of mayhem.) Golf was for the future, if ever. (I played in the officers' tournament in 1957 and won a booby prize for most strokes on a single hole. If I ever took up golf, I vowed, I would take lessons.) I knew enough about baseball, hockey, and football and saw enough films to keep up my conversational end about such things. But they seemed not enough to keep the mind alive. Peter Cook (in *Beyond the Fringe*), speaking as the miner who 'didn't have the Latin for the judgin',' uttered a line that could have been applied to lunch-time conversation in the bank cafeteria: 'If you were searchin' for a word to describe the conversations what go on down the mine, "boring" would spring to your lips.'

I don't think my reaction had much to do with cultural differences between Holland and Canada. The Dutch watch movies and spectator sports as avidly as Canadians, for example. Perhaps class differences played a role, but I had no idea of the class background of most of the officers I encountered. Perhaps it was simply the case that bank officers had adopted tastes, hobbies, and interests that they found satisfying and that did not get them into trouble.

Doubtless it was a comment on the life of corporation man that none of these activities was intellectually demanding or thought-provoking.

My spare time activities were chess, swimming, philately, reading, and, increasingly, listening to recorded music. I derived enormous pleasure especially from chess. After winning the club ladder championship in 1956 I was selected for the team that represented the club in matches with other island clubs. For the next few years I played at the VCCC at least once a week, once gaining the Marinker Trophy for most tournament wins in the course of the year. I also regularly played at their homes with a couple of men who could not bear the smoke-laden air of the club, a Dutch-born barber, Syrt Wolters, and a retired man of Belgian stock, Max Enke. The latter was a stickler about making tea, heating the pot, measuring the tea carefully into a tea ball, and steeping it for five minutes exactly. (I still make it this way, and now Cornelia does too.) His chess was less precise.

Swimming was my sport of choice. In the winter I swam mostly in the Crystal Gardens pool, but at some point, encouraged by Jack, who had become active in the YMCA, I joined the Y and used its pool regularly. Once the weather got warm enough we swam off Willows Beach or in Cadboro Bay, two bodies of water that were unpolluted and not too frigid. The lakes near Victoria (Beaver, Elk, Thetis, Prospect, Langford, Shawnigan) were warmer but, as none of us yet drove, hard to get to unless Father was willing to give us a ride. On the 1956 Labour Day weekend I entered the Elk Lake–Beaver Lake swim and finished fifth of nine competitors. I consoled myself with the thought that I had used the breast-stroke while the higher finishers had done the crawl, and that I had beaten Peter. Sibling rivalry was alive and well.

A continued interest in collecting stamps owed a good deal to Opa Reitsma. My first album had been a birthday gift from him, and he may have felt a responsibility to make sure that it was kept up to date. For three or four years after we left Holland he regularly sent me mint sets of Dutch stamps as they were issued, as well as First Day covers whenever he felt energetic enough to go to the Post Office to arrange for them. When he indicated around 1956 that he was having increasing difficulty in moving around, I asked the Cazants whether they could help me. Drawing on sums of money I sent to him from time to time, Meneer Cazant supplied me with mint stamps into the 1970s, years after I had ceased to be an active collector.

I spent more time in reading than I did on all the other pastimes combined. My tastes were catholic, but I read mostly fiction borrowed from the Victoria Public Library. I particularly enjoyed the mysteries of Dorothy Sayers, Rex Stout, and Ellery Queen, and the novels of Sinclair Lewis and P.G. Wodehouse. Lewis was better than any other author I've ever read at making me dislike what he disliked: cant, hypocrisy, bullying, the notion that might makes right. Wodehouse was another batch of muffins altogether. Him I loved for his good humour. He wrote much that was negligible, but at his best he was brilliantly inspired. Periodically I reread *Joy in the Morning,* one of the most nearly perfect comic novels I know.

My interest in classical music was new. For my sixteenth birthday I had received a portable record player, and during my last year in high school I bought a few popular 78s and 45s. My first LP was *Rock around the Clock* with Bill Haley and the Comets, which I gave to myself on my seventeenth birthday and which remained one of my favourite albums until Harold Ridgway sat on it at a party a couple of years later and broke it. The second LP I bought was 'something completely different,' however: piano sonatas by Mozart and Beethoven, performed by Jose Iturbi. Next I got Beethoven's Pastoral Symphony and Bizet's suites of orchestral music from *L'Arlésienne* and *La jolie fille de Perth.* I can't remember what brought about this improvement in my taste. Mother, though she had once played the piano and knew the works of the major European composers, listened only to church music of often dubious quality. Father liked a few lush works, such as Rachmaninov's Second Concerto and Widor's Fifth Symphony (oddly romantic choices for one so unsentimental), and agreeable fluff of the kind composed by Ketelby and Leroy Anderson, but showed little interest in anything else.

Whatever the reason, I began to borrow albums from the public library and liked most of what I heard. A recording of Chopin's

First Concerto, with Alexander Brailowsky as the soloist, was a real ear-opener. The interplay between piano and orchestra in the first movement was delightful, the concluding rondo was graceful and spirited. (Although I no longer think of it as a 'great' concerto, the equal of Beethoven's Fourth, say, or the Mozart K. 488, I still listen to it with delight.) I expanded my horizons: to the noble cadences of the Brahms Violin Concerto, the brightness of Ravel's Concerto in G, the driving rhythms of *The Rite of Spring*. I enjoyed almost all instrumental music, though not as yet opera or other vocal works. Over the years little else has given me as much pleasure as music.

Literature and music, except perhaps for best sellers and the hit parade, were little discussed by bankers. Politics were even less so. The Progressive Conservatives and Liberals were both safe, but it was even safer not to express a preference. Social Credit was slightly suspect because of attempts the party had made in Alberta, twenty years earlier, to interfere with banks. In British Columbia the party seemed sound, however, having formed the government since 1952 without doing anything bankers could object to. The left-wing Co-operative Commonwealth Federation (CCF), on the other hand, was well beyond the pale.

My interest in politics was growing. In 1957 Mother, who liked John Diefenbaker's style, bet me a dollar that his party would win the federal election. She didn't know what she was talking about, said I, and took her on. I lost, of course, and in 1958 I declined to enter into a similar wager, a Tory victory being a certainty. This was the first Canadian election in which she and Father voted, both casting their ballots for A.deB. McPhillips, a lawyer with a penchant for mixing metaphors. His creations were eagerly seized on by the Liberal *Victoria Daily Times*. 'Let us not foul our nest with a mess of pottage,' he once implored his fellow members of Parliament. 'What happened to the old mailed fist,' he thundered on another occasion: 'Did it go down the drain?'

The most important political events of the time were the Suez crisis and the Hungarian uprising, both late in 1956. The latter allowed even bankers to state their views without courting controversy: it was one more instance of Soviet bullying and aggression.

The Suez affair was another matter. Influenced by attitudes current in Victoria, I supported Britain, France, and Israel. Then it became clear that the U.S. and Canadian governments took a different view of the attack on Egypt. Evidently, the crisis was one about which bankers were unwise to venture an opinion.

Religion was also a subject on which it was inappropriate for bankers to express strong views, although we were expected to favour it in a general way, and being a churchgoer did no harm at all. I had been confirmed in the Anglican Church in early 1954 but did not become actively religious until three years later. I can't recall what triggered this, but sometime during 1957 I came to believe that I was a sinner who had been saved by Jesus Christ. I had no sense of the supernatural, however. Although I prayed earnestly, I had to take it on faith that I was talking to God. I did not *feel* anything. I was already frugal, industrious, and sober (bankerly virtues all), but now, taking seriously St Paul's dictum that 'the love of money is the root of all evil,' I put aside the interest in money making that had consumed me for a year or so. I also ceased to swear and began to read the Bible and various devotional books and periodicals.

I particularly liked C.S. Lewis's *Mere Christianity* and *The Screwtape Letters*. Reading them emboldened me to take on H.V. O'Reilly, a doctrinaire atheist whose letters appeared frequently in the *Victoria Daily Times*. After my first letter was published, he wrote to me directly, and soon each of us was trying to make the other see the error of his ways. We kept this up for at least a year; I can't recall who first tired of it.

For a while I took part in another struggle. While browsing in the book department of Eaton's, I saw a copy of Bertrand Russell's *Why I Am Not a Christian*. I placed a devotional book in front of it. The next day Russell had reappeared. I hid him again; he popped up again. This went on for a week or two. Then he was gone: sold or returned? I hoped the latter. (Years later, I read the book. It seemed quite sensible.)

Fairfield United became my church. I joined it in 1958 and for three years taught Sunday school there. Mother, however, who had encouraged me to attend that church, herself became disillusioned with it. She liked the choir she sang in and the people she met, but she disliked the doctrinal liberalism of its ministers. The fundamentalist radio preachers she had begun to listen to, with their fanciful analyses of the prophetic books of the Bible, were more to her taste. The horns of the Beast, the whore of Babylon, the number 666: these seemed to hold the key to history and politics.

Among her favourites was Alberta's Premier Ernest Manning, who broadcast from Calgary. I cared little for him, but he seemed reasonable alongside the likes of Billy James Hargis, based in Tulsa, Oklahoma, and Carl McIntyre, broadcasting from New Jersey. These linked their religion to a virulent anti-communism that saw a Red under every bed. Mother, who took them seriously, feared that the world was in danger from a conspiracy that was linked to heterodoxy and unbelief. For several years she received mail from the John Birch Society, an ultra-right American outfit which claimed that virtually every country, not excluding Canada and the United States, was on the brink of a communist takeover. She tried to persuade us of the world's perilous condition, and got querulous when we disagreed.

(Occasionally, over the years, I have pondered her religious development. Her background was *hervormd*, akin to a liberal Presbyterianism, but before 1952 she rarely attended church. By the early 1950s she was reading books about religion, however, and in Victoria she became a regular churchgoer, first Anglican and then United.

There was nothing in this to predict her turn to North American–style fundamentalism. I have been tempted to find the reason for it in her uncertain health and in her awareness – to which she never gave voice – that emigration had created more problems than it solved. The religion she embraced in middle age promised that her health would be restored and that material blessings would be showered on her, if only she would serve God in exactly the right way. The uncritical reading of the Bible provided by the radio preachers fostered in her a doctrinaire faith as well as a strong desire to convert those near and dear to her. As she had always been anti-communist, this aspect of fundamentalism she found highly congenial.

The pressure she put on those around her to embrace the true faith was not as great as the pressure she put on herself. The trouble with her religion was that the benefits she so fervently prayed for simply did not come, for which she then blamed herself. Evidently she had not got the formula right. For two decades she wrestled with this conundrum until finally, in 1974, a serious illness seems to have persuaded her that 'the struggle naught availeth,' that 'the labour and the wounds' were indeed vain. She stopped going to church altogether, stopped troubling her husband, sons, and siblings about the state of their souls, stopped taking an interest in matters that had for years been important to her. This was a relief to us; it was also just a bit sad.)

Although I did not share Mother's brand of Christianity, my religion *was* evangelical. This meant, as I saw it, that I ought to tell other people about my faith and should even, when the occasion arose, seek converts. The bank offered little opportunity for this. Discussing religion with customers was out of the question, and none of my fellow workers showed the slightest interest when I broached the subject. Ruth looked at me in a peculiar manner, and suggested that religion was a private matter. I did not fully agree with her, but I was happy to abandon the topic: I had found that when I tried to talk about my religious life I felt ill at ease.

What religion mainly did in my case was to reinforce a censoriousness that came all too easily to me. It is an unlovable trait, of course, but at least once it was justified. The occasion was a dinner at the Victoria Golf Club, where an assistant general manager dispensed inspiration straight from head office. I sat next to a man, barely into his twenties and thus only four or five years my senior, who had drunk more than was altogether prudent. Even before the soup had been served, he began to complain about his salary. It was much too low for the needs of his young family, he explained at tedious length, but no one in the bank seemed to care about this. Gesturing towards the man from Montreal, seated at the head table among a covey of branch managers, my neighbour whined: 'Look at him, he must earn at least thirty thousand bucks. I get about three!' Put off by the smell of liquor on his breath, the tone of his voice, and the banality of his story, I asked him with some acerbity why he had married on so small an income. Surely no one at head office had asked him to? He pondered this, then smirked lubriciously: 'Well, you've got to say one thing for marriage. It beats paying for it every Saturday night!'

In May 1958 the bank assigned me to a two-week executive training course at Vancouver's main branch. We junior officers were booked into the Alcazar, a run-down hostelry at the corner of Homer and Dunsmuir which we predictably called the Alcatraz. Our meal allowance was more generous than our accommodation, which probably cost the bank less than two dollars a night: we got three dollars on weekdays, when we lunched free of charge in the main branch cafeteria, and five dollars on Saturdays and Sundays. I managed to save almost half of my meal money, using it to buy stamps from a dealer on West Pender Street. The year before, I had bought a new stamp album, and I was eager to fill in the empty spaces.

Of the course I remember next to nothing, and of the other trainees only that I had no wish to spend my free time with them. Instead, I took advantage of the opportunity to poke around Vancouver. Jack and I had spent the 1957 Labour Day weekend in and around the city while staying with friends in New Westminster, but beyond the Pacific National Exhibition and Mt Seymour we had seen little of the area. (I do remember being surprised, as we looked down on the city, to see that a thin blanket of smog hung over it.) This time I walked around a lot, exploring Stanley Park, playing at the Vancouver Chess Club, visiting the Vancouver Art Gallery. Its pride and joy were a number of works by Emily Carr, a Victoria artist who since her death in 1945 had become something of an icon. (Some of her paintings I liked, but her apparent obsession with forests and totem poles bored me.) I attended a track meet at Empire Stadium, and on Sunday I went to church twice, Anglican in the morning, United in the evening.

Vancouver was a sprawling place, difficult to get around without an automobile, and its architecture seemed mostly forgettable. But the setting impressed me, as it must everybody, for Burrard Inlet and the North Shore mountains make up a magnificent vista. (I used to think that I would like to live in Vancouver because it offers a compromise between Victoria's beauty and Toronto's cultural riches. Now I am no longer sure: the city seems to be choking on its success.)

Not long after my return to Victoria I resigned from the bank. A personnel officer urged me to reconsider, promising rapid promotion and salary increases, but he didn't change my mind. I had not strayed from my choice of chartered accountancy as a career and had decided to stick with my plan to go to university. Ruth said that I should; similar advice came from Bob Wright. I ran into him in 1957 and, upon his asking, told him what I was doing. He pulled a face: 'You're too smart for that, Mike. Go get that college degree you were talking about.'

The only thing arguing against this was that a B.Comm. degree took five years of study and would be costly. Was it worth it? I asked a customer, an elderly chartered accountant. He suggested that I talk to his younger partner, Gordon Holms. I wouldn't be a worse C.A. if I were to enter articles right away, Holms told me, but he recommended I take a degree: 'At university you'll be rubbing shoulders with the same people you'll be meeting as clients later on. That will be a big advantage.'

This settled the matter. I had started my studies in the fall of 1957 by means of a correspondence course in mathematics; the following spring I applied for admission to Victoria College and began to plan my first year. Four courses (English, a language other than English, a laboratory science, and mathematics) were compulsory for all first-year students; Economics 100 was a prerequisite for Commerce. Knowing that chartered accountants were in demand in Latin America, I chose Spanish for my language. The lab science all but chose itself. Since I had dropped science after grade ten, physical geography was the only appealing option. Because I had already completed my mathematics course I had room for one elective. I phoned a high school friend, John Lancaster, for advice. He didn't hesitate: 'Take psychology. It's a snap!'

In August I spent two weeks as acting second officer in the branch at Richmond Avenue and Fort Street while the incumbent was on vacation, returning to 1200 Government Street for my final two weeks as a banker. On my last day, the manager said nice things about me, everybody applauded, and I walked away with a Parker 51 pen and a lot of memories, most of them good. I had not been eager to go to work in the bank but had found it better than bearable, and I had saved almost a thousand dollars. My fees would be around $200, books might be another $100, and incidental expenses surely not much more. Mother said that, as Jack had graduated from Vic High and, having taken a job with the provincial government, was now paying board, I would not have to pay board for at least a year. I would have more than enough money for my needs.

Helping Father and Mother financially had been a source of satisfaction even as it bolstered my sense of independence. No need to kick over the traces: I knew I could make it on my own. I had learned to do more than one task simultaneously, which would prove very useful. Perhaps most important, when I left the bank I was more disciplined in my work habits than when I entered it. The bank took two years of my life, but on the whole the years were well spent, better than in the military service I would have had to perform had we stayed in Holland.

By September 1958, at the age of nineteen, I may have been as assimilated as I would ever be. In the bank, even more than in school, the pressure was towards fitting in. There was no advantage in sounding like a foreigner. I didn't have much of an accent when I graduated from high school, and two years later next to nothing was left. What I still had was difficult to place, except to other Dutch immigrants. More than one customer asked me whether I was from England, which pleased me inordinately!

We had become Canadian citizens late in 1957. Our parents took the oath of allegiance on 19 November, and, being under age, we, their sons, were part of the package. The naturalization took place at the Court House on Bastion Square; all of us attended. The ceremony was unimpressive, but the result was the same as it would have been after the most grandiose event imaginable. We were officially Canadian.

Had anybody that day asked me whether I was Dutch I would have said: 'No longer.' Was not Prime Minister Diefenbaker insisting there should be no hyphenated Canadians? Victoria was my city; Canada (of which I had so far seen almost nothing), my country; English, my language. I even dreamt in it. I spoke Dutch with Mother and Father and some of their friends, but that seemed irrelevant to what I felt about Holland and Canada. Born there, I now belonged here. My brothers, I think, were of much the same view, Peter perhaps a bit less, and the younger ones, from Joe on down, rather more. Our parents, on the other hand, were still expatriates. This did not seem to trouble them; they had expected nothing else. It was enough that their sons belonged here.

The truth was more complicated. Although we didn't know it, my brothers and I had dual nationality. Minors when our parents abjured *their* allegiance, we remained Dutch nationals even as we became Canadian citizens. (Jack discovered this when he was almost drafted into military service while studying at the University of Utrecht in 1964–5.) As well, I misjudged quite completely the weight and persistence of childhood experience. Awareness of this did not come to me until I visited Holland in 1961, however. On that November day in 1957 I believed myself to be unequivocally Canadian.

4

College Days

Victoria College occupied a small campus on Lansdowne Avenue at Richmond, a fifteen-minute bus ride northeast of the downtown core. The Young Building, formerly the Provincial Normal School, was a dignified but shabby edifice built early in the century and reminiscent of a once-prosperous pensioner fallen on hard times. Of more recent vintage was the Ewing Building, nondescript bordering on ugly, which housed the library and the administration. A crowded, smoke-filled hut served as cafeteria. The grounds were well kept, and from the upper storey of the Young Building the view south was spectacular. When the University of Victoria completed its move to Gordon Head in the mid-1960s it left the view behind. This must have struck both students and staff as a pity.

Founded in 1920 – an older, McGill-linked institution had closed in 1915 – the college was affiliated with the University of British Columbia and offered the first two years in Arts and Education as well as the first year in Commerce. It listed a few third-year courses; degree programs would soon follow. With some 850 students and fifty professors the college was still tiny, but explosive growth was just ahead.

Frosh week was a mildly humiliating but mostly gentle introduction to the year. First-year students wore funny hats and placards stating name, age, and telephone number, but there was little or no hazing except at the Frosh Dance, where a kangaroo court tried uppity frosh and inflicted punishment. The next year freshmen experienced more hazing, however, and a glass door in the

Ewing Building was shattered during a scuffle. The principal decreed that hazing must cease. This had the effect of moving it off campus. In 1960, I seem to recall, sophomores chained two freshmen to a sign in the Roundabout, a traffic circle (no longer in existence) on Douglas Street, north of the downtown area.

The prevailing mores discouraged conspicuous application to one's studies: the ideal student was the all-rounder. Although fraternities and sororities were banned, there were many clubs. I joined the swimming team, the bowling and chess clubs, and the InterVarsity Christian Fellowship (IVCF). Sometimes I went to the Jive Club, grooving with old friends like Wendy Love and Jean Warren to the strains of 'Rockin' Robin,' 'Sea Cruise,' Elvis Presley's 'All Shook Up,' and Jerry Lee Lewis's infectious 'Whole Lot of Shakin' Going On.' I had a mild crush on one of my regular dancing partners, someone I had met in my psychology class, for much of the first term but never asked her out, for reasons I am now unable to fathom.

As I try to make sense of my life, only a few events (war, emigration, parenthood) loom larger than my undergraduate education. It may sound trite, but my studies liberated me. The process began in first year. Most eye opening among my courses was psychology. W.H. (Bill) Gaddes, tall, lean, and earnest, introduced me to ways of seeing human behaviour that challenged my still orthodox faith. Mother may have realized what was happening better than I did. At one point she was angered to learn that I was reading an article by Brock Chisholm, late of the World Health Organization. She knew of him because he had retired to Victoria and his letters appeared occasionally in the newspapers. As a result he was one of her *bêtes noires*, less because he counselled parents against teaching children to believe in Santa Claus than because he was a prominent agnostic. She phoned Gaddes to complain; somehow he managed to set her mind at rest. My mind continued hard at work, however.

Also intellectually disturbing was English, two hours a week of composition under the watchful eye of Caroline Burridge, and one of literature (poetry, short stories, drama, and one novel, *Brave New*

World) with John Grube. Burridge was a recently retired Oak Bay High teacher pressed into service because the college was short of staff to teach the sections in first-year English. Patient and endlessly helpful, she did a superb job. She had studied, I later learned, at the old Victoria College associated with McGill, where she had been a classmate of my grade ten French teacher, Mary Hamilton. They were remarkable women: intelligent, accomplished, and passionately devoted to teaching.

Grube, still in his twenties, cultivated a world-weary image but was clearly enthusiastic about his subject. I came to love it too, although some of the material made me uncomfortable: the bishop's comments about miracles in *Saint Joan*, for example, the depiction of religion in *Brave New World*, and the moral collapse of the missionary in Maugham's short story 'Rain.' Implicitly, sometimes explicitly, treasured beliefs of mine came under attack. But my outlook widened as I read these works, as well as Eliot's religious poetry, the witty drama of Sheridan, Arthur Miller's unflinching portrayal of a human being as commodity, and much else. I wrote an essay comparing the patriotism of Kipling and Wilfred Owen. From it I took a lasting admiration for Owen's poetry and a new awareness of the moral dilemmas posed by colonialism and war.

Psychology and English began a gradual process of reconsideration of my religious faith. Economics 100, economic history, the one course I had to take because I was in pre-Commerce, began to change my life in another, no less profound way. G. Reid Elliott, although a painfully shy lecturer, was puckishly provocative. 'Canadians can criticize their politicians but not their employers,' he once said or, more accurately, muttered: 'In the Soviet Union it's the other way around.' Another of his *mots* was: 'In almost every socialist there's a fascist struggling to break out.' I so much liked writing (voluntarily!) twenty-odd short papers for him, on subjects ranging from medieval money to the Colombo Plan, that I paid a visit to the counselling office. Might I be suited to something other than accountancy?

Aptitude tests indicated that I would make a fine chartered accountant, but also that I would do well in front of a classroom. As a consequence I did some research on university teaching. (The lower levels of teaching didn't attract me: I didn't want to spend my working life surrounded by children or adolescents.) There would, I found, be lots of openings in the 1960s. I also found that professors earned relatively little, given the length of their education: a full professor in western Canada earned roughly the same as the manager of the Government Street branch. But this weighed less heavily than the freedom that academics seemed to enjoy. Having spent two years working in a bank, I did not disdain money and I had no desire to be poor. Recalling the biblical warning that a camel was likelier to pass through the eye of a needle than a rich man to enter into heaven, however, I had no wish to turn my life into a means towards the making of money. A modest competence would suffice.

Without as yet committing myself to university teaching, that winter I abandoned thoughts of chartered accountancy. I have never regretted this. I would have made a good C.A. technically, and I would almost certainly have become materially wealthier than I am now. But I would not have liked arranging my life and opinions so as to attract clients or keeping my mouth shut for fear of losing them.

To give myself time for my extracurricular activities *and* do well in my studies I drew up a schedule that covered every waking hour. Classes, study, church, my clubs and pastimes: everything had its place. This methodical approach brought me without cramming to full readiness for my exams. I was rewarded with the watch (my first) that went to the top student in the college, and a scholarship worth $300.

It seems fitting at this point to thank those who donated the scholarships I won throughout my student years. Without them I would have had to take part-time jobs, to the detriment of my studies, my activities, or both. Still, I did need a summer job to help finance my education. In May 1959 I went to work for the division of examinations of the Department of Education, 'the Department' as we called it.

In charge of the summer staff was Alex Sokalski, the magistrar (this latinate title had been coined in the early 1950s by another magistrar, Peter L. Smith, now a professor of classics at the University of Victoria). A recent UBC graduate in French, Alex veered unpredictably between the wish to be liked and the need to crack the whip. His assistant, an intense psychology student named Ken Bull, didn't worry about *his* popularity. He served as magistrar in 1960 and 1961. As he was a fault-finder *par excellence*, no one was sorry to see the end of his tenure.

More congenial than either Alex or Ken was Rob Taylor, a second-year history student and an accomplished amateur actor. We commenced a friendship that continues to this day. Peter Wilkinson, a future Anglican clergyman, I knew already as one of Jack's classmates. Rob, Peter, and I became the nucleus of a small circle that also included Jack, Martin Bergbusch, Ron Poole, and occasionally Horace Mayea, like Rob a fine amateur actor. We went to movies, listened to records – *At the Drop of a Hat*, by Michael Flanders and Donald Swann, was a favourite – and discussed art, literature, politics, philosophy, and religion.

In the course of arguing with the others I worked out the view, which I still hold, that enlightened self-interest dictates taking the needs of other people seriously, and that those who are well-endowed materially or intellectually must assume some responsibility for those who are not. After all, our wealth or other attainments are realized in, and owe much to, our social setting, so it is appropriate that we at least partially repay society. (At one point I tried to read Ayn Rand, knowing she held a very different view, but her ideas and prose both put me off.)

However, my conviction that one must have some care for others remained largely theoretical. I had little or no experience of working-class people, to say nothing of the genuinely poor. When I read Wells's *The New Machiavelli* I recognized something of myself in its protagonist and his friends: 'Directly any of us socialists of Trinity found ourselves in immediate contact with servants or cadgers or gyps or bedders or plumbers or navvies or cabmen or railway porters we became unconsciously and unthinkingly aristocrats.' I was no aristocrat, of course, nor a socialist. But I *was* irremediably middle class and something of a snob.

The Legislative Assembly having risen, we used the committee rooms and the office of the sergeant-at-arms in the Parliament Building. The office of the Premier, the ebullient W.A.C. Bennett, was nearby, and we saw him in the halls from time to time. When passing a potential voter, 'Wacky' would flash a toothy smile and boom: 'Good morning [or afternoon], my friend.' I had a low opinion of Social Credit by this time, but it would have been churlish and perhaps unwise not to return the Premier's greetings in kind.

By mid-May some twenty students were on hand, three-quarters of them women. The Maplemen – we worked in the Maple Committee Room – did both clerical and physical work. Most of the women worked in the Cedar Committee Room and were called Millies because of the process called 'milling' that they carried out, examining the transcripts of students to determine what they needed for graduation, and correcting errors. In charge of the Millies was the Mill Mom, in 1959 my high school classmate Joanne Dawson.

Exams were compulsory in grade thirteen, the equivalent of first-year university, offered by large schools outside Victoria and Vancouver. A lot of students in grades eleven and twelve took recommendations, available to those in accredited schools who had grades of C+ or better in the examinable subjects. Students in non-accredited (some public and all private) schools had no choice but to write exams, as did everyone who applied for scholarships. The pressure mounted as the baby boomers entered the highest grades in growing numbers. By the summer of 1965, my last in the Department, things were getting out of hand. One evening the registrar and I contemplated the intricate arrangement of tables in the Central Junior High School gymnasium that had enabled us to cram in every grader for grade twelve English. 'This can't go on much longer, Mike,' Harry Evans said, lighting what may have been his sixtieth cigarette of the day from the butt of the fifty-ninth: 'We've got to get rid of exams. But first we've got to find a pedagogical reason.' Departmental exams were abolished a couple of years later, I gather, but I will bet the government did not admit that the logistics had become unmanageable.

We shipped blank exams and supplies such as logarithmic tables all over the province, then got Central ready for the teachers who began marking right after Dominion Day. Marking, scaling, entering grades on the transcripts, determining who had graduated, photocopying documents, and mailing them: everything had to be completed within four weeks to enable those with failures to apply for a supplemental exam in mid-August.

The enterprise required careful management and pinpoint timing. Nominally in charge was the assistant registrar, J. Ross Hind – J.R., as we called him. Amiable to a fault, he was also a ditherer. The contrast with Harry Evans was immediately noticeable in the way they walked. J.R. sauntered, whereas Harry, a wiry workaholic, always moved on the double, cigarette hanging from his lower lip. In July he simply took over. Able to explain things quickly to the rankest tyro and to anticipate bottlenecks with uncanny skill, he was one of the most competent persons I have ever worked for. Under his watchful eye the 'Central operation' went like clockwork.

Of all the processes carried out at Central, scaling was the most fascinating. From Walter Burgess, a UBC math student who worked in the office of tests and measurements, I learned how scales were devised to compensate for exams that were too easy or too hard, to secure the desired grade distribution and failure rate, and to eliminate the marks of 49 and 48 per cent so as to discourage some appeals. Walter's explanations cured me of the notion that in themselves exams provided an accurate gauge of how much students knew. The results evidently had to be adjusted, using criteria that were in part subjective.

At the end of July, having mailed out the exam results and transcripts, we returned to the Parliament Building. (In August 1961 there was a special session of the Legislature to take over B.C. Electric. This forced us to clear out the committee rooms, only to reverse the move when the session ended two days later. The curses we Maplemen rained on Wacky Bennett were probably outnumbered only by those from B.C. Electric shareholders.) Teachers marked the supplemental exams at home; everything else was done at the Parliament Building. Before Labour Day the results and revised transcripts went out. By the second Friday of September most of the staff had gone, leaving the Maplemen to mop up.

Many of Victoria's best students, especially its women, had summer jobs in the Department. The group was homogeneous (white and mostly the daughters and sons of professional and managerial people) and cohesive, meeting after work at picnics, pot-luck dinners, beach parties, literary evenings, and concerts in the Butchart Gardens. Almost everyone's favourite social event was 'Christmas in August': gifts could not cost more than a quarter, and the ones most appreciated and admired were entirely home-made. A real *esprit de corps* existed, also a private vocabulary consisting of terms used in our work and a private slang intended to baffle the uninitiated, terms such as M.N., coined by Glenys Parry and meaning *mauvaises nouvelles*, and N.T.G.A.A., not too good at all.

Putting bright people to work at routine tasks had one major drawback: attention tended to wander. The Maplemen often played Botticelli, a memory game, while working. It may have been the inattentiveness this fostered that caused the great exam snafu of 1961. Right after 9:00 one June morning the telephone rang off the cradle: in several Victoria schools (luckily nowhere else in the province) the sealed exam envelopes for one course contained the exams for another. By truck and private car we got the right exams out, and before 10:00 everyone had them, but it was an embarrassing blunder all the same, the kind that might prompt a query from the minister of education. Ken spent a good deal of time seeking to identify the bunglers. One person had filled the envelopes, another had checked them, a third had carried out spot checks while sealing. Without a record of who had done what, however, Ken's efforts turned up no names. That was just as well: his mood was truly sulphurous.

As I think of those summers another thing sticks in my mind: the parsimony of the provincial government. It paid no overtime: civil servants were supposed to take compensatory time off. For us there was no slack, however. Overtime was expected from everyone, and some of us accumulated 100 hours or more. Because we were not covered by provincial labour legislation we did not get time-and-a-half, but were paid as though we had worked the hours in September, October, and, in the case of a particularly industrious Mill Mom one year, November!

The government's cheese-paring style was most clearly manifested in the truck we drove. Battered, unwieldy, temperamental – it would not stay in gear when one tried to brake on the engine – and quite possibly dangerous, the 1949 Ford pick-up spent the academic year in the vocational shop of the high school in Nanaimo, returning to Victoria every May as if to summer camp. Harry said that he would not be allowed to replace the vehicle unless it broke down totally or someone piled it up. It was still in use in 1965!

By the fall of 1959 only Steven, Jan D., and I lived at home. Peter had withdrawn from college to take a job with an engineering firm in Vancouver, Jack was studying physical education at George Williams College in Chicago, and Joe was working in a logging camp on the island well north of Victoria. All three must have been glad to leave, for the atmosphere at home was often tense. Mother had become a zealous fundamentalist, attending a Pentecostalist and a conservative Baptist church before settling eventually for the Christian and Missionary Alliance. Father, on the other hand, was as irreligious as ever. He was not aggressive about this, and he was no atheist nor even an agnostic. He believed in God, but he simply didn't care about organized religion, and he didn't think God cared about him.

Mother's deity cared intensely about many matters, among them the spiritual welfare of members of her family as well as the minutiae of our personal behaviour. She no longer drank so much as a thimbleful of beer, for example, having decided that God commanded abstinence from alcohol. I did not drink in any case, but found it surprising that Father went along with Mother's new practice, at least at home. 'God wikt, maar je moeder beschikt' (God proposes, but your mother disposes), was his comment on her teetotalitarianism and other aspects of what he regarded as her religious obsession. That he should joke about these things distressed her.

They quarrelled a good deal, usually converting a present difference into an argument about some ancient grievance. Around this time, in the diary that I began to keep in the summer of 1959 and fitfully kept into the 1970s, I opined that they were drifting towards divorce. In this I was wrong: having been married for a quarter of a century my parents needed each other for many reasons, of which familiar disagreements were not the least important.

Mother and I also quarrelled. What she objected to in my case was not my lack of religion but rather its increasing liberalism. My opposition to capital punishment was a typical cause of conflict between us. I can't recall whether my attitude was prompted by something I had read, or whether I found the punishment repellent in itself, but either way I saw no need to hide my opinion. That I argued with her she found annoying, but her irritation was as nothing compared to her fury when I wrote to a U.S. religious periodical to which she subscribed, controverting its claim that the death penalty was the Christian answer to murder. Revenge belonged to God and not to human beings, I argued; the deterrent value of capital punishment was unproven, miscarriages of justice did occur, and the act of execution degraded everyone associated with it. (I continue to believe that fully civilized countries do not execute people.) Mother was angry and sad, taking my letter as evidence that I was moving towards apostasy.

As a result of my own differences with Mother, my sympathies lay more with Father. I realize now that this was unfair. Mother's indifferent health affected her more than I realized. As well, she was haunted by a sense of lost opportunity. She sometimes envied her sister, Phiet, who had earned a doctorate and made a name for herself as a classicist while being married and raising a child. Mother was far from being a feminist, but she suspected, I think, that she might have done more with her life than being a wife and mother.

To make matters worse, Father was stuck as a relatively ill-paid draughtsman with the B.C. Forest Service, even though since 1956 he had been a member of the Architectural Institute of British Columbia. His efforts to be upgraded were unsuccessful, and being nearer sixty than fifty he was too old to look for another job. It bothered Mother a good deal that he received neither the professional recognition nor the larger salary she desired for him.

Although I worried about them occasionally, I didn't spend a lot of time trying to make sense of my parents' lives. My studies were too demanding. In the fall of 1959 I registered in courses in English, history, philosophy, psychology, and Spanish. English was a survey from Spenser to Austen, taught by the debonair head of the English department, Roger Bishop, and the acid Grant McOrmond. Along with *Pride and Prejudice* – does anyone doubt that Austen is among the best novelists ever? – seventeenth-century poetry greatly appealed to me. I enjoyed reading Milton aloud and found spiritual sustenance in the works of Donne and Herbert.

I also liked the Cavalier poets, especially Suckling and Marvell. Their *insouciance* was at odds with the cautious way in which I conducted my own life, but perhaps I admired it all the more for that. 'To His Coy Mistress' was a particular favourite. (In 1982, en route from Munich to Geneva and killing time in Zürich's Kloten airport, I came across Marvell's gem, side by side with a German translation, in the *Neue Zürcher Zeitung*. In middle age I found the poem more poignant than it had been when I was twenty: 'But at my back I always hear / Time's winged Chariot hurrying near: / And yonder all before us lie / Deserts of vast Eternity.')

Philosophy was a historical survey taught by an anthropologist, Roy Watson, the college not yet having a trained philosopher. Not surprisingly, he stuck close to the text. Spanish I remember mainly because of my classmate Leslie Millin, feisty and armed with a fiendishly sharp tongue. Once he saw me eating a sandwich with dark turkey meat. 'What's in that sandwich, Mike?' Les exclaimed. 'Dinosaur's afterbirth?' As he had lived in Mexico for a while, his Spanish was better than anyone else's. He also played the guitar and sang Mexican songs, which made him a great asset at parties.

The courses I liked most were Mental Health and Europe since 1500. Bill Gaddes taught the former in his customarily lucid fashion, but he had a greater impact on my life outside the classroom than within. Early in the fall he asked whether I would take the Wechsler-Bellevue intelligence test, which he said he had for curiosity's sake been administering over the years to students who had done well in Psychology 100. It would take several hours to complete, he warned, but these could be spread out.

Feeling flattered by his request, I said I was willing to spend the time if he was. My score was very high. A November 1959 entry in my diary sheds light on my thinking at the time: 'Finished my IQ testing on Saturday morning ... Almighty God, guide me into thy path, that I may do thy will. I am becoming increasingly interested in history. So many interesting books have appeared about the Second World War that I think I should like to write a history about it. I'd probably have to find a historian wife, though; it won't be a job for one man alone. All the research that would be necessary!' I cringe a bit as I read this now, but that was the way I thought as an earnest and devout twenty-year-old. More important in the long run was that the seemingly objective evidence of my high intelligence – I had not yet learned to question the idea of 'intelligence' as a measurable absolute – turned out to be the final push I needed to commit myself to an academic career.

Another person who influenced me in this was my history instructor, R.H. Roy. He once spoke feelingly about his sense of utter loneliness during the last days of the Second World War, silhouetted on a dike in the northern Netherlands, aware that a German 88 mm gun could blow him and his tank crew into oblivion on what might be the final day of hostilities. I enjoyed working on my essays, one on Calvinism and the other on Nazi Germany, so much that I made an appointment with him in March and asked whether he thought I might make a good historian.

He encouraged me in a cautious way: there was a lot of competition and not much money in the field, but for those who liked history, as I seemed to, and who liked to talk to people, the occupation was highly suitable. Cheered by this, I decided to become a history professor. Interest and enjoyment determined my choice: I enjoyed figuring out what had happened in the past and telling others about it. If an assessment of social utility played any part in my decision I am unaware of it. But then, no such assessment had influenced me in earlier choosing chartered accountancy, either.

In my second year I was even more active in extracurricular activities than in my first. Chess, music, the Jive Club, IVCF, and bowling took a good deal of my time, but none more than music. I became vice-president of the Listening Club, which held weekly noon-hour concerts of recorded music and organized the spring concert.

Victoria offered limited opportunities for hearing live music, although I recall hearing the Dutch organist Feike Asma at Christ Church Cathedral and a performance of a choral work by Mendelssohn, probably *Elijah*, at one of the larger United churches. I recall one *really* big event, a Victoria Symphony concert in March 1960 featuring Glenn Gould in Beethoven's Third Concerto. Tickets were scarce: for a decade Gould had been the most prominent Canadian pianist, renowned for his recordings, noted also for his eccentricities.

The program opened with melodious gloom and continued with romantic doom: the *Tragic Overture* followed by *Francesca da Rimini*. Gould appeared after the intermission. From my diary:

It was time for the great man. He strode in, sat down on a very dilapidated bench, crossed his arms and legs, and wiped his face only twice during the introduction by the orchestra. His music was pure joy to hear but to enjoy him most you have to close your eyes. His histrionics are rather distracting, and even then I'm told they're not as bad as they used to be. Why he doesn't get his hair cut or doesn't buy a decently-fitting pair of pants is a riddle. He hums and beats time, and is almost as fascinating to watch as to hear.

It seems that I was a keener critic of personal appearance than of music.

Victoria still lacked professional theatre, but at the college the Players' Club did good work: I remember a fine performance of *You Never Can Tell* in which Rob Taylor appeared (as the waiter). The Langham Court Theatre offered amateur drama from time to time, and I went to see *The Mouse Trap* there: a most engaging piece of fluff. The Intimate Stage was active during the summer, bringing together students from UBC and Victoria College. Several of them were friends of mine, and in 1959 I helped with the lights for a production of *Look Back in Anger* that starred my old friend John Gilliland and my co-worker Margot Thompson. Osborne's play was realistic, and some of its language I found raw and offensive. I was not the only one: during the intermission several members of the smallish audience expressed displeasure. (The venue was the Victoria Art Gallery, where no more than 100 people could be seated.)

Of the relatively few films I saw, *Ben Hur* appealed to my religious sensibilities while offering, in the chariot race, one of the most memorable of action scenes. *I'm All Right, Jack* was a brilliant satire on postwar British society, featuring a strong cast headed by Ian Carmichael and Peter Sellers. But I liked most Jacques Tati's whimsical *Les vacances de Monsieur Hulot*, which is still among my all-time favourites. Having seen it more than a dozen times I know the perfectly executed sight gags by heart: the table-tennis game and its effects on the card players nearby, the funeral where a leaf-covered inner tube is mistaken for a floral offering, the impromptu fireworks display and Hulot's inept efforts to end it, and on and on. I start laughing before they happen; I'm smiling now as I think of them.

Sometimes I watched television at a friend's house. I was little impressed: 'Standard of average program seems low,' I wrote in my diary: 'Stereotyped formulas are obvious, and one or two shows made less sense than the commercials. If this is what the public wants, it doesn't say much for the taste of the public.' Still, I enjoyed *The Valiant Years*, a documentary about the Second World War, and a tongue-in-cheek crime show called *77 Sunset Strip*. And the 1960 World Series, of which I saw scattered innings on a set in the Men's Common Room at the college, produced a magic moment. In the seventh game, the New York Yankees rallied to tie the game in the ninth only to lose, 10-9, when the Pittsburgh Pirates' Bill Mazeroski homered to lead off the bottom of the inning. Until the Blue Jays' Joe Carter hit one in the ninth inning of game six in 1993 it was the only time a home run decided a World Series.

I read more than ever: mainly novels, poetry, and drama but also economics, history, and biography. In 1959 my reading included Alan Paton's novels *Cry the Beloved Country* and *Too Late the Phalarope*, which I found 'intensely honest and moving, and hauntingly beautiful; at the same time ominous.' I also read Trevor Huddleston's *Naught for Your Comfort*. Whether I had an opinion on *apartheid* before reading these authors I can't remember, but they led me to see the institution as profoundly evil and almost certain to end in civil war. I didn't think that outside pressure or intervention would make much of a difference to this, and for years I opposed economic sanctions on the grounds that they were more likely to hurt black South Africans than to lessen the resolve of whites to maintain their privileges. It seems now that I was mistaken.

Fairfield United Church continued to loom large in my life. A new minister, Harry Johnston, encouraged my interest in biblical scholarship as well as my desire to be useful. I taught Sunday school, helped with the cub pack for a year, and was active in two youth groups. I also organized my social life around the church. Among the friends I made there was David Leeming, a mathematics major who may have owed his tendency to take charge to his father, a local school trustee. He (or his parents) owned an impressive collection of LPs, both classical and humour. It was at their house at the top of Bond Street that I first heard the comedy of Victor Borge, Tom Lehrer, Bob Newhart, and Anna Russell.

David was one of two people who accompanied me to the Glenn Gould concert in 1960. The other was Carolyn, the oldest daughter of Jim McCammon, the mining engineer to whose Akela I played Baloo in the Fairfield United cub pack. She was quiet and reserved, but as I got to know her better I found that she stood up for herself in argument and was very intelligent (she later took a Ph.D. in chemistry in minimum time). Early in 1960 we became sweethearts. This made for an enjoyable spring and summer, but by the fall she had grown impatient with the restrictions that going steady imposed and we broke up. As I continued to be fond of her and she still liked me, we made a successful effort to remain friends.

Upon completing my second year I wanted to transfer to UBC to enter Honours History, but I lacked a required introductory course in Canadian history. As I couldn't afford to take time off for summer school, I would either have to take the course by high school correspondence or read up the subject by myself and write an exam in the fall. Neither was an appealing way to start a notoriously demanding program. Moreover, it would cost more to live in Vancouver, and my hopes for higher summer earnings were dashed when Rob Taylor became assistant magistrar. I sought advice from the head of History, Sydney Pettit, who suggested I stay in Victoria for a general degree. My grades would get me admitted to any graduate school, he said. I decided to stay.

For $275, money saved by not going to Vancouver, I bought a 1950 Morris Minor – I had got my driver's licence in 1958. I could afford the running costs if I operated a car pool, I calculated. Alas, I forgot to budget for repairs. I had to replace the battery and the generator, and would have replaced the ring gear had I had the money.

Unexpectedly costly, the car nevertheless paid for itself by saving me a lot of time. Jack also found it useful. He had transferred to Victoria College after finding that he liked his academic courses at George Williams more than his courses in physical education. He turned up in September with contact lenses, a Chicago accent (soon lost), and a newly acquired agnosticism.

Was I moving in that direction? Some of my IVCF friends may have thought so, for that fall I forsook them for the more liberal Student Christian Movement. In fact, it was the IVCF's unabashed evangelicalism more than its conservative doctrine that drove me away. Well before the end of second year, it had begun to embarrass me to sing hymns at lunch-time on Fridays. Sundays were a different matter, and I continued to be a faithful church attender throughout 1960–1. At the same time, my views became steadily less conservative. As I had never deeply felt my faith, my increasing lack of concern for dogma probably pointed to my eventual loss of religion.

I took three courses in history, two in English, and one in German. Sydney Pettit, who taught a third-year course on medieval Europe and a fourth-year course in European intellectual history, combined the manner of a Trollopian archdeacon with the method of a Dickensian schoolmaster. Woe betide those who took notes while he lectured, and those who failed to copy down his dictated summary! Much more relaxed was Anthony (Tony) Emery, an Oxford graduate who taught Tudor and Stuart Britain. A charming dilettante – his real interest was art history – he was the most amusing lecturer I have ever had: a bewhiskered man with a fine sense of humour, an equally good sense of timing, and a disarming self-deprecatory chuckle. He was an entertaining after-dinner speaker, as I would learn at UBC's 1963 academic symposium. At some point he spoke about the importance of genetics. 'So, girls,' he said, 'before you decide to marry that boy you love, look carefully into his genes.' The pun was daring for those times, and loud guffaws rewarded him.

With Ann Saddlemyer, a newcomer who compensated for youth with a show of self-confidence, we read works by Butler, Conrad, Hardy, Hopkins, Housman, Shaw, Wilde, Yeats, and her beloved Synge. I preferred Butler, whose novels *Erewhon* and *The Way of All Flesh* I still treasure; Wilde, whose wit delighted me; and Housman, whose elegant pessimism comforted me as I came to terms with disappointed love. He is still a favourite of mine.

I tried my own hand at poetry, and laboriously produced three stanzas, written in blank verse, linking autumn and the possibility of nuclear war. I submitted this to Julian Reid, a friend who edited a poetry journal of some kind. He returned it after a few days. For a rookie my poem wasn't bad, he said, but it was a bit hackneyed. Could I work on it some more? Or perhaps try some other theme? I thought about it for a while, then decided not to bother. Prose, not poetry, seemed to be my *métier*.

Grant McOrmond, knowledgeable if acerbic, lectured on the Romantic period. It seemed an odd choice for him, because, of the five poets whose work mainly engaged us, Wordsworth, Coleridge, Keats, Byron, and Shelley, he seemed to have much use only for the last two. These he discussed with real *élan*. Dealing with the works of the others he was conscientious but uninspiring.

Having become interested in German history, I abandoned Spanish in third year in order to study German. (When I first visited Spain, a decade later, I could still read the language, but conversation was out of the question. An unexpected benefit from having studied Spanish as well as French is that I can decipher descriptions in *Italian* museums.) During the summer, with Mother's help, I had worked my way through the introductory German text; that fall I registered in the advanced first-year course. J.B. MacLean's punctiliousness about grammar didn't interfere with my delight in sampling the work of Goethe, Heine, Rilke, Thomas Mann, and others.

I was invited to join the Creighton Club (named after the eminent

Toronto historian Donald G. Creighton), consisting of a dozen third- and fourth-year history students, and late in the session presented a paper on the German resistance to Hitler. The president of the club was David Alexander, a quiet-spoken man who was endowed with a subtle, wide-ranging intellect. He was clearly the star of what was the college's first graduating class, and his presence in several of my classes reassured me that I hadn't blundered by staying in Victoria.

Active in the Creighton Club, the Listening Club, the SCM, chess, debating, and the Jive Club, I earned an activity award for the second year in a row. Added to six courses and my church work, however, they made life too hectic and exhausting. By January I was looking for a rest or at least a change. Outside the registrar's office I read a notice offering a year's study in Germany, paid for by the German Academic Exchange Service (DAAD), and applied. The news that I had won a fellowship reached me hours before the last meeting of the Creighton Club. I arrived at the old army hut that housed the Faculty Club full of excitement. Tony Emery asked me whether the Germans would send someone in exchange. 'They had better not!' Pettit snapped and strode off. Emery laughed: 'Two things I dislike, prejudice and Germans.'

Father sounded like Pettit. 'Je hebt gemasseld, Chiel' (You've been lucky, Mike), he said. 'En ik hoop dat je er plezier van zal hebben, maar heb niet het lef om met een Duitse vrouw terug te komen.' He hoped I would enjoy it, but I shouldn't try to return with a German wife! He needn't worry, I told him. Excited as I was about the prospect of going abroad, I had misgivings as well. My war-born prejudice against Germans lingered. It was to indulge my interest in the Second World War and the Nazi period that I was going to Germany, not to look for a mate.

Rob Taylor and Peter Wilkinson had decided against a third summer at the Department of Education, so I became assistant magistrar even though J.R. knew that I would not be back in 1962. The new Maplemen were Gordon Shrimpton and Martin Petter. J.R. thought highly of Gordon and asked Ken to groom him for the magistrar's job. I liked him but got along better with Martin, a history student with tastes similar to mine. He, like Rob, became a lifelong friend.

One of the new women attracted me. Endowed with an expressive face, a throaty laugh, and a ready wit, Sandra McKeachie was hard to ignore. She intended to major in English and history, and thought of becoming a writer (she became a journalist and later taught journalism). Within weeks of meeting each other, Sandy and I were love-birds.

In order to spend more time with her, I signed up for the acting crew of Intimate Stage, which she had already joined. The group's director and guiding spirit was Tony Nicholson, a thirtyish travel agent with a peremptory manner. He wanted to do a musical, Sandy Wilson's *The Boy Friend*, but after ascertaining that he was woefully short of singers and dancers he chose two short plays instead, *The Bald Soprano* and *The Ghost Sonata*. Sandy landed the female lead in the Strindberg play, in which I got a walk-on part. Then the male lead begged off. Looking for a replacement, Tony's eye landed on me. Had I acted before? he asked. 'Never,' I replied, confident that he would now move on to someone else. 'Good,' he said instead, 'the part is yours.' 'But what about my lack of experience?' That didn't matter, he replied: so long as I was averagely intelligent I could learn my lines, and he would teach me how to act. More than a little intrigued, I accepted his challenge.

I didn't like the play. The language was turgid, the motivations of the characters unclear, the relationships among them utterly confusing. I much preferred Ionesco's crisp absurdities. (Jack and I still savour one exchange from *The Bald Soprano*: 'The heart has its reasons.' 'They also say the opposite.' 'The truth lies somewhere in between.') But I swallowed my distaste and learned my lines, including one very long monologue, playing the part of Arkenholtz with a minimum of histrionics.

We put on three performances of our double bill before sell-out crowds at the art gallery. Some of the audience may have been a bit confused: one of Victoria's theatre critics had written, with a presumably jocular reference to the titles of the two plays, that we were planning a musical evening! It was a source of considerable satisfaction to me that I didn't suffer from stage fright – it helped that, without my glasses, I could hardly see the audience – and didn't fluff my lines. Martin Bergbusch said that I was a sensitive version of myself; Tony conceded that I was 'all right.' Neither he nor anyone else suggested that I had a future on the stage, however, and apart from graduate-school skits I haven't appeared on it since.

And yet: lecturers have to hold their audiences, just as actors do. That distant three-performance turn has served me well in the classroom. I might have been no Kean, but I was adequate, and I built on this when, some years later, I began to lecture. I like to speak to people, the more the better. No doubt I ham it up from time to time, but that is deliberate: I want my students to pay attention.

Before the *Ghost Sonata* went on stage, Sandy and I had broken up, though happily we continued to speak to each other. For a time we had got on famously and had begun talking about marriage, even picking names for our children. One weekend in July, while rehearsals of the play were already well along, we visited her parents in Nanaimo (dreary, but not yet the horrible example of urban sprawl it is today). Afterwards they told Sandy that we seemed to be getting too serious about each other. When she imparted this opinion to me I said they might be right: the talk of marriage and children was beginning to give me cold feet. I suggested we see less of each other. Her parents' observation probably made it easy for her to agree to this: she was not much of a rebel.

Was I chickening out? I was. I was unready for marriage, either emotionally or in the mundane sense of being able to provide for a family. I liked female company a lot, however, and I suppose I got my share and more. My Dutch background was far from being a hindrance. If anything, it was an advantage. I don't know whether it had mattered to Carolyn, for example, but it disposed her father favourably towards me. As an officer with the Royal Canadian Engineers he had spent several months in Holland in 1945, waiting for repatriation, and he had warm memories of his contacts with the civilian population there. Who knows? perhaps a bit of this had rubbed off on his daughter. In Sandy's case, my background gave me a touch of the exotic that she found appealing. She liked to refer to me as 'Latin,' pronounced in the French fashion, which was her shorthand for 'Latin lover.' This betrayed ethnic as well as geographical confusion, but I managed for once to suppress my annoying habit of correcting obvious error in others.

On the first day of September 1961 I sailed from Montreal on the S.S. *Arkadia* of the Greek Line. Leaving Victoria the day before, I had flown to Vancouver by Viscount, then by DC-8 via Toronto to Montreal (my first jet flight). Over Lake Superior we passed through towering clouds that formed 'an unreal Grand Canyon, most delicately coloured, first pink, then mauve, finally a mysterious grey white.' On arriving in Montreal I checked into the Laurentian Hotel; early the next day I took a taxi to Pier 42. At 11:00 the ship cast off.

The first people I met on board were my cabin-mates, John Hill and George Hynna. They promptly invited me to have a beer. It was to be the first of many: like me, both were planning to attend Freiburg University. John had completed his third year in Honours German at McMaster; George, a modern languages graduate of the University of Toronto, was taking a year out before entering Osgoode Hall law school.

Altogether there were ten DAAD fellows, drawn from nine universities. So far, I had known few Canadians my age who had not been born and raised in or near Victoria. Now I met several, some with perspectives very different from mine. John, for example, insisted Canada should not be a satellite of the United States, and should follow its own course in international affairs instead. As I was pro-American at that time, we got into more than one argument during the year that followed.

On 9 September we approached the Dutch coast and the North Sea Canal. 'I saw Wijk aan Zee from a distance,' I wrote in my diary: 'Was fascinated to see the Dutch countryside again, mixed with a certain pride, longing.' Seeing the breakwater at IJmuiden, on which I had often walked in 1949 and 1951, proved particularly evocative. Happy memories of summer holidays came to my mind, then others crowded in: school days, my old friends. I paced along the deck nervously, feeling apprehensive, edgy: was *this* where I belonged?

At the quay in Amsterdam, Tante Phiet was waiting for me, accompanied by her daughter, Flora, and her ward, an Indonesian girl named Greet (Oom Jef, a heavy smoker, had died of emphysema some years earlier). In her creaking Citroën 2CV we drove to her flat on the Tintorettostraat in the southern part of the city. My aunt and I talked late into the evening, mostly about family matters. It struck me that she seemed to believe Father to be doing better professionally than in fact he was: the first (but not the last) indication I got that Mother had been misrepresenting to her relatives how we were faring in Canada. Tante Phiet was a more relaxed and erudite version of Mother, and decidedly more liberal in her political and religious views. During the year that followed I learned to like her a lot.

The next day, Sunday, I really went home, or so it felt. Tante Phiet had a day-long meeting of classicists in Baarn, and I hitched a ride with her. She dropped me off at Emmalaan 11A, where the Schoute family welcomed me warmly and poured coffee. When I looked around the living-room with its huge fireplace, scores of memories rushed in. This was where I lived for the first twelve-plus years of my life!

The Schoutes showed me around the house, to which they had made a number of changes: bathroom renovations, new walls upstairs that had increased the number of bedrooms, the replacement of the old coal furnace with one that burned oil. The house was basically as I remembered it, however, and the principal rooms downstairs were unaltered. The house *did* seem smaller than before, and so did the garden: a universal experience when people return to childhood haunts.

Baarn itself seemed smaller, too. Late that morning I walked to the Kettingweg, where I was meeting the Cazants for lunch. I stopped to contemplate the Wilhelminavijver, thinking of the many happy hours I had spent around or on it. I also paused at Father's war memorial near the railway station. Even so, the walk didn't take anywhere near the twenty minutes I had anticipated.

The lunch was agreeable: one of Mevrouw Cazant's cousins, a professor at the University of Geneva, and his Swiss-born wife were visiting, and the conversation, in Dutch and French, flowed easily. After lunch the academic couple opted for an afternoon of reading while the Cazants and I went for a hike in the woods of the Royal Domain. It was a gorgeous late-summer day, and we walked for several hours, Mevrouw Cazant and I chattering happily about the events of the last ten years, while Meneer Cazant made the occasional waspish comment: just like old times. At the end I was somewhat out of breath. I hadn't walked this much since caddying at the Victoria Golf Club half a dozen years earlier. (North Americans walk less than Europeans.)

Several days of discovery in Amsterdam followed. Then, just before I was due to leave for Freiburg, I spent a weekend in Hilversum with the Hennus family, friends of Father's whose son, Michiel, was my age and with whom I had stayed just before our departure in 1952. On Sunday, Michiel and I dined in Baarn at the home of my old friend Willem Hendrik de Beaufort, now, like Michiel, a law student in Leiden. They seemed keenly interested in hearing about Canada, and I handed around copies of *Beautiful British Columbia*, but more as a traveller returning from distant places than as a visitor from abroad. Yet I did not feel fully at home.

Intrigued by my ambivalent feelings, I spent more time in Holland, that September and throughout the year, than I had originally intended. My plan had been to find a place to stay in Freiburg and then meet George, John, and several other DAAD fellows in Munich for the *Oktoberfest*. Instead, after finding a room, I returned to Holland. I visited Tante Pieta in Doorwerth, sitting around and reading, schmoozing with my cousins Thera and Ineke, playing chess with Tjitte, wandering down to the castle in gorgeous sunshine. A few days later I stayed with the Cazants. While in Baarn I lunched with my old friend Louise Hasseley Kirchner and was impressed to hear that she had been elected president of the women students' association at the University of Utrecht. The next day I was in Utrecht myself to lunch with my cousin Maja and her fiancé, Aldo Voûte, both students at the university. In Utrecht, too, I visited Opa's sometime companion, Mevrouw den Ouden, as well as Tante Gesien and her family. I looked up Father's other two surviving sisters, Tante Toos and her twin sister, Coba, both living in Ede, and his favourite cousin, Marie Raisig, in a nursing home in

Laren. At Tante Phiet's place I saw Oom Kees and Tante Tück, who were about to move to a small town near Osnabrück (they became German citizens in 1965). I was taking part in a family festival and loving it.

Everyone made me feel welcome, but none more than Tante Phiet. I stayed with her for a few days in early October, just before I went to Paris. One evening she took me to the Concertgebouw, a building of which I have several delightful memories. Wilhelm Backhaus played Beethoven's Fourth Concerto; the orchestra also performed a piece by Hans Henkemans (married, Tante Phiet said, to our cousin Amy Knappert) and Bartók's Concerto for Orchestra, a work new to me but one that I immediately liked. Afterwards I got Backhaus, Henkemans, and the young conductor, Bernard Haitink, to autograph my program, which I still have.

Over Christmas and New Year's I was in Holland again. In the course of a Boxing Day dinner with the Wentink family – Johan Wentink had been Father's friend and occasional collaborator – I learned that architecture had proved very remunerative since 1952 and that one of the Wentink children was preparing himself to join Johan's practice. It was unsettling to realize that Father would have done better by staying in Holland than by emigrating.

(While writing this memoir I asked Father whether he had ever considered a partnership with Wentink. Not really, he said. Why not? 'Ja, zie je, Chiel, Johan was eigenlijk meer een zakenman dan een architect,' more a businessman than an architect. The answer struck me as less than persuasive. Since Father was not well-endowed with business skills, he might have done worse than link himself to someone who apparently had them in abundance. But Father did not trust business people generally – his distrust of contractors was monumental – and for all I know he might not have trusted Wentink as a partner, even though he was a friend.)

During my stay with the Cazants over Christmas I chummed around with Mevrouw's nephew, Boudewijn van Oort. His father, an architect like mine, had left for Canada approximately when we did; Boudy, an amiable and athletic physicist, had graduated from Carleton University and was attending Oxford as a Rhodes Scholar. His Dutch was at least as good as mine, but we spoke

English with each other, feeling just a bit superior to those around us.

It was cold, and we went skating in places I found hauntingly familiar, among them the moat around Groeneveld castle. We also attended concerts together, in Hilversum and Amsterdam. Returning by train one evening we found that all the second-class compartments were crowded, so we took refuge in first class. When the conductor inspected our tickets he informed us we were in the wrong carriage. Speaking English, we feigned not to understand him. Pointing to the tickets he said, 'Second class,' then, waving about him, 'this is first class.' Finally and emphatically, returning our tickets: 'Now you go to second class.' Suitably chastened, Boudy and I slunk off.

I visited Holland again at Easter and in late June, Tante Phiet, Tante Pieta, and the Cazants providing me with my *pieds à terre*. Perhaps I outwore my welcome with them, although no one ever said so, but I found that I could not get enough of my native country, familiar and strange at the same time. Or was I homesick for my family and friends more often than I knew, and was going to Holland a way of coping with it? Did I regret that we had emigrated? At times I did. Once I woke up, realizing that I had been dreaming in Dutch. I had not done so for years, and it led me to speculate about what it would take to make the country of my birth mine again.

I knew that in an important sense it had ceased to be so: I had too many ties now to Canada or, more accurately, Vancouver Island. By comparison with its open spaces, moreover, Holland seemed pokey. Yet in some ways I felt more comfortable in my country of birth. It was tidier, and things seemed to be organized more effectively. Moreover, the Dutch class system made more sense to me. Taking my cues from relatives and former classmates, I knew where I belonged: in the upper middle class. In Canada my position was and would be more ambiguous. Social class meant (and means) less in this country, and the status of professors was less clear cut than in Holland.

I have visited Holland many times since, and uncertainties continue. I am now more solidly rooted in Canada than I was in 1961–2, and it would be difficult to re-adapt to Holland, even assuming that Cornelia and our sons wanted to live there. Yet my sense of where I belong socially is stronger there than here. Politically, however, I am more at home in Canada. Here I am somewhat left of centre; in Holland I find myself somewhat to the right. This owes as much to the different ways the countries have developed, I imagine, as to my personal history. Netherlanders are less inclined to regard the government as an enemy than Canadians (themselves friendlier to the state than their American neighbours), and tolerate a degree of bureaucratic interference with their lives that sometimes strikes me as excessive even when I can see the reasons for it. With much of its densely settled population living below sea level, on land that has been reclaimed from the water and must constantly be safeguarded against it, Holland, more than Canada, is a collective and cooperative achievement. This has exacted a price, paid in the coin of personal freedom of action (though not of expression). It is a price I am somewhat reluctant to pay. As well, during the last three decades the Dutch welfare state has become generous to a degree that I'm inclined to regard as unwise.

I am not tempted to return permanently to Holland, then, though political upheaval in Canada might force me to. Could I thrive there if I did go back? I hope that I will never need to find out.

Freiburg im Breisgau, tucked into the Black Forest twenty kilometres east of the Rhine and sixty north of the Swiss border, was founded early in the twelfth century. It flourished as a commercial centre and proved it by completing its great red sandstone *Münster* with its octagonal tower by the sixteenth century – earlier than most other cities in Germany. The old town, with its narrow streets and romantic old gates, was picturesque, the Black Forest supplying a verdant backdrop.

Water rushed through open gutters along the streets. These were the famous *Bächle*, a picturesque waste-disposal system and a hazard to careless or inebriated cyclists and pedestrians. Broad paths wound their way up the Schlossberg, offering vistas of the rooftops of Freiburg, the cathedral, and the hills beyond.

With its 10,000 students, the university dominated the city. Dating from 1457, it counts Ulrich Zasius and Erasmus of Rotterdam among its early teachers. In this century it has been the home of the philosopher Martin Heidegger, the historian Gerhard Ritter, and the chemist and Nobel laureate Hermann Staudinger. There were university buildings in various parts of Freiburg, but the main ones were near the town's core, among them the late-nineteenth-century library and, of similar vintage, *Kollegiengebäude* I, which contained lecture halls and faculty offices. The sixteenth-century *Alte Universität* housed classrooms and social facilities; on the other side of the Bertholdstrasse stood the modern *Kollegiengebäude* II. Built in the 1950s, its many lecture rooms included the largest of the university, the Auditorium Maximum or Audi Max. In front of this building reposed a curvaceous Henry Moore bronze: *Die Liegende* (Reclining Figure). Its large holes had earned it the nickname by which it was popularly known, *Die Emmentaler Venus*.

My monthly stipend was DM 350 (almost $90 at the time), of which I hoped to spend no more than a quarter on a room. However, I found when I arrived in mid-September that affordable single rooms near the university did not exist. I solved my problem by agreeing to share with a pre-med student from Dartmouth. Frank Ruch was a burly, easygoing Pennsylvanian with German roots who was taking time out to improve his command of the language of his ancestors before commencing medical studies back home. He had been in Europe since the late spring and intended to stay in Freiburg for one semester only. That was fine with me: I thought I would have little trouble finding another roommate (or room) when I got to know the place better.

After a couple of days of riding around on Frank's motorcycle, checking rooms in Freiburg and several surrounding villages, we settled for one on the Komturplatz, a twenty-minute walk from the university and with a choice of two streetcars to Bertholds-brunnen, the fountain at the intersection marking the town centre. Although a bit cramped, the room was well furnished, and the rent (DM 75 each) was reasonable enough. Our *Wirtin* (landlady) seemed pleasant, and she undertook to change the bed linen regularly and keep the room clean.

Frank and I got along together but did not become close friends.

Philosophically we were far apart. He thought eugenics might have value and once called himself a Social Darwinist, though when I said that sounded like 'might is right' to me he changed the subject. As well, I disliked one of his best friends, a frat rat from Kansas who professed admiration for the novels of Ayn Rand. Still, Frank was a good talker, and I appreciated the excellent Telefunken table radio that he contributed to our establishment. He loved opera, his proud boast being to have attended a performance at La Scala. Not until 1982, when I saw *La Cenerentola* there, was I able to follow suit.

The semester did not begin until November, so I had time to travel. First I went to Holland, then, in early October, I took the train from Amsterdam to Paris to spend two weeks with distant relatives, Robert and Tétard Mégerlin – Tétard's maternal grandmother was a Brutel de la Rivière – and their five children. Robert was an importer and prosperous: their huge two-storey apartment at 61, rue d'Auteuil, near the Bois de Boulogne, said as much. The oldest child, christened Norbert but known as Pouky (all Mégerlin children answered to nicknames), studied at the École Polytechnique. I knew him dimly from a visit he had made to Baarn in 1947; he was almost exactly my age. His oldest sister, Biquet, aged twenty, was beginning to study medicine at the Sorbonne; Patsy, two years younger, was preparing to take her *baccalauréat*. The other two were in lower grades.

On my first evening I was taken for a tour of major landmarks, all of them floodlit: the Arc de Triomphe, the Madeleine, Notre Dame. In *La Rondine*, Lisette tells Ruggero that first seeing Paris is like first seeing the ocean. She was very nearly right: more than once I pinched myself to make sure it wasn't all a dream.

Paris is at its best in the fall and the spring – I spent a further ten days there in April – when the weather is mild and the number of tourists within reason. With a Michelin *Guide Vert* I explored the many museums, art galleries, churches, and everything else that makes Paris so marvellous to visit.

Staying with the Mégerlins largely shielded me from Paris's cost. Usually I took a bag lunch and returned to the rue d'Auteuil in

time for dinner. The *carnets* of Métro tickets were heavily subsi-
dized, I imagine, and the museums I visited rarely cost more than
two or three francs at most. Only when I bought a coffee did I get
a sharp reminder that the city was far from cheap. Still, I had no
real reason to think up the witticism Jack coined when he visited
Paris three years later. A tourist needed to know only two French
phrases, he once said to Robert. Which were those? Robert wanted
to know. 'On m'a volé,' Jack answered, 'et on m'a volé encore une
fois.' Robert and Tétard were still chuckling about that one when
I saw them in 1975.

Convinced that my cultural horizons needed expanding, Tétard
bought tickets for me: Van Cliburn in the Brahms B-flat-major
Concerto, Zino Francescatti in Beethoven's Violin Concerto, and
my first opera ever, *Rigoletto*, with Mady Mesplé as an affecting
Gilda. To that point the closest I had come to opera was a concert
performance of Kurt Weill's *Down in the Valley*. Verdi's masterpiece
was the real thing. I was thrilled by the music, the acting, the sets,
the costumes. 'Opera is tremendous,' I gushed in my diary: 'I
wouldn't have missed this for anything.'

Over the years opera has become one of my few passions. Although I have difficulty expressing my feelings, I find it easy to
respond emotionally to opera. The playfulness of the exchanges
between Papageno and Papagena or Cherubino and Susanna, Des-
demona's haunting last aria, the audience knowing what is about
to happen, the sublimity of Wotan's farewell to Brünnhilde, the
passion of the second act duet between Octavian and Sophie, or
the deep emotions of the third act trio with the Marschallin, the
frenzied energy of the first act's final scene in *Turandot*, the sad yet
hopeful guillotine-punctuated 'Salve Regina' that ends *Dialogues
des Carmélites* and invariably brings tears to my eyes: I love it all
more than I can easily say. Combining drama and music, at its best
opera is to me the highest form of art.

I saw my first ballet, *Swan Lake*, in Paris and decided I could take
ballet or leave it, an attitude that hasn't changed since then. Seeing
a strip show was another first. Upon hearing that *le striptease* did
not exist in Victoria or Freiburg, Tétard decided I must take the
opportunity offered by Paris. She gave me some money and sent

Patsy along to protect me from prostitutes (she needn't have worried: I was too frugal and fastidious to be tempted). We went to a dimly lit *boîte* on the Boulevard des Capucines, featuring half a dozen strippers. Their naked bodies aroused me, but most of the acts were perfunctory, and Patsy opined that she could easily do better herself. As she was both beautiful and shapely I regarded her with speculative interest. Smiling, she shook her head. Oh well, back to the bodies on display.

Parts of Paris resembled an army camp: soldiers or policemen with automatic weapons guarded public buildings. One day, as I emerged from the Métro near the Pont Alexandre III, dozens of police officers were lining the road. A Citroën limousine surrounded by motorcycle cops swept by. The profile of the man in the back seat was unmistakable: President de Gaulle. The security was no idle precaution. The troubles associated with the Algerian war had not yet ended; the FLN, the Algerian National Liberation Front, and the OAS, the Secret Army Organization, were forces to be reckoned with. Whether any plastic bombs exploded while I was in Paris I can't recall, but I do know my relatives worried about them. One evening in October, during a stroll through the Marais with Tétard and Biquet, a foolish impulse led me to slip into a doorway and peek out, murmuring: 'Je suis plastiqueur, moi.' My companions had a fit. I must never do this again, they said: if a policeman saw me he might shoot first and ask questions later.

Late in October, just before the term began, I visited the Kachel family in Reutlingen, an industrial town south of Stuttgart. They were acquaintances of my mother's family; she had stayed with Herr and Frau Kachel and their son, Dieter, in 1931 when she was convalescing from depression. By the time I visited them, old Herr Kachel had died, leaving the family pharmacy business in the hands of his son. The pharmacy on the Marktplatz (in an eighteenth-century building that had escaped war damage) had been run by Kachel fathers and sons for five generations!

I was the guest of the aging Frau Kachel but had my most interesting conversations with Dieter. An athletic-looking man of about forty years, he had spent three years as a private and non-commissioned officer in the *Gebirgsjäger*, the mountain troops, seeing his first action in the Ukraine offensive of 1942. Invalided to Greece from the Crimea just before the Russians overran the peninsula, he had later fought in Yugoslavia and Austria before being captured by the U.S. Army. That was by design. Determined not to fall into Russian hands, he and his buddies had commandeered a truck at gunpoint and driven west.

Dieter said he would have been ashamed had he been posted to a country like Holland, where his family knew people and where the Germans had been unwelcome. But in Ukraine they had been greeted like liberators, at least initially. Hostile to communism as well as to the Soviet Union, he thought Germany might have accomplished something good in the east. As he saw it, however, the SS and other German elements had soon ended this possibility by terrorizing the population of areas like Ukraine.

He said he had learned two things from the Nazi period: 'nie wieder Krieg' (never again war) and no more politics. He had been asked to run for local office by the CDU, the Christian Democrats, but had declined: politics was a *Schweinerei*, a dirty business best avoided. Once he had belonged to a political party, the NSDAP, and that had been a mistake. He would not make another. As for war: he fervently hoped his son would not have to fight as he had had to. He had survived, but he was the only one of twelve *Kameraden* with whom he had started out in 1942 to have been so lucky.

In a way Dieter's remarks established what in time I came to recognize as a pattern. The handful of people in their forties or older with whom I talked about the Nazi era had all belonged to the party, but claimed that they had joined it only to get ahead (in Dieter's case to study pharmacy at the university in nearby Tübingen). None admitted to knowing about the extermination camps; all said they had never thought of themselves as National Socialists. This confirmed what I read in Golo Mann's history of recent Germany: 'Astonished and incredulous, the Allies found that in a country ruled by National Socialism for twelve years there were actually no Nazis at all! It was as if the whole thing had been a play like *The Captain of Köpenick*, murderous as no evil prank (*Unfug*) in history had ever been before but a prank all the same, a fraud in which hardly anyone wanted to admit having been complicit once it stood exposed.'* When Nazi Germany collapsed, most people's reasons for joining the party vanished. Nothing fails like failure.

Back in Freiburg on All Saints' Day, I attended a performance of *Tannhäuser*. Freiburg had opera in repertory, but this was a special event: my student ticket was DM 9.60 ($2.40) instead of the usual DM 3.00. Rarely have I spent money better. The renowned *Heldentenor* Wolfgang Windgassen sang the title role and Hildegard Hillebrecht sang the role of Elisabeth. Their voices were thrilling; the Pilgrim's Chorus made me weep with joy. *Tannhäuser* is no longer my favourite Wagner, but at the time it was the most beautiful piece of music I had ever heard: 'as much a religious as a musical experience.'

Music moved me more and more, religion less and less. In December I noted in my diary that I hadn't attended church for three months and didn't miss it. I ceased to be a Christian that year, painlessly and without a struggle or any speculation as to what was taking place, lapsing into an unaggressive (I hope) form of agnosticism. Upon my return to Canada I still attended church from time to time, but as a social rather than a religious duty.

Yet aspects of Christianity influence me to this day. My moral sense, which includes a disapproval of greed and ostentation, a mistrust of great wealth, a concern for social justice, and a conviction that I should deal with others as I would have them deal with me, stems largely from the Christian religion. I feel no need to try to persuade others of my agnosticism: live and let live. However, I *am* hostile to all forms of fundamentalism, finding them intellectually disreputable, morally repugnant, and intolerant in their very

---

* Golo Mann, *Deutsche Geschichte 1919–1945* (Frankfurt 1961), 195 (my translation).

essence. At the same time I have no use for atheism. It is silly to pretend to certainty where it is impossible to have it.

Having decided not to seek academic credit for my German year, I was free to do pretty well as I pleased. I signed up for five courses but attended most of them fitfully at best. In the winter semester my favourite course was Germany from 1871 to 1914, taught by Hans-Günter Zmarzlik. An energetic man some forty years of age, he was one of Freiburg's rising stars: not long afterwards he was appointed to the chair in *neue und neueste Geschichte*, recent and contemporary history.

In the summer semester, May through July, I took his course on Germany from 1914 to 1945, which was even more interesting than the other. Zmarzlik's most provocative idea was that Social Darwinism had contributed to the rise of National Socialism and had found its logical expression in that movement. With its emphasis on 'the survival of the fittest,' allegedly rooted in biology, Social Darwinism not only increased tolerance for Nazi policies designed to isolate and exterminate the 'unfit,' the mentally handicapped, psychiatric cases, homosexuals, Gypsies, and Jews, but shaped these policies from the very outset.* Having written his *Habilitationsarbeit*, the second doctorate commonly required from German academics, on this subject, Zmarzlik was impressively knowledgeable. (The German first doctorate is less demanding than the North American Ph.D.) To this day I find his arguments persuasive. With its pseudo-scientific justification of the oppression of the 'weak' by the 'strong,' of those who have not by those who have, Social Darwinism is one of the most evil ideologies to have emerged during the last two centuries.

I attended classes by the medievalist Gerd Tellenbach and the political scientist Ludwig Bergstraesser, two of Freiburg's grand

---

* See H.G. Zmarzlik, 'Der Sozialdarwinismus in Deutschland als geschichtliches Problem,' *Wieviel Zukunft hat unsere Vergangenheit?* (München 1970), 56–85.

old men, but their words have left little or no mark on my memory. The same is not true of Martin Heidegger, emeritus professor of philosophy. On the evening of 31 January 1962 he gave his annual lecture. Taking the advice of a friend, I turned up at the Audi Max at 6:00, enduring a lecture on parapsychology in order to avoid the mad struggle for seats that broke out an hour later.

At 8:15 Heidegger walked in and after a brief introduction began to speak. I listened intently for a while, then, while he was still lecturing, I scribbled some notes:

Heidegger is a 70-year-old man with sparse grey hair and a florid face who leans against the lectern and directs hoarse words into the microphone. He is talking about 'time' and 'being' (the lecture title is '*Zeit und Sein*') and juggles them about without seeming to say anything comprehensible. I am reminded of Golo Mann's description of the man: '*Martin Heidegger mag man den Poetischeren nennen, aber er trieb Wortgaukelei, ein Miteinander von Tiefsinn und geistigem Betrug.*'*

The Auditorium Maximum is jam-packed with students, many of whom have been here since 5 o'clock. Whether they consider it worthwhile is doubtful. Their faces show everything from close attention to complete boredom, and several have left the lecture hall. It has not visibly bothered the little man in the charcoal-grey suit; he is still expostulating hoarsely about the meaning of time and being. He qualifies everything he says and is careful to define, using, however, terms which need further definition and so he keeps chasing himself through a never-never land of words. So this is one of Germany's most respected philosophers?!

When philosophy has become something of which the educated layman can no longer make sense, what is its purpose? Is philosophy going the same way as the arts and disappearing into a morass of private meaning which a layman can never penetrate? The little man has done

---

* 'One may call Martin Heidegger the more poetic, but he played word games, a mishmash of profundity and spiritual deception.' Mann, *Deutsche Geschichte*, 49. The comparison is with Karl Jaspers. Mann refers only obliquely to Heidegger's Nazism, an aspect of his past scarcely if at all spoken of in the 1960s.

something to answer the latter question. At the beginning of his address he said that contemporary philosophy is just as little immediately accessible as contemporary art or poetry or theoretical physics.

He did not win me over. Famous as he was, Heidegger sounded to me like a b.s. artist.

'I can read what I please, a luxury I haven't had since 56–57,' I wrote happily in my diary in the late fall. German history and novels in English and German – among them *I Claudius* and *Claudius the God, Buddenbrooks*, and Theodor Plievier's *Stalingrad* – were my main fare, and my reading knowledge of German improved steadily.

My spoken German benefited greatly from my membership in World University Service. WUS had two purposes: to bring together German and foreign students and to raise money for projects in the Third World. Somehow I became assistant social convener, in effect the dogsbody to a smooth operator named Jürgen Friebe. Compensation for the drudgery (envelope addressing, stamp licking, and so on) was that I became part of the executive, an exclusively German-speaking group.

WUS, a.k.a. *Wandern und Saufen* (hiking and boozing), had weekly meetings, as well as outings and parties. Many were the agreeable hours I spent with Minna, Renata, Annetraut, Axel, Ursula, Armin, Albrecht, Karl, Dieter, Hans-Peter, Ulrich, Hans, Jürgen, Werner, and the other *WUS-ler*: lunching in the Mensa, the university cafeteria, or the Studirter Igel, a student-run restaurant, drinking in the Ratsstüble, a *Kneipe* (tavern) near the university, or in Sprichs Weinkeller, and perhaps above all, hiking in the Black Forest. The trails were well marked and passed by the doors of inns, so that hunger and thirst were never a problem, and the scenery was unexcelled.

In January I bought skis and boots in order to be able to join other *WUS-ler*, among them John Hill, George Hynna, and Fred Schroeder, a DAAD fellow who had graduated in classics from the University of Toronto, on the Feldberg, the highest point in the Black Forest. Here I began, haltingly and with much falling and thrashing about, to learn to ski.

Was it in a *Gasthof* off one of the slopes or in the *Alte Universität* that George told a joke that still ranks among the best I've ever heard (and seen)? A Swede, a Frenchman, and a Canadian are bragging about their respective countries. Showing a muscled arm, the Swede says, 'This is Sweden, the land of men who get things done.' The Frenchman exhibits a well-shaped calf: 'This is France, the home of culture.' The Canadian says that Canada has brawn too: big deal. We lack culture: who needs it? 'But in Canada,' George said, slowly unzipping his fly, 'in Canada,' reaching into his trousers, 'in Canada,' hauling out his shirttail with a dramatic flourish, 'you can buy a shirt like this for $2.95!'

WUS raised money by way of functions such as Caravan, a sale of goods from developing countries, and student dances. Most ambitious of these was the *Ball der Nationen*, which drew 1500 to the city convention centre to dance to the strains of the U.S. Seventh Army Swing Band, its presence a credit to Jürgen's persuasive skills. Having helped to organize the tombola, a raffle of donated door prizes, I spent much of the evening counting coins and rolling them, an underrated skill I owed to my years in the bank.

After drinking too much at one WUS dance, I passed out in a washroom in the *Alte Universität*. When I woke up at around 3:00 a.m. I was locked in. Fortunately, I was on the ground floor, so I climbed out into the courtyard, only to find that its gate was locked as well. My plaintive calls for help roused a caretaker, who turned me over to two cops waiting outside. My DAAD identity card seemed to satisfy them. Did I know the way home? In something like the local dialect I said: 'Doch, um die Ecke und immer das Strässle gerade aus' (Sure, around the corner and right on to the end of the road). Grinning, they started me on my way. My first hangover was a blockbuster. For several days afterwards I abstained.

Not only did Freiburg turn me into a social drinker, it made me a culture vulture. I saw plays by Anouilh, Scribe, Ibsen, Brecht, Frisch, and Sheridan, heard a performance of Mozart's *Requiem Mass*, and attended recitals by Stefan Askenase, Geza Anda, and George Neikrug. And I frequented the opera, savouring everything I heard and saw: *Die Entführung aus dem Serail, Hoffmanns Erzählungen, Der Fliegende Holländer*, and a work rarely performed in Canada but popular in Germany, Flotow's *Martha*. (I was in the

Freiburg Opera again in 1985 for a performance of *The Queen of Spades*. Either the company's production values had fallen or I had become more demanding: I left after the first act.)

One evening the Freiburg Philharmonic featured Clifford Curzon in the Brahms D-minor Concerto, a favourite of mine. (The closing bars of the first movement never fail to thrill me: it is as if someone, after repeatedly failing in trying to do a very difficult task, has finally and triumphantly got it right.) An even greater luminary than Curzon was the composer Paul Hindemith, who conducted a program that included his own *Nobilissima Visione*. 'Tremendous,' I wrote in my diary.

Not only culture but politics engaged my attention. In November, the WUS executive asked me to attend a conference on European unification in Stuttgart-Hohenheim. It was held in the clubhouse of a *schlagende Verbindung*, a fencing fraternity. (I witnessed a chilling demonstration of the 'sport.' The duellers wore helmets and masks so blood wouldn't flow; when they duelled for real it usually did.) The conference participants favoured German *and* European unification but judged both to be remote in time. That was a generally held view. Speaking in Freiburg in January, the well-known journalist Sebastian Haffner said about German unification: 'Die Frage hat jetzt einen Nullpunkt erreicht' (The issue was at the bottom of the agenda). Hoping that the military balance would shift towards the West so that unification could be forced on the Russians, he urged his listeners not to allow the matter to drop off the agenda altogether. He did not think it likely that an American-Soviet *rapprochement* would serve as the means for unification, nor did he think that East Germany would collapse.

No more potent symbol of Germany's division existed than the Berlin Wall, erected by the German Democratic Republic (GDR) in August 1961. I saw it for the first time in March 1962. Our DAAD-organized bus trip began in Stuttgart where, the night before we left, John and I attended a performance of *Madama Butterfly* with Martina Arroyo in the title role. (She defined that role for me until, more than twenty years later, I heard Yoko Watanabe sing it.) Mindful of delays at the border, DAAD had booked us into a hotel in Hof in northern Bavaria for one night. That evening I got a chance insight into Middle Eastern politics. George, John, and I were playing poker with two Turks and an Iranian. The latter was drinking beer; the Turks drank apple juice. When I tactlessly inquired whether Islam had relaxed its ban on alcohol, the Turks, looking pointedly at the Iranian, hastened to assure me that it had not. He seemed crestfallen, then brightened: 'But you Turks aren't good Muslims either.' Bridling, they asked him what he meant. 'Your country is not against Israel!'

In Berlin we stayed in the Hotel am Zoo, a venerable hostelry on the Kurfürstendamm. Wide and tree-lined, the Ku-damm reminded me of the Champs Élysées. However, the ruined nineteenth-century church tower, flanked by a modern church, is nothing like the Arc de Triomphe. The latter celebrates military success; the former starkly recalls crushing defeat.

Only seven months old, *die Mauer* (the Wall) was already a tourist attraction. Our tour bus stopped in the Bernauerstrasse, site of many escape attempts, some with tragic endings marked by wooden crosses. Later we heard a lecture on the iniquity of erecting the Wall. Forays into East Berlin reinforced my negative image of the GDR. I was struck by the huge red banners denouncing West German revanchism and American imperialism, cheering on the Cuban revolution, and urging people to make ever greater efforts in the pursuit of socialism and of peace. Like advertising executives, the GDR authorities appeared to believe that slogans become reality if repeated often enough. War damage was more evident in the East, while the consumer goods on display were drab and unfashionable. This confirmed my belief that capitalism was more effective economically than communism, certainly in providing consumer goods. Still, communism had a good side: it cost next to nothing to take the U-Bahn (subway) from the Friedrichstrasse to the Alexanderplatz. The apartment buildings on the nearby Karl-Marx-Allee were massive and ugly, but the heart of the city, Unter den Linden, with its neoclassical buildings, was attractive and unpolluted by commercialism.

The day after we returned to Freiburg, John and I joined Fred Schroeder for two weeks' skiing in Kandersteg, in the Berner Oberland. Fred, who on skis slightly resembled a large teddy bear, was generous, endlessly good-natured, and always eager to share a joke: a splendid companion. The three of us enjoyed ourselves to the full. In good weather a ski resort can hardly help but be delightful, and but for one snowfall near the beginning of our stay it was sunny throughout.

At first I swallowed a lot of snow, but as the days passed I found growing pleasure in the sport, sliding down the slopes at increasing speeds, with wind in my face, carving turns with mounting confidence. Within a week I was descending from the Stock, more than a kilometre above Kandersteg, without falling more than once or twice. (One minor source of regret is that I haven't been on downhill skis since a holiday in the French Alps in 1982. Ski trips are troublesome to arrange, and Cornelia doesn't like the sport. In recent years I have stuck to cross-country skiing, less exhilarating but no doubt better for my heart and limbs.)

The evenings John, Fred, and I spent in the company of several female students, one of whom invited me to visit her and her family in Siegburg, near Bonn. Margot Depiereux was a pharmacy student two years my junior who behaved as though she were an older sister. (For the last twenty-five years she has lived in Berlin. The most fascinating letter I have received during the last ten years was her account of the breaching of the Wall in 1989.) Her father, Hans Depiereux, was a *Notar*, a practitioner of a remunerative branch of the law concerned with real property. His wife, Marianne, though for my taste perhaps a bit too eager to correct my German, was warm-hearted; Margot's older brother, Stefan, who studied economics, was also thoroughly amiable. They were excellent hosts, and Siegburg was a good base for excursions to Bonn and Cologne, where I particularly enjoyed the cathedral and the art gallery.

It was in Cologne, too, that I attended one of the most enjoyable social gatherings of my life. The occasion was the birthday of the wife of one of Hans's friends, a professor of medicine at the university. I was a late addition to the guest list, and underdressed at that. I had not brought a suit along, and Marianne quickly abandoned the attempt to fit me into one of Stefan's: he was 10 cm taller and 10 kg heavier. A telephone call was needed to ensure that I would be welcome even in a sports jacket.

On the way to Cologne, Hans repeatedly instructed Stefan to

drink no more than two or three glasses of wine so that he could pilot the Mercedes home, and Marianne drilled me in exactly what to say when meeting our host and hostess as well as the guest of honour, a Monsignor. A printed place-card – 'Mr Kanada' – marked my seat at the table reserved for the younger generation. The food and wine were excellent, but the mood was slightly sub-dued until the Monsignor and his attendant priest took their leave. That marked the start of the serious celebrating. Repeatedly, the manservant descended to the cellar for more Moselle and Rhine wine, and only Stefan restrained himself. He did, however, join lustily in the student songs. Periodically, the professor and his son, members of the same *Verbindung* (to which Hans also belonged), rose, bowed elaborately to each other across the room, and drank. If this comes with academic life, let me have more of it! I thought happily, not yet knowing that in Germany, as in Canada, professors of medicine have significantly higher incomes than other academ-ics. Except for poor Stefan, everyone in our car floated home in a golden, vinous haze.

Margot's parents offered information that I didn't know how to interpret. Over a bottle of Moselle after dinner one evening, Hans claimed he had been starved nearly to death while a prisoner of war in France in 1945. Marianne added that he had weighed less than fifty kilos – his normal weight was seventy-odd – when he returned from captivity. Until the publication in 1989 of *Other Losses*, James Bacque's study of the postwar fate of German POWs, I didn't understand what Hans was talking about. Bacque greatly exaggerates the number who died, but he *is* right about the de-plorable treatment of POWs by the Americans and the French.

Frank left Freiburg at the end of February as planned, and I moved into a room on the Pochgasse in Zähringen, a quiet village five kilometres north of the downtown core that had gradually turned into a suburb. I owed my new abode to Ulrich Wankel, the presi-dent of WUS, who was leaving to continue his medical studies elsewhere. All good rooms passed from student to student much as do heirlooms from parent to child, and this room was very good indeed. It was large and airy, and at DM 50, breakfast included, the price was more than right. If I missed the last streetcar, which left Bertholdsbrunnen around midnight, I would face a long walk home. No matter: I had lucked in, and I knew it.

Aside from its distance from the university, the location was convenient enough. It was but a short walk to the streetcar stop, and there were several good shops in the village. One was a bakery which had fresh bread just before noon. One of the great pleasures in life is to eat *Bauernbrot*, still warm from the oven, slathered with sweet butter and jam.

Sometimes I lunched in the company of my landlord and landlady, Friedrich and Anna Flamm. He was a retired prison guard, she a farmer's daughter who had brought some land into the family. They breakfasted long before I did and went to work on their property, but I quite often saw them at midday, when *they* ate their hot meal. They were friendly and eager to talk with me, a bit of an exotic from their point of view. I, in turn, was eager to talk with them. Not only were they agreeable people but, having been born in the previous century, they had witnessed a lot of German history.

They called me Herr Horn until I demurred: they must call me Mike. 'Aber das können wir nicht, Herr Horn: Sie sind ja Akademiker und wir sind einfache Leute' (But we can't do that, Mr Horn; you are university-educated and we are ordinary folk). I insisted. They compromised, calling me Herr Mike.

The Flamms were no admirers of the Federal Republic, though they conceded that it was much better than the Third Reich. What of the Weimar Republic? 'Ja, wissen Sie, Herr Mike, das war auch Quatsch!' (You know, Mr Mike, that was foolishness too!). To these aging Germans the golden age was *die Kaiserzeit*: the era of the Hohenzollern empire. It was no democracy, of course: military and foreign policy were not subject to parliamentary control. But, assuming they knew this, it clearly bothered the Flamms not at all. Much like Canadians then and since, they treasured peace, order, and good government, and these, in their view, the empire had provided.

Were they wrong or naïve? Quite possibly. But is it not possible that Europe in our century would have been a happier continent if imperial Germany had survived or if, indeed, it had prevailed in 1914 (as it probably would have if Britain, like Holland, had remained neutral)? We cannot know what would have happened in that case, of course, but we *can* guess with a high degree of certainty that Adolf Hitler would never have been heard of and that we would have been spared much misery and evil.

Friedrich Flamm gave me some insight into the workings of the Nazi party at the lower levels. A good Roman Catholic, he had declined to join the party after 1933. Then he was passed over for a promotion he thought he had coming to him. When he asked the reason he got the answer that only party members could expect to be promoted. Fine, he said, and joined the NSDAP. Not long afterwards his superior said he had heard Flamm was still attending Mass. 'Na, und?' (So what?), Flamm asked. Well, it wasn't right for party members to be conspicuously devout. Flamm told me he had said he didn't mind belonging to the party, but he would continue to go to church. 'Und wissen Sie, Herr Mike, man hat mir nichts getan. Nichts!' (And do you know what, Mr Mike, they did nothing to me. Nothing!). Nazi control of personal life, he implied, was far from total.

When the summer semester began in May, Fred and George had transferred to the Free University in Berlin, while John and I were joined in Freiburg by Eric Tiessen, a UBC history major who had spent the first semester in Cologne. The three of us, often joined by Eric's American girlfriend, spent a good deal of time in each other's company. One such occasion was a weekend visit Eric, John, and I paid to the RCAF base at Baden-Soellingen, about an hour's drive north of Freiburg. We were the guests of Cpl Bill Waldron and his family, whose acquaintance I had made in April when I was spending the Easter weekend on the island of Texel with Tante Phiet, Flora, and Greet. One day I spotted a station wagon with British Columbia licence plates and introduced myself. The result was an invitation to the base, subsequently extended also to Eric and John.

The visit was very enjoyable, though we all drank too much in the mess on Saturday evening. We stocked up in the PX on peanut butter, instant coffee, and cigarettes, and looked around the base with interest. I wanted to take a close-up photo of a CF-86 Sabre, but two military policemen intervened: 'Those planes are classified, buddy.' Surely the Soviets had learned all they needed during the Korean War? I countered. Neither of the cops seemed to appreciate this reminder that the equipment was badly obsolete. 'A wise guy, eh?' one of them said and threatened to expose my film. I beat a hasty retreat to Bill's car. 'What was that about?' he wanted to know. I told him. 'All those guys are assholes,' he dismissed the MPs: 'It comes with the job.'

I spent a fair amount of time away from Freiburg. In June I took the opportunity to spend two weeks in Berlin, at a cost of a mere DM 50, to take a course offered by the *Ministerium für Gesamtdeutsche Fragen* (Ministry for Intra-German Relations). Taught by a refugee from the GDR, the course offered a critical view of dialectical and historical materialism. Among the readings was Wolfgang Leonhard's fascinating *Die Revolution entlässt ihre Kinder*. Leonhard, a member of the *Gruppe Ulbricht* that reached Berlin from Moscow in April 1945, had fled to Yugoslavia four years later, having become convinced that Stalinism was antithetical to socialism. I found his book engaging, not only because of the story it told, but also because of Leonhard's commitment to humanist values that are not infrequently subverted even in the West: equality before the law, for example, and freedom of expression. Leonhard, who by 1962 lived in the Federal Republic, was an idealist without a secure home.

In the course of one of several forays into East Berlin I bought a few books, among them official histories of the Communist party of the Soviet Union and the *Sozialistische Einheitspartei Deutschlands* (Socialist Unity Party of Germany), the East German ruling party. These turned out to be works of fiction rather than of history. I got more out of *Der dialektische Materialismus*, by R.O. Gropp. My marginalia indicate that I was a critical reader: comments such as '*Unsinn!*' (nonsense), '*falsch*,' and '*stimmt nicht!*' (wrong!) abound. But I learned something all the same: Marxism is unsound as philosophy and deeply deficient as economics, and it fails as a blueprint for a new society, but it has some continuing validity as a critique of capitalism.

I treated myself to an orgy of opera, concert music, and theatre. Staged at the Deutsche Oper by Wieland Wagner, *Tristan und Isolde* had simple and effective sets but was too static for my taste, and too long. *Carmen* was more enjoyable: psychologically believable and immensely tuneful, it is the work that I would use before all others to introduce neophytes to opera. I also liked *Aïda* and *Ein Maskenball (Un Ballo in Maschera)*, despite the latter's creaky plot. At the Komische Oper in East Berlin I saw *Die Zauberflöte*, staged by Walter Felsenstein and conducted by Kurt Masur: 'joyous, very *lebenslustig*, well acted and sung.' Lorin Maazel led the Berlin Philharmonic in works by Schubert and Schumann, and I attended a performance of *My Fair Lady* in a German translation. All of this cost me a good deal of money, but in my diary I justified the expense by reminding myself that once I was back in Victoria I would have to do without such pleasures.

In East Berlin I saw two plays performed by the Berliner Ensemble in the Theater am Schiffbauerdamm, shrine to Brecht's memory. *Der aufhaltsame Aufstieg des Arturo Ui*, questionable as history, was great as political satire. *Die Dreigroschenoper*, with its stirring musical score by Weill, I enjoyed even more. I was not an uncritical spectator, however: 'I don't agree with Brecht's thesis that the bourgeoisie knows only relationships of interest & has lost the capacity for spontaneity,' I wrote in my diary. There was a commotion when the audience became aware that Sophia Loren and Vittorio de Sica were in their midst: 'Everybody clapped and cheered.' From where I sat I could see only that he had white hair and she did not.

One evening I joined two other course participants at the Sofia, an East Berlin restaurant. The prices, although high, were more than reasonable for us with our smuggled East German currency, bought at an exchange rate of six or seven Ostmark to one Deutschmark. Afterwards we went dancing. Rock 'n' roll was *verboten*, but, *pace* Cuba, Latin American rhythms were not. Lutz and Bärbel were dancing a spirited cha-cha when a waiter asked them to cease. Did they think decent people enjoyed watching such bourgeois decadence?

The Wall was nearing its first anniversary. The reason for its construction had been the GDR's wish to end the drain of educated East Germans and to protect the East German economy. But it was an obstacle to others besides those wanting to flee. West Germans and foreigners passed easily into the East, the sole constraint being that we had to leave by midnight. West Berliners could not visit East Berlin, however, nor could East Germans visit West Berlin. At a party in Fred Schroeder's residence I met a student whose parents lived in Leipzig. They were visiting East Berlin to see their son; using binoculars they could wave at each other across the Wall. Some reunion!

Towards the end of July, I made a foray into Switzerland. I had twice visited Basel, where I enjoyed the Kunstmuseum – one of my favourites among the smaller galleries of Europe – and the view from the cathedral over the Rhine, and I had gone skiing in the Berner Oberland in March, but I had not got to know any Swiss people. Then the Adrians, friends of my parents who lived in Bern, invited me to spend a week with them at their cottage in Merligen on the Thunersee. They were very hospitable, the scenery was magnificent, and the weather gorgeous. When not hiking or swimming I sat in the shade, reading the *Alexandria Quartet*, feeling at peace with myself and the world.

One day I accompanied Hans Adrian, a curator in the national museum, on an overnight trip into Bern. Its site high above the Aare, its arcades and fountains, and its view of the Alps make it one of the most attractive capital cities in Europe. It is one I always enjoy revisiting, if only for the fountains, especially the grotesquely charming *Kindlifresserbrunnen*, the fountain surmounted by an ogre who is making a meal of several presumably naughty children.

At the beginning of August I returned to Freiburg, packed my bags, had a last drink or two at the Ratstüble with several *WUSler*, still in town though the term had ended, and bid farewell to the Flamms. Eric and I were sailing from Amsterdam on the seventh. On the early morning of the fourth we said our goodbyes to John and got on a northbound train, transferring to a ship in Mainz. Down the Rhine we steamed to Koblenz, past castles and grapevine-covered hillsides. When we passed the Lorelei I joined in singing Heine's lines: 'Ich weiss nicht was soll es bedeuten, / dass ich so traurig bin ...' Actually I knew why I was sad: my European year was near its end.

We spent two days in Amsterdam as Tante Phiet's guests, and I proudly showed Eric around the city, of which I had grown very fond during the year just past. On the evening of 5 August we saw *Some Like It Hot* in homage to Marilyn Monroe, news of whose death by suicide we had just heard. Having seen this film (Billy Wilder's best, in my view) in Freiburg in a dubbed version, I was eager to see the original. Dubbing, an irritating form of cultural vandalism, is used only for children's films in Holland. No doubt this is related to the Dutch tendency, forced on them by linguistic and geographic necessity, to acquire several foreign languages.

We embarked on the *Arkadia* on the seventh. A shipboard romance with a nurse from Edmonton who taught me how to do the twist made the days pass quickly. Our ship docked in Montreal on the sixteenth. Eric and I said goodbye, whereupon I spent the day with Louise, wandering around downtown Montreal. We went our separate ways that evening from the airport, she to Alberta, I to Vancouver. The next morning I was back in Victoria.

Glad to have been away, I was also glad to be back. I had seen many art galleries, museums, and churches and enjoyed a feast of music and drama beyond Victoria's dreams. I had met my Dutch relatives and got to know my native country better. I had learned to speak German. Most important of all, I had lost my prejudice against Germans. Nothing can excuse or explain away the great evils committed by Germany from 1933 to 1945, especially the never-to-be-forgotten horror of the Holocaust. That said, the Germans I had met were, like Netherlanders and Canadians, ordinary people trying to get on with their lives. The students I had known had been toddlers during the Nazi era. Its evils were not *their* fault.

Not all things German had caught my fancy, of course. For example, I disliked what I came to regard as a characteristic tendency to officiousness displayed by not a few people in uniform, particularly policemen and streetcar conductors. But that was not a large complaint.

On my way back from the Thunersee in early August I had

spoken with a woman my age, a secretary who had been holiday-
ing in the Berner Oberland. She complained that as a German she
wasn't liked in Switzerland. Since the war Germans weren't very
popular anywhere in Europe, I said, less than diplomatically. She
sighed. 'Ja, das stimmt. Aber ich kann ja nichts dafür dass ich
Deutsche bin. Man soll mich doch für mich allein akzeptieren.'
(That's true. But I can't help being German. People surely should
accept me for myself alone.) I had learned to accept Germans that
way.

As for Holland, I liked it enormously and had enjoyed seeing
relatives and old friends. But although I felt at ease, I never felt
altogether at home. Had my attitudes changed? Probably. Certainly my affections had. In February 1962, in the course of a dark,
rainy afternoon in Freiburg, I had written in my diary: 'I'm looking
forward to going back [to Canada]. This is not my land, even
Holland isn't really my land anymore, though I could make it mine
again if I stayed there long enough. Victoria and Vancouver Island
are my land. That's what I'm used to and there I've made real
friends – people with whom I feel entirely comfortable.' Granted,
I wrote that while I was feeling homesick. But home *is* where the
heart is.

During my absence from Victoria it had become possible to take
an honours degree at the college, but I couldn't satisfy the requirements in one year. Once more I accepted Sydney Pettit's advice to
settle for the general degree. Perhaps to console me, he took me
for a drink in the Snug, the lounge of the Oak Bay Beach Hotel.
This was a favourite haunt for faculty members, recent graduates,
and a few older students, as well as artists such as Richard Cicci-
marra and Fenwick Lansdowne. I had never passed through its
door before I went to Germany, but was to do so often in the months
and years to come. It was the closest thing in Victoria to a German
Kneipe.

Not having worked that summer, except for the last three weeks
upon my return, I was short of money. Fortunately the vice-principal, the amiable and ever-accommodating Robert Wallace, had
allowed me to carry over a $250 scholarship. To this I added a small

bursary and a loan from the provincial government (the only time I had to borrow for my education), so that I could cover my college expenses as well as pay a modest amount of board to Mother. I really couldn't afford to keep Joe's Chevy on the road (he being in Zeballos on northern Vancouver Island), but I drove it nevertheless: I had even less time than money.

Two of my six courses were in history: British imperialism with Jack Ogelsby, a newcomer from the United States, and a seminar in which I did bibliographical work for Ogelsby and read historiography and philosophy of history with Tony Emery.

I took recent literature in English with the department's new star, John Peter, a South Africa-born novelist with a sharp mind and an even sharper tongue. One of his ploys was to ask whether anyone had read some book or other, then, after a few seconds of silence, he would continue sarcastically: 'But of course you haven't. You're Canadian undergraduates: you haven't read *anything*.' This sort of remark might today be regarded as unacceptable. We didn't like it much, but put up with it, knowing it to be very nearly true. And perhaps some of us began to read more widely as a consequence.

We studied English and American authors only. Canadian and other 'colonial' writers apparently did not merit attention. In the Freiburg University library a few months earlier, John Hill had found a thesis on Hugh MacLennan written by a German scholar. To that point I, an English major, had never even heard of Mac-Lennan! Doubtless Peter *had* read him and other Canadian authors, but his course gave no evidence of it.

In fact, I don't think that there *was* a course in Canadian literature at Victoria – this may have been typical of Canadian universities in the early 1960s – whereas Freiburg had more than one. I remember meeting the man who taught them in 1961–2, a visiting scholar from the University of Manitoba. His German students seemed to find Canadian authors more interesting than did his students in Winnipeg, he said. I registered this information noncommittally, but thought to myself that the Canadian students had better taste than the Germans. My own attitude to Canadian literature resembled my attitude to the country's history: I knew little and cared less. This view, I believe, was common among Victoria students of the time.

I studied ethics with Ted Bond, an intense man with a Vandyke beard that he stroked incessantly as he lectured. The essay I wrote for him, on 'Free Will and Determinism,' was probably my best piece of work that year.

German Romantic drama, with J.B. MacLean, comprised two plays each by Lessing, Goethe, and Schiller, and exposed me also to that splendid work of scholarship Barker Fairley's *Study of Goethe*. MacLean made us write summaries, in German, of its chapters, one a week: a challenging and valuable exercise. My sixth course, in classical studies, was part history, part literature, and largely forgettable.

As if six courses were not enough to keep me busy, I joined the executive of the graduating class and the governing council of the Alma Mater Society (AMS), wrote a column, 'Bull by the Horn,' for the weekly *Martlet*, helped edit the annual *Tower*, and presided over the Creighton Club. I rejoined neither the college chess club nor the Victoria City Chess Club, however, a consequence of a chance encounter on the eve of my departure for Germany the year before. An older member of the VCCC was staying at my hotel in Montreal, and we met in the lobby. After the usual courtesies he said: 'I've been watching you, Horn. You're not good enough to take chess as seriously as you do. Remember, it's only a game.' I had decided that he was right. I did attend the Jive Club from time to time, however. The twist was big that year, and the Beach Boys were beginning to make a splash.

I was also active in the debating society and was a representative in intercampus debates that year. In October I was one of two members selected to partner two debaters from England who were visiting Canadian campuses from coast to coast, the subject being the British entry into what was then called the European Common Market. Opinion in Britain was divided on the subject; so was opinion in Canada. I had no strong views one way or the other, but had learned to debate whatever proposition was assigned to me. My partner was Alan Andrews, an arts student from Leeds, who preferred the negative on this question. He believed that Britain's entry into Europe, whatever it might mean for Britain, would be calamitous for its former colonies, especially those in Africa. The debate was well attended, the event having received considerable attention from the media and one of the judges being Leslie Peterson, the minister of education.

Alan and I lost, and I thought no more about the debate until, in 1985, his path and mine crossed again. By this time he was a professor of theatre at Dalhousie University and about to join the Academic Freedom and Tenure Committee of the Canadian Association of University Teachers, which I had joined the year before. He reminded me of the debate and added that he believed, even more strongly than in 1962, that he had been right. By turning its back on former dependencies, he said, Britain had effectively condemned many of them to extreme poverty.

The most time-consuming of my activities was my work on the AMS council. Student government is sandbox government, but some issues had more than ephemeral importance. One of these was student drinking. Provincial law prohibited drinking by minors, then anyone under the age of twenty-one, and a college regulation banned alcohol on campus. Neither rule was closely observed. Once I went to the Snug with a young woman, some months shy of her twenty-first birthday, who offered her mother's driver's licence as proof of age. The waiter regarded it, then her, pensively: 'Are you related to Dean Whitlow of Christ Church Cathedral?' Hilary beamed: 'He's my father.' 'Oh well, I suppose it's all right then,' the waiter said. My friend Simon Wade, who did *not* look older than his years, said that he had started drinking at the Snug at age eighteen.

Although the usual policy was one of *laissez-faire*, so many empties littered the Gordon Head gymnasium after the Homecoming dance in October 1962 that Principal Harry Hickman, a gentle teacher of French, felt compelled to act. He summoned the AMS council to a meeting. Flanked by his acting vice-principal, Hugh Farquhar, and the dean of women, the mathematician Phoebe Noble (now famous as a gardener), he asked us to cancel dances for the remainder of the academic year. Noble, perhaps the toughest-minded of the three, said that drinking by veterans in the late 1940s, when she had begun teaching, had been all right because 'men who had fought had earned the right to drink.' We had not. Hickman and Farquhar nodded assent; we groaned.

In the end we reached a compromise: dances, yes, but no longer on campus. In the aftermath, the council asked me and another member to examine provincial liquor legislation as it affected students. *My* attitude had been shaped by my year in Germany, where university students drank with few restrictions. Persuading my partner that British Columbia's laws needed an overhaul was like kicking in an open door. We drafted a petition asking that the drinking age be lowered to eighteen and that liquor licences be granted to dance halls and night clubs. The council endorsed it, but dropped the matter when the UBC Alma Mater Society declined to join us. They believed that there were more important matters on the agenda, such as university funding, and that pushing for a relaxation of the liquor laws would alienate a still-significant segment of public opinion. Doubtless they were right.

A footnote came in March, near the end of the academic year. For the last meeting of the Creighton Club the executive organized a dinner, to which we invited all the history faculty as guests. A geographer, Eric Ross, spoke about the first prohibition legislation in the British Empire, passed in his native New Brunswick in the 1840s. In honour of the topic we served sherry before dinner and a glass of wine with. This was foolish, as I should have realized: we were in the Gordon Head cafeteria, and the manager reported us.

The next day I found a message in my mailbox from Principal Hickman: would I please attend on him at my earliest convenience? That meant 'now.' As I walked over to the Ewing Building I wondered what he would do. He was stern: 'After our chat with the AMS council, which you attended, you should have known how wrong this was.' I was lucky that faculty members had been there, he added, since he might otherwise have been tempted to suspend me and perhaps also the other members of the executive, Susan Dickinson and Sandra McKeachie, as an example to the entire student body. Instead he was suspending the club. This seemed pointless to me, the academic year being almost over, but I prudently kept my opinion to myself. (When I tell today's students this story they think I've made it up.)

More important than student drinking was the future of the college. I know now that the College Council, pushed by the local business community, had come to favour a full-fledged university. The faculty were split; the students were in the dark. The AMS council lost some of its ignorance in November when a history student, Colin Ross, came to a meeting to inform us that his room-mate, whose father taught at the college, had heard that the chairman of the College Council was drafting a new act. We decided that we needed to know more, and the AMS president, Alf Pettersen, Colin, and I arranged to meet with the chairman, Judge Joseph B. Clearihue. A jovial man in his early seventies whose own interest in higher education was of long standing, Clearihue seemed surprised that students might also be concerned about the issue. He did not instruct us to mind our business, however. Instead he shared with us his strong belief that independence offered the best guarantee of the long-range welfare of Victoria College, and promised that he would let us see the final version of the act he was drafting for the provincial government's consideration.

The AMS council was satisfied with this, but the graduating-class executive was not. In December I accompanied the class president, Sue Dickinson, and the social convener, Bruce Warburton, to a meeting with the minister of education. An urbane lawyer, Leslie Peterson was one of the few members of the government for whom I had any use, and I listened intently to his answer to our question: would we get Victoria or UBC degrees? 'He didn't want to commit himself,' I wrote in my diary, 'but after a while made it pretty well clear that the degrees would in all likelihood be UBC, since the session starts on 26 January, and it's very unlikely that a Victoria University Act will be available by that time.'

When the session began, Premier Bennett had a report from UBC's president, John B. MacDonald, which recommended that his institution be the only one with professional and graduate faculties, that Victoria College remain an undergraduate college but with degree-granting powers, and that a similar college be founded in Burnaby. To many Victorians this was a letdown. More pleasing was the Universities Act of 1963, which provided for universities in Victoria and Burnaby equal in status to UBC. It would come into effect on 1 July; we of the class of '63 would receive the last UBC degrees awarded in Victoria.

Continued uncertainty surrounded the name the college would assume. Many liked 'Victoria University,' and the Alma Mater Society ordered beer mugs with that name on it (I still have mine). Alas, such an institution already existed in Toronto. Tony Emery told me that one of his 'more unworldly colleagues' had proposed the name 'Juan de Fuca University.' 'The short form will no doubt be Fuca U,' Emery said with a pleased smirk. This proposal predictably went nowhere; the more prosaic 'University of Victoria' became the compromise choice.

The government had chosen a new course for higher education, but its funding policy was unchanged. Every year UBC's budget submission was cut. In 1963 the cut was said to be larger than usual, and the UBC Alma Mater Society launched the 'Back Mac' campaign – the reference was to President MacDonald – centred on a petition urging more generous treatment of higher education. Our students collected 20,000 signatures to add to the 200,000 gathered by students from UBC. However, I doubt that the petition had much effect. In common with other Canadian universities, those in British Columbia have never received enough money to allow them to rise much above a decent mediocrity.

Aside from the 'Back Mac' campaign, the only other overt sign of student activism in 1962–3 was the anti-calendar. One February evening in the Tally Ho on Douglas Street, a popular student drinking spot, a young political science instructor, Lionel Feldman, argued passionately that too many of the faculty were unproductive and should be dismissed. 'He was unnecessarily bitter,' I wrote in my diary, 'but he's at least partly right. He advised us to get to work on an "anti-calendar" for next year, warning future students against certain professors and courses.'

Thinking that such a consumers' guide to courses might be a good thing, I moved at the next meeting of the AMS council that we produce one. The motion passed, on the understanding that I would take charge of the project. I recruited an all-star editorial board, consisting of a past president of the AMS council, John Anderson, a future president, Olivia Barr, the director of publications, Don Shea, Sue Dickinson, and, last but not least, the inimitable Daniel O'Brien.

A bit of a roughneck who, surprisingly, studied classical literature, Dan had a fertile imagination as well as an offbeat sense of humour. Many of his fancies found expression in the *Centurion*, a campus magazine that he edited with his sidekick, Bob 'Toad' Bell. Dan wrote about half of the material and drew many of the cartoons. My favourite shows one man supine while another looms over him with a tray of beer glasses. The caption: 'You wouldn't hit a man with glasses, would you?' Dan would, I thought, save us from taking ourselves too seriously.

Course evaluations are commonplace today, but in 1963 they were not. Looking for models, we found only Harvard's *Confidential Guide to Freshmen* and Stanford's *Scratch Sheet*. Ours, in fact, may have been the first in Canada. Tony Emery, who wrote in support of our project in his column in the *Times*, told me that his was a minority view in the Faculty Club and that Sydney Pettit had insisted with particular force that students had no right to evaluate professors. Ted Bond said that some of his colleagues feared that 'instructors would have to turn their lectures into entertainment sessions and mark leniently in order to get good mention, and that heads of departments and deans would rely upon the anti-calendar as a basis for promotions and salary increases.'

I had no answer to such concerns, although I thought them far-fetched. But I did reassure the AMS president-elect, Larry Devlin, worried about lawsuits, and Vice-Principal Farquhar, eager to prevent bad publicity for the college, that we weren't just trying to 'get' certain professors. This was not entirely candid: one or two of my fellow editors had pet hates. But I thought that I could control them. As for myself, I had no reason to carry on a vendetta against anyone. Not all of my professors had impressed me, but most were knowledgeable and challenging, and several were excellent, among them Ted Bond, Bill Gaddes, Jack Ogelsby, and Ann Saddlemyer. Tony Emery was *hors concours*: brilliant though unsound. The high school mentality I once complained about in my *Martlet* column pertained to the students far more than to the professors.

The students who completed the questionnaires – we had a 60 per cent response rate – generally liked their courses and instructors. John Peter was arrogant, many students wrote, but that was okay: he had a lot to be arrogant about! In spite of his sarcasm his ratings were high. Criticisms were usually constructive. Sydney Pettit fared well, but many of the respondents suggested he stop dictating his lectures. (Neither Sue, who edited the history reviews, nor I foresaw how much this would anger him.) Only one course was panned by virtually everyone who had taken it. I could understand why, having studied physical geography with the professor in question. He was the only truly unsatisfactory instructor I had at the college. But I toned down the review all the same.

Under the title of 'The Students' Report,' the anti-calendar appeared just in time for registration in September. Several professors were unhappy. 'Dan, Sue and myself put up with quite a lot of nastiness one way and another at the beginning of term,' Olivia reported to me early in 1964. Most annoyed of all, she claimed, had been Pettit, who had 'refused to sponsor Sue's honour essay' when she tried to upgrade her degree and 'would not allow Dan to take [Medieval] History 304.' (That summer I, too, would feel his displeasure. In the Snug one evening he met my greeting frostily: 'I do not care to remember you, Mr Horn. Please leave.') There would be no anti-calendar in 1964. No graduating student wanted to invest the time, Olivia said, and others were unwilling to risk professorial wrath.

We were ahead of our time. Today student course evaluations are ubiquitous. Where we intended ours simply for the guidance of students, however, today's documents are often used to guide decisions about tenure and promotion (as some of Victoria's faculty had feared!). This is very probably a mistake. Student evaluations are a reliable guide to student likes and dislikes and in that way they are useful to other students, who may like and dislike much the same things. Evaluations are less reliable, however, in identifying 'good' and 'bad' teaching and differentiating between the two. Easy graders may be more popular than those who are tough; amusing lecturers are better liked than the humourless. I had one professor I thought of as bad when I took his course, and who was so regarded by many of his students, about whom I later changed my mind. He was far from being a 'good' (i.e., entertaining) lecturer, but he knew his subject and he made me think.

In retrospect I feel ambivalent about the anti-calendar. If I could do it all over again, I don't think I would bother to spend the time. We meant well, and I hope we did no harm, but I doubt that our document repaid the effort we devoted to it. I doubt, too, that similar documents elsewhere have done much good over the years. (Sour grapes have no part in this opinion: student reviews of my courses have always been positive, but I'm no longer sure that this is greatly to my credit.)

As I neared graduation I still wanted to be a professor, or, perhaps more accurately, I wanted to be nothing else. Chartered accountancy had ceased to attract me years earlier. Perhaps law should have appealed to me: several acquaintances, among them Harold Ridgway and David Skillings, had entered or were entering the UBC law school. But my view of that subject, gathered in a high school course, was largely unfavourable. I had seen enough of business people while I worked in the bank to know I didn't want to spend my working life among *them*. My summers in the Department had inoculated me against the public service. Journalism seemed facile. I had never considered medicine (the sight of blood made me feel queasy), high school teaching (I had no desire to spend my life among adolescents), or architecture (Father's complaints about contractors who cut corners and clients who wouldn't pay had scared me off). University teaching promised me a life doing things I enjoyed: talking, reading, and writing. And although I realized that its financial rewards were not large, this didn't trouble me.

I applied to Berkeley and Stanford, the two top institutions on the West Coast, with UBC and Toronto as backups. Lining up money was just as important as getting into graduate school: I had no wish to borrow in order to qualify myself for a profession so modestly remunerated. So I applied for several fellowships, the most generous of them offered by the Woodrow Wilson Foundation. Its selection committee interviewed me at the University of Washington in January. When my fifteen minutes were up I won-

dered whether my performance had been good enough. David
Alexander, waiting for me when I emerged, told me not to worry:
he had won a Woodrow Wilson Fellowship in 1961 with grades
lower than mine.

Over a pitcher of beer we talked about graduate studies and
about life in the United States. He disliked the country's political
conservatism, regretted having gone to Washington, and told me
he planned to take his doctorate in Britain and then hoped to return
to Canada. (He later taught at Memorial University of Newfoundland, making a key contribution to the study of the region's economic history. News of his untimely death in 1980 came as a shock.)
However, Ruth and Rod Williams, with whom I was staying, expressed no wish to return to the Canada they had left in 1961.
Victoria was very agreeable in its way, they said, but they preferred
the greater opportunities offered by the Seattle area.

Berkeley and Stanford both required me to take the Graduate
Record Examinations. My scores in the verbal, quantitative, and
history tests were all gratifyingly high, assuring my admission to
any graduate school that set store by them. Then I read a brochure
about the new Massey College in the University of Toronto. It
sounded enticing, but was Toronto as good as Berkeley or Stanford? The advice I got was contradictory. Tony Emery and Sydney
Pettit recommended Toronto; Jack Ogelsby and Reg Roy favoured
Stanford. When I phoned Howard Lim during the Christmas break
– he had won a Woodrow Wilson Fellowship in 1962 and was
studying psychology in Berkeley – he dismissed Stanford as a
'school for rich undergraduates where graduate students don't
rate' and recommended his own university. What made up my
mind, paradoxically, was Toronto's requirement that I do a make-
up year before entering the M.A. program proper (I lacked the
equivalent of a Toronto honours degree). Surely this indicated a
high standard?

It played no part in my choice that the University of Toronto
was in Canada. My patriotism was local, not national. In early 1963
I wrote in my diary about the prospect of union with the United
States: 'Unless the attitude of the Canadian public changes so as to
allow the acceptance of a somewhat lower standard of living, union

will sooner or later turn out to be the only solution to Canada's economic problems: unemployment, trade deficit, and lack of a strong secondary industry. I'm not wildly enthusiastic about the idea, but consider it the logical conclusion of a development which has been taking place ever since Confederation.'

Still, some aspects of American society bothered me, the same ones that had troubled David. One was the obsession with communism, which I thought excessive. It was hard, I suppose, for me to believe that a system that couldn't even produce attractive or functional consumer products was a serious threat to our way of life. I also deplored the inability of conservative Americans to distinguish between revolution and reform, opposing both in the name of 'freedom.' 'They talk of freedom,' I wrote in my diary, 'but their "freedom" is the freedom of the strong to oppress the weak.' (I had identified what Noam Chomsky has called ' "the Fifth Freedom," understood crudely but with a fair degree of accuracy as the freedom to rob, to exploit and to dominate, to undertake any course of action to ensure that existing privilege is protected and advanced.')* My own preference was for government action to modify the undesirable aspects of the market economy and to help its victims.

This forced me into the middle of the economic and political road. I recall a rip-roaring argument in the early spring with Brian Belfont, a prominent UBC radical, who had come over for the day to participate in an academic symposium at the Gordon Head campus. Having been a delegate to UBC's own symposium at Parksville a week or two earlier, I was given the task of entertaining three visitors from Vancouver, and ended up dining with them at a Chinese restaurant before they headed home. How we got on the topic of Fidel Castro's Cuba I can't recall, but I attacked its record on human rights and civil liberties. Brian's view was that the economic and social needs of the masses outweighed the bourgeois privileges I favoured. (Another of the UBC visitors was Wendy Dobson, now a prominent economist. I don't remember whose side she took in the debate but imagine it was mine.) Hostile to com-

---

* Noam Chomsky, *The Culture of Terrorism* (Boston 1988), 1.

munism, and suspicious of democratic socialism, I heartily approved the welfare capitalism that I had seen in West Germany
and Holland.

This got me into trouble with Mother, distressed by my loss
of religion as well as my political liberalism. I found out at some
point that she was telling acquaintances that she thought I had become a socialist, or worse. My views got me into trouble, too,
with the mother of a personable amateur actor and dancer with
whom I went out that spring. During the campaign leading to the
federal election on 8 April 1963, Sharon's mother one day referred
to the federal NDP leader as 'that socialist-communist Tommy
Douglas.' When I pointed out, perhaps patronizingly, that there
was a difference between the two, she looked at me searchingly
and changed the subject. 'Are you a communist, Mike?' she asked
me some weeks later. I demurred. 'Then are you a Nazi?' she
continued. That was just as bad: what made her think so? It turned
out that my support for public health insurance had blown my
cover.

Her mother's objections to my views led Sharon to stop going
out with me in June. She didn't need the trouble I caused her, she
explained apologetically. (A few years later she married Lorne
Priestley, with whom I had served on the AMS council in 1962–3.
Television heartthrob Jason Priestley is their son.)

I took a strong interest in the 1963 federal election, the first one
in which I voted (living in Germany, I had been unable to vote in
1962). Nuclear weapons loomed large, the Diefenbaker government having fallen over the issue of equipping our armed forces
with nuclear warheads. As well, the Cuban missile crisis was still
fresh in memory. In October 1962 the United States had served
notice that it would use military action to prevent the warheads
that were intended for Soviet missiles installed on Cuba from
reaching the island. I thought the American action justified but
feared its consequences. On 22 October I wrote in my diary: 'If
neither side backs down we may have a nuclear war on our hands
within a week. But can either side afford to back down, or rather,
does either side feel it can back down? ... I feel pretty sick.' In the
Snug the evening before American warships were scheduled to

intercept the Russian freighters carrying the warheads, I had a second beer, one more than usual: it might, I said, well be my last.

The Soviets retreated and the crisis passed. It left its mark on me, however. 'The chances for another major war are so great that most people looking honestly into the future are forced to concede it is virtually inevitable,' I wrote in the *Critic*, the publication of the Debating Society: 'The war to end all wars may well start within ten to twenty years.' Still, I rejected Diefenbaker's stand against nuclear weapons in favour of Lester Pearson's lukewarm acceptance of them: 'Our government seems honour-bound to take the warheads ...' I doubted that this would make the world a safer place but, believing the nuclear genie to be out of the bottle to stay, adopted a fatalist position: *if* the end were nigh we might as well face it fully armed. On domestic issues I more clearly preferred the Liberals, led by Pearson, to the Conservatives or the NDP. Attracted by what I saw as the Liberal party's sensible reformism, I voted for its candidate, David Groos.

Within two weeks of the election I was writing my finals. The results did not matter a great deal – I already knew I had won a Woodrow Wilson Fellowship – but were pleasing all the same: I stood at the head of the graduating class. Convocation, a splendid fancy-dress parade, took place on 27 May. Chancellor Phyllis Ross, President MacDonald, and Principal Hickman looked particularly grand. The grad dance was at the Crystal Gardens that evening. I thought I looked spiffy in my tuxedo, and Sharon was ravishing in a white gown. After passing along the receiving line we joined Larry Devlin, Colin Ross, and their dates at a table, parked our mickey of rum under it, and danced into the small hours.

I felt great. My college years had been gratifying: I had excelled in my studies while becoming a BMOC. No longer was I the immigrant boy looking on that I had been in my high school years. Fitting in with a vengeance, I had become a member of the student inner circle.

My sense of accomplishment was reinforced by my being appointed magistrar, Gordon Shrimpton having taken a job that he found more congenial. Unlike him, I enjoyed being in charge and stayed through the summer of 1965. Supervising and planning was often interesting and sometimes exhilarating. As well, I wrote an updated edition of the 'bible,' the compendium describing the summer's work in detail. The major change had been the move to computer-assisted processing of marks, but there were many others. I ensured the efficacy of the new version by giving each section to a newcomer for comment: was my account crystal clear?

What stands out most after thirty years are the people with whom I worked, some of whom are still good friends. One in particular, Dan O'Brien, was responsible for more than one happy memory. One summer he arranged an elaborate contest that asked the question: 'Who is greater: Dusty Springfield or the Beach Boys?' The latter were at the height of their powers: 'Fun, Fun, Fun,' 'Help me, Rhonda,' and 'California Girls,' were great dancing and sing-along songs. Dan set the thing up as a sort of Olympic skating competition, with people listening to various songs and then rating them out of ten. The Beach Boys won with ease.

Dan's sense of humour was excellent, but his language sometimes caused offence. Harry Evans and J.R. were reconciled to a notice stating 'God damn your bloody eyes if you disturb this pile' only after being told that the expression was adapted from *Billy Budd*. Stronger language prompted an anonymous complaint to Harry, and he asked me to suggest to Dan that he tone down his language. 'Who complained?' he wanted to know. I said I had no idea but imagined it was one or more of the Millies. 'I'll fix them,' he growled.

Every Friday was awards day: during the afternoon coffee break those who had distinguished themselves in some way were honoured by a friend, by me, or by the group as a whole. For two or three noon hours Dan had worked busily and secretively in the Maple Room with scissors, glue pot, and felt pens. On Friday he presented the Millies with the product of his labours: an elaborate cardboard chastity belt named 'Little Hercules.' Attached to it was a screed: 'Little Hercules was made in Canada, in the hope and expectation that none of the Millies will be.'

One day that summer I got a phone call from Harry: how was Dan? 'Fine,' I said, somewhat mystified: how should he be? 'What about his leg?' 'It seems to be all right,' I said cautiously. Harry expressed satisfaction and rang off. I turned to Dan. 'Harry asked about your leg. I didn't know there was anything the matter with it.' 'There isn't,' he said, then explained. The day before, while on departmental business, he had spotted the deputy minister, Dr English. Wearing jeans torn at one knee, Dan was below the minumum standard of dress for even casual employees of Her Majesty's government, so he had immediately assumed an exaggerated limp. Dr English had asked him what was the matter; Dan replied that he had fallen, ripping his pants and hurting his leg. The solicitous English had evidently relayed this news to Harry.

Alas, Dan later became deeply immersed in the Victoria counterculture and never re-emerged. The last time I saw him was in 1969 in the Snug. Dressed in black leather, he described himself as a 'fascist hippie' and seemed less good-natured and more truculent than the inspired eccentric I had once worked with. After that I lost track of him. Years later I was distressed to hear that he had died as a result of a drug overdose.

Another work-related memory concerns the great door-plate hullabaloo. While working overtime one evening, the Millies spent their coffee break unscrewing ten or twelve plates and redesignating our rooms as well as several nearby offices. This was intended to amaze and amuse the Maplemen, but because none of us noticed the changes when we arrived at work the next morning and had to have them pointed out to us, we rather spoiled the fun. Around 9:30 Harry phoned: had any Maplemen been working overtime? None, said I: only the Millies. Later that morning he summoned me. He came from a meeting with the deputy ministers of education and public works and the deputy provincial secretary, he told me. The subject had been a serious breach of security. During the night someone had monkeyed with several door plates near the legislative chamber, and the security staff were at a loss to explain how it might have happened. Premier Bennett would be furious when he heard of the incident, so if any of the Maplemen *had* been in the building and I were covering for them, now was the time to come clean.

Everyone could relax, I said: the Millies had done it. Harry swore. Apparently this hadn't occurred to him. How many had been working overtime and who? 'All of them.' He swore again: the miscreants included not only the Mill Mom, the sober-minded Julie Banfield, but also his own daughter, Pat, and Marilyn Wallace, the daughter of the deputy provincial secretary. During our tea break that afternoon Harry read us a stern lecture on appropriate behaviour.

Observing Ken Bull had persuaded me that people work better if you jolly them along than if you abuse them. They must also be well-trained before they begin a job. For three summers I gave my pedagogical and organizational talents full rein. We got things done without snafus, and the people I worked with were still talking to me at the end. I could have done much worse.

Early in September 1963 I packed most of my belongings and set out for Toronto. I had few regrets. Freiburg had spoiled me. After my year there I knew Victoria for what it was: a cultural backwater, its symphony orchestra amateurish, its art gallery small and underfunded, its bookstores (in that pre-Munro era) a feeble joke, its professional theatre non-existent. The movie houses, like the pubs were closed on Sunday. Concerts and other manifestations of high culture *were* permissible on that day, but the tickets for them had to be bought during the week: no box office was allowed to open on the sabbath!

One Sunday in the late fall I had gone to the Royal Theatre to see a travelling ensemble of the Canadian Opera Company perform *La Bohème*. Its skimpy production values, compared with those of a performance I had attended in Paris in the spring, jarred me; even more disturbing was the vocal inadequacy of its Rodolfo. Yet that low-budget *Bohème* was the only opera performed in Victoria all year. Nothing illustrated more starkly the limitations of the city I still thought of as home. Unquestionably beautiful, and a great place for outdoor activities such as sailing, tennis, and golf, Victoria was culturally bush league. It was time to leave.

5

Canada and the United States

My introduction to Toronto took place on a warm, muggy, mid-September evening. A bus took me from the airport to the Royal York Hotel, a taxi to Massey College, where I arrived around 10:00. A porter let me in, gave me my keys, and pointed me to my quarters. 'I have a large study–sitting room and an adjoining bedroom of generous proportions,' I wrote in my diary: 'I'm pleased.' I unpacked my bags, and then, my body on Pacific time, sank into a suede-upholstered chair and read until 2:30.

When I woke up it was too late for breakfast, so I walked up to Bloor Street to get a bite to eat and look for a convenient branch of the Bank of Montreal. They were my first steps in an exploration of the city that continues to this day.

At first Toronto did not impress me. Its setting was humdrum compared to Victoria's or Vancouver's, and its architecture did not make up for the setting. The neo-Romanesque City Hall was attractive; so was the Georgian Osgoode Hall nearby. The adjacent University Avenue, however, was wide, windswept, and sterile, the Champs Élysées as they might have been designed by a banker. At its head was the Legislative Building, squat, businesslike, not at all like Rattenbury's ornate contribution to Victoria's skyline. The clean but unprepossessingly tiled subway stations, somewhat resembling huge public toilets, best typified Toronto: livable, not beautiful. Not that I saw at once all there was to see. I qualified my initial judgment when I discovered the ravines that give the city much of its charm. In 1965–6, when I had a car, I finally saw the lakeshore bluffs in Scarborough: a most agreeable surprise.

Founded in 1793, Toronto had over many decades become the cultural centre of English-speaking Canada and the financial powerhouse of the country. The 1961 census counted 1,824,481 in the city and five boroughs. Still, utility wires strung on poles along the streets hinted at a continuing oneness with smaller communities.

Toronto's downtown core was dedicated to the worship of money. The Stock Exchange on Bay Street was its main temple; subsidiary shrines clustered around it in the form of brokerage houses, trust company offices, and bank buildings. Tallest among these was the head office of the Canadian Imperial Bank of Commerce, which had dominated the skyline for three decades. That was about to change: much larger buildings in the international style were in the making. The first and bleakest of them, looking as though designed for Darth Vader, was the Toronto-Dominion Centre, begun in 1964; others soon followed.

The best of the new buildings was the twin-towered City Hall, designed by the Finnish architect Viljo Revell and completed in 1965. (The large public square in front, with its pool and its splendid Henry Moore sculpture, would become an important centre of civic activity.) Revell was not the only foreigner to touch Toronto. An army of newcomers, so far mainly from Europe but increasingly also from Asia, were altering the face and image of 'Toronto the Good.'

The climate was anything but good. September was unpleasantly humid. October, probably Toronto's best month, brought crisp, sunny days, but the period from November well into March was unlovely: dark and dreary, snowfalls alternating with thaws that quickly turned the city into a soggy mess. Spring arrived at last in April, a good two months later than in Victoria.

In compensation for the climate and weather there were the Art Gallery of Ontario (AGO), the Toronto Symphony, and Sam the Record Man. Sam's was the biggest eye-opener: in Victoria no store discounted records. (Q: Why did God create WASPs? A: Because *somebody* had to buy retail.) But I enjoyed the AGO, and the Toronto Symphony subscription series tickets I bought proved to be a source of great enjoyment. My second-balcony seat in Massey Hall, though hard, was cheap, which also excused the lack of amenities in the building. Among many fine performances I heard there I recall with greatest vividness the *War Requiem*, with Lois Marshall and Peter Pears. Their voices, Britten's music, and the poetry of Wilfred Owen added up to a deeply moving concert. As well, I remember hearing Mstislav Rostropovich with the symphony one evening thirty-some years ago, then walking to the nearby Colonial Tavern where Oscar Peterson was playing. Eat your heart out, Victoria! I thought as I sat down and ordered a bottle of beer.

Over the years Toronto has grown on me to the point where I cannot easily imagine living anywhere else in Canada. Only one other city, Montreal, offers both opera and major league baseball, and neither Cornelia nor I is ever likely to work there or move there in retirement. However, when we do retire I doubt that we will stay in Toronto. Cornelia loves southwestern Ontario, and the West Coast still calls to me, especially in winter. Probably we will divide the time between the two.

Like the city, the University of Toronto was notable for its size more than its appearance. The older buildings had some charm, but typical of the newer was Sidney Smith Hall, bland and uninspiring. Massey College was different. An architectural historian has called it 'simply among the best buildings in Canada.'* (It is ironic that one of the worst, the Robarts Library, was soon to be built within a stone's throw of Massey.) Designed by Ron Thom, the college was brick and concrete, the warmth of one mitigating the coolness of the other. Seen from outside, the college was elegant but somewhat forbidding. This impression changed as one passed through the gate into a tree-filled quadrangle, a slender bell tower rising from a pond at the southern end. Most of the public rooms were near that pond, but below ground level in the northwest corner was a chapel designed by Tanya Moiseiwitsch in the Byzantine style. Above it the Round Room, an austere space intended for meetings and dissertation defences, conjured up thoughts of the Spanish Inquisition.

Admirable as the college was architecturally, one feature elicited a lot of criticism. None of the windows had screens. This gave free

---

* Michael McMordie, in *The Canadian Encyclopedia* (Edmonton 1988), 2: 1312.

entry to flies and mosquitoes, and prompted questions as to what Thom had been thinking of. Screens had probably never occurred to him, I suggested to some other junior fellows over a pre-dinner drink. After all, houses built in Vancouver and Victoria didn't have them. How do you keep insects out? someone asked. Simple, I replied: earwigs and wasps were the only insects one noticed much, and the former didn't fly while the latter rarely enter houses without a good reason. This comment brought smiles and laughter that I was quite unable to interpret. I asked for an explanation and for the first time in my life heard about WASPs. In Victoria, then the most WASPish town west of New Brunswick, no one I knew had ever used the term!

From the outset the college faced criticism of its function and goal. Was Vincent Massey, Canada's first native-born governor general, trying to recreate the Oxford of his youth? 'Oh, to be in England, now that England's here,' one wag said, while another derided the college as 'Half Souls'.' Some people characterized as silly the academic gowns worn at dinner and the Latin grace said before and after by the don of hall, in 1963–4 a mathematician visiting Toronto from a Welsh university. 'Nos miseres et egentes homines ...,' John Rigby intoned in his precise way: 'We wretched and needy men ...' Neither wretched nor all that needy, I thought when I found out what the words meant, but it *sounded* good. Two years later a visiting scholar from Oxford, Bob Ogilvie, made the most appropriate response to the words: he founded a dining club and gave it that name.

The High Tables at which four or five students rubbed shoulders with the Master, the senior fellows, and several guests, also came under attack. Yet they served their purpose in introducing us to another, larger world. Among other men – the guests were all men in those days – I met Michael Pitfield, later clerk of the Privy Council, the English philosopher A.J. Ayer, and, in the quad one evening, the economist John Kenneth Galbraith, who stayed there long enough so that I could fetch my copy of *The Affluent Society* for his autograph.

Massey's choice of Robertson Davies as Master didn't help the college's image with the sceptics. Dandyishly dressed, with long, greying hair and a full beard, the journalist and author was no typical Canadian. Some people, including some who lived in the college, were put off by his appearance and manner. The beard, the Edwardian jackets, the mellifluous voice, the careful choice of words: who did he think he was?

I got to know Davies slightly better than most of the junior fellows, as we students were called, because for several months his second daughter, Jennifer, and I went out with each other. I greatly appreciated the occasional invitation to dinner, with its opportunity to hear her father talk when at his ease. I gleaned an impression of someone, at bottom shy, who had made an elaborate artifact of himself, had wrapped himself in a cloak of mannerisms. Behind this he seemed tolerant, witty, and wise. And at all times he spoke with intelligence, flair, and an unequalled sense of timing. In a nation of hemmers-and-hawers he was an Eisengrim of the spoken (and written) word.

He was his own man, his intellectual independence shored up by considerable wealth. The way he and his family lived suggested as much: a Jaguar in the garage, furniture and rugs that were expensive in an understated way, a superabundance of books. Once, while admiring her father's many first editions, I asked Jennifer tactlessly how he could possibly afford them all. Neither journalists nor professors, I thought, earned anywhere near enough. 'Well, you know,' she said in an offhand manner, 'Daddy has a private income.' She didn't elaborate, and I didn't ask. A few years later, when he sold the *Peterborough Examiner* to the Thomson chain, some Southam Fellows, journalists on study leave who were attached to the college, estimated the price at four to eight million dollars. They had no way of knowing, of course, how much of this was net.

The hall porter was as uncommon in his way as the master. Norman McCracken was a retired sergeant-major of the Queen's Own Rifles of Canada, a stocky man with a brush cut, a parade-ground voice, and a magnificent waxed moustache. More important to the effective functioning of the college, however, was Davies's secretary, the super-competent Moira Whalon.

Several senior fellows, who with Davies governed the college, were much in evidence. The librarian, Douglas Lochhead, was a poet and a connoisseur of paper and printing. The bursar, Colin Friesen, had left an assistant bank manager's position to join the college and seemed to be enjoying the change. Robert Finch, a courtly French scholar and poet, had a suite of rooms above the gate; the sinologist Bill Dobson, a superb raconteur, had a study in the college. Vincent Massey's son Lionel often lunched in the college, and President Claude Bissell turned up regularly. So did Maurice Careless, a historian, John Polanyi, a chemist, and Tuzo Wilson, a jovial geophysicist who liked to illustrate the theory of continental drift by pushing the grease on the surface of his soup about the bowl with his spoon.

Ernest Sirluck, a professor of English who in 1964 became the dean of graduate studies, rarely lunched at the college but did turn up at other functions. I won't easily forget my first meeting with him. It was during the fall of 1964, at one of the sherry parties that Robertson and Brenda Davies held to entertain groups of junior fellows. Among the other guests were a few senior fellows and a clutch of presumably suitable undergraduate women from the nearby residences of Trinity and University Colleges. I was chatting with one of these young women when Sirluck joined us. What the subject of conversation was I can't recall, but at some point he said to me in a matter-of-fact tone of voice: 'I think that's the silliest thing I've heard anyone say in at least a month.' I supposed he knew whereof he spoke, but I resented the remark all the same, not least because he made it in the presence of a woman I'd just met and to whom I'd taken a liking.

A year later he redeemed himself in my eyes. As a result of bad advice given to me by a member of the graduate faculty office staff, I had been short-changed $500 in fellowship money. I appealed to Sirluck. A few days after writing to him I got a telephone call from the secretary of the faculty: 'Dean Sirluck wishes to see you next Tuesday afternoon at 1:30.' As I took my seat he looked at me, fortunately without recognition, and said: 'Mr Horn, I have made enquiries and find that your complaint is justified. I will arrange to have $500 paid to you during the second term. Next time don't rely on a junior member of my staff for an opinion on a matter as important to you as this.' I thanked him, shook his hand gratefully, and left his office, no more than ninety seconds after I had entered it. He might be tactless, I said to myself, but he was also fair.

Over us all hovered the Visitor. In his seventies, his skin stretched over finely chiselled features, Vincent Massey was a patrician to the core. He made some effort to get to know the junior fellows, but his manner was very much that of the grand seigneur. This inhibited discussion, although I do recall taking part in one rewarding conversation with him. On 20 February 1967 I joined three other junior fellows, the mathematician Derrick Breach, and two students of English, Bill Dean and Ian Lancashire, in a visit to Batterwood House in Port Hope. It was Massey's eightieth birthday, and we were bringing him gifts from the junior fellows. He offered us a glass of sherry, and we then touched on several topics before settling on Marshall McLuhan 'whom Massey considers a bit of a charlatan.'

Was he right? I felt unsure. After reading *Understanding Media* some months earlier I had noted in my diary: 'An entertaining book, though scarcely well-written. I have the feeling that obfuscation is used to appear profound. But perhaps he just writes badly.' A few years later Jack drew to my attention the book *Het avondrood der magiërs* (The Twilight of the Wise Men) by the Dutch essayist Rudy Kousbroek. Massey would have liked, I think, Kousbroek's compelling critique of McLuhan as ignorant of European history and hostile to clear thought. (That Kousbroek has never been translated into English is a source of renewed surprise to me whenever I read one of his essays. At home in at least four modern languages, he is lucid, humorous, erudite, and invariably thought-provoking. Among Canadian writers only Robert Fulford comes close.)

Wearing an academic gown gorgeously trimmed with red, Davies welcomed the junior fellows at a sherry party early in term. Some sixty-five of us resided in the college; twenty-five or so non-resident fellows, mostly married men, had study carrels in the basement. Most of us were at the party, looking each other over, trying to size him up. He told us that we were rarely privileged and hoped we would benefit from our association with each other and the college. He hit the right notes with one exception. Mealtime conversation might sink to the discussion of 'women and horses,' he feared, so he undertook to post a weekly topic to which we might turn if none suitable should occur to us. Some men quickly began to offer their own invariably ribald suggestions alongside the authorized version. Within weeks the latter ceased to appear.

The opening ceremonies took place on 4 October. Afterwards I had too much to drink but did not disgrace myself beyond asking Raymond Massey how he liked hospital life, a reference to his television role in *Dr. Kildare* (never having seen the show, I owed this question to Jennifer). Other highlights of the year were the Christmas dance and the Christmas Gaudy. The dance was enlivened by a skit written by two or three of the junior fellows and directed by Brenda Davies. The Gaudy featured seasonal music and a poem written for the occasion by Robert Finch, but the star was Davies himself. His first of many annual College ghost stories was richly amusing; later Gaudies always played to a crammed hall.

The college was run from the top down. A protest against the rule requiring female guests to leave by 11:30 got nowhere (most junior fellows learned to circumvent it when necessary without causing umbrage). A student association of sorts finally took form in 1965–6, but it did nothing when in 1967 two non-renewals caused a mild stir. Few of us cared that no one thought of soliciting our views. If we were far from the vanguard of the student revolution, this was because we did not wish to spend the time, or to risk our fellowships (which were substantial in value, as our fees did not come close to covering the cost of room, board, and services such as the library, open for use around the clock). Mostly we were left alone to spend our time as we chose. The college was a graduate student's dream.

Now and then I saw DAAD acquaintances such as George Hynna and Fred Schroeder, or Victoria friends like Les Millin, Bruce Warburton, and Elsie Wollaston. Of these people I saw Fred most frequently, and it was in his company that I carried out the only political canvassing I have ever done.

When I phoned Fred, soon upon my arrival in Toronto, he invited me to his parents' home on Oriole Parkway for a drink but said we had to do some work first. The man who enjoyed the uncertain benefits of our labours was Mark MacGuigan, later a federal minister of justice, who in 1963 was running for the provincial Liberals in Toronto–St Patrick. Every householder we managed to contact expressed a preference for the Progressive Conservative candidate and eventual winner, Kelso Roberts, and after an hour or so we gave up and headed for Fred's place for an evening of beer and talk. Having done a year of law he had recently switched to classics, a subject he now teaches at Queen's. He spent a large part of the evening telling stories, most of them amusing, some almost horrifying, about his year in law and his summer job with a downtown firm.

Fred was a fine raconteur; so were his older brother, a naval officer, and their father, Walter Schroeder, a justice of the Ontario Court of Appeal. For several years I enjoyed Christmas dinner with the Schroeders, and I visited them regularly. When I saw Algonquin Park for the first time, in the late summer of 1966, it was in the company of Fred and of Margot Depiereux, who was touring North America and was the Schroeders' guest while in Toronto. What I saw of the park impressed me but little: it looked like Vancouver Island without mountains. What *did* impress me (and Margot; Fred was blasé) was a violent thunderstorm that hit early that evening as we were driving back to Toronto. The downpour was so heavy that we couldn't see anything at all and were forced to stop at the side of the road until the storm passed. I have experienced this only once or twice since.

Though not limited to it, my social life in Toronto centred on the college, where I quickly made new friends. With David Trott, a soft-spoken UBC graduate who studied French, Mark Levene, and Stuart Niermeier, two students of English from Winnipeg, I rented a TV set. Mark was a slight, intense man with a keen sense of humour. Stuart, blond and much larger than Mark, was devoted to three things: Anglo-Catholicism, the poetry of Tennyson, and the *Goon Show*. The last of these reinforced his innate sense of the ridiculous. Once he entered the Common Room looking crestfallen.

He had bought a tapered shirt, he explained mock-plaintively, 'but it tapers the wrong way.'

Others with whom I got on well included Derrick Breach, a rumpled mathematician from New Zealand who introduced me to a complicated board game called Diplomacy and to several commercial art galleries, Bill Dean, an outspoken Australian who had switched from law to English literature, and John Paynter, a UBC graduate who arrived at Massey in 1965 after two years at Oxford. I remember with particular affection Ken Windsor, a thoughtful and humane historian who threw unexcelled parties. He taught for some years at the University of New Brunswick, where he helped to start the journal *Acadiensis*, before dying in an automobile accident overseas: a sad loss.

Arnold Bruner, a Southam Fellow who later became a lawyer, was not a close associate, but I worked with him in a small way to break up a hate-mail ring working from a downtown hotel. He wanted to approach a young Netherlander who worked there: could I help? On some pretext I invited the man to the college for a drink; Arnold joined us and steered the conversation around to anti-Semitism. Soon our guest was talking a mile a minute about the extracurricular activities of three people who worked with him. Upon being assured his name would not be disclosed, he agreed that Arnold should take up the matter with the hotel management. Arnold later told me his intervention had abruptly ended the activities of the three.

Socializing at Massey usually involved a good deal of drinking. The Common Room got a liquor licence early during the college's first year, but most of the drinking took place in junior fellows' rooms. The pre-dinner sherry party quickly became a tradition, and the effect of several glasses of fortified wine on empty stomachs often meant that dinners were rather noisy and jolly, especially on Friday and Saturday evenings.

Aware that alcohol affected my work in the evening, I usually limited my intake to a couple of small glasses of sherry before dinner, or a beer in the Common Room at 10:30. There were exceptions, of course: scheduled celebrations such as the Founders' Gaudy and the Christmas Dance, or unscheduled ones such as the termination of Jay Ford's engagement to Peggy Atwood, then still a mere graduate student and not yet the well-known poet and novelist Margaret Atwood. Jay was the college wit during the first year, among his brainchildren being the Rosemary Speirs limerick contest, and that evening he was at his bonhomous best. Several of us joined him in an evening of congratulatory boozing of which my memories are understandably a bit vague, although I do remember Bob Abra, a journalist in his forties who considered himself a survivor of the war between the sexes, assuring Jay repeatedly that he would not regret having broken off the engagement, that, indeed, he would look back on this day as the happiest of his life. I had formed no strong opinion of Peggy during the few times I had met her, but when I read her first novel, *The Edible Woman*, a few years later I decided she had had the last laugh.

I liked the college and its archaisms. They added a certain style to our lives as well as an aura of élitism which I found gratifying. What was objectionable, though it did not occur to me to think so then, was the exclusion of women from membership. Granted: in the 1960s women were still relatively uncommon in graduate and professional programs. But they did exist, and were probably of higher average intellectual quality than the men, having survived a sterner selection process.

A reader of Massey's memoirs looks in vain for an explanation of why women were excluded, but Claude Bissell writes in his biography of Massey: 'A residential college, it was assumed, must be confined to one sex, and Vincent never had any doubt about which sex should have the priority.'* Female graduate students resented their exclusion. Early in the fall of 1963 one of them, Rosemary Speirs, led a band of mostly female picketers around the quad. The Master left his study to speak with her, walking slowly, his grey mane inclined towards her russet hair. She later told me that he had advised her to find someone who would do for women what Vincent Massey had done for men, advice she found unhelp-

---

* Claude Bissell, *The Imperial Canadian: Vincent Massey in Office* (Toronto 1986), 295.

ful. Massey surely had a right to decide what to do with his family's money? I said. Conceding this, Rosemary countered that the university ought not to have offered land and support to a college that excluded women. Unsure how to answer this, I changed the subject. (In 1974 the college opened its doors to the first group of female junior fellows, one of whom, Cornelia Schuh, later became my wife. Female senior fellows were next, and in 1988 Ann Saddlemyer, who had taught me at Victoria College more than twenty-five years earlier, became the first female master. Civilization as we know it has not collapsed.)

Rosemary was one of a number of women I dated while living in Massey College. With one of them, an undergraduate from Nova Scotia, I had a brief but passionate fling in February and March of 1964, at last losing a virginity that had become increasingly irksome to me since my loss of religion two years earlier. The earth did not move for me nor, so far as I could judge, for her. In this as in so many ways a neophyte simply did not shine. (Among my favourite Woody Allen lines is one from *Love and Death*. Praised for the quality of his love making, the hero modestly admits: 'I practise a lot when I'm alone.' I guess I hadn't practised enough.)

My only serious romantic involvements of those years took place in Victoria, in the summers of 1964 and 1965. Neither lasted more than a few months. The former ended when Judy, with whom I had been planning to spend the Christmas holidays, wrote in November 1964 to tell me that she had made up with a previous boyfriend. As I had seen this coming, I bore her no ill will and remembered with gratitude the most romantic journey of my life to that point, three days spent with her while we crossed Canada on a CPR train in early September. As well, the following May she introduced me to Wendy, who became her successor in my affections.

My affair with Wendy came to an abrupt end in the autumn of 1965, when I backed out of an engagement to marry her in the next year. Ready, or so it seemed, to accept the idea of marriage in the abstract, I took fright when she introduced concrete details such as china patterns, flatware, and linen into the discussion. The more I thought about it, the more I feared that raising a family on a professor's salary – in 1965 middle-class families with two incomes were still unusual, though becoming less so – would not leave enough money for travel and books, which were very important to me.

One who advised me to end the engagement was Jack. After graduating from UBC in art history he had spent a year at the University of Utrecht before coming to Toronto in 1965 on a Woodrow Wilson Fellowship. Having him around was a tonic: I could talk with him about things I would discuss with no one else, and I trusted his judgment. When I spoke of my misgivings he told me not to second-guess myself. If I had doubts, I shouldn't get married.

In 1963–4, my make-up year, I took four courses. Two were surveys in Canadian and American history, courses I was forced to take because so far I had studied neither. Both numbered several hundred students, and I found the lectures alienating. Soon I stopped going to them altogether. Fortunately, both courses had tutorials of about a dozen students each: there was more money for teaching here than at Victoria College. My tutor in the Canadian course was Ramsay Cook, friendly and looking younger than his thirty-two years. Although I was predisposed to find Canadian history dull, I enjoyed my tutorials with him. I wrote both my essays on aspects of the history of British Columbia, learning many things about which I had been ignorant. I had not been eager to take the Canadian course, but as the year went on I was increasingly glad I had been compelled to do so.

My tutorials in U.S. history with Patrick White were also interesting, but my seminar in German history was a disappointment. Robert Spencer was uninspiring, and only one of the other students was able to read German! My other seminar, on European intellectual history, was with John Cairns, billed as one of the department's rising stars. I liked him a lot and turned to him in a bout of disillusionment with my studies. He suggested that I complete the M.A. before throwing in the towel. If I still wanted to quit then, he added, I might give some thought to the Department of External Affairs, where my foreign languages would prove useful.

Soon afterwards I discussed this with someone well-placed to give counsel. John Roberts, a junior officer in the Canadian embassy in Paris, was visiting the college as a guest of a Southam Fellow, Robin Green. John warned me against External Affairs. He was about to get out and into politics, he said, having reached the conclusion that External Affairs would not allow him to do anything on his own before he was at least forty-five. (He later ran for Parliament, in time becoming a member of Pierre Trudeau's cabinet, and at one point made an unsuccessful bid to become the federal Liberal leader.) I took his comments seriously: probably they were what I had wanted to hear all along. My decision to continue studying was made easier when I won a $2500 fellowship.

In 1964–5 I took three courses, Kenneth McNaught's on the American Left, Harold Nelson's on recent international relations, and A.P. Thornton's on the British Empire and Commonwealth, adding to this a research paper for McNaught. He and Nelson were effective seminar leaders, Thornton less so. But he had a superb prose style and a gift for coining a phrase. Of the Arab-Israeli conflict he once said: 'Two wrongs don't make a right, and two rights make nothing but trouble.' Fascinated by the essay I wrote for Thornton on the unification of South Africa, I wanted to do a Ph.D. under his supervision. He said I should go to that country to examine the sources on the subject that interested me, apartheid. The South African Ministry of Education took months to reply to my inquiry, however, and when they did reply they all but told me to get lost. Perhaps that was just as well: my tactlessness might have got me into trouble.

In 1965–6, my final year of courses, I took comparative North American institutions with Craig Brown, Canadian intellectual history with Cook, and Canadian government and politics with Jack McLeod. That my program focused on Canada in this way was an accident. I wanted to take the course with Cook because I had enjoyed my undergraduate seminar with him, and McLeod's course was my outside minor. I would have preferred a course in political theory, but the graduate director of the political science department, noting that I had not taken the subject as an undergraduate, would not give his permission.

Taking the course with Brown was entirely fortuitous. I was

supposed to do a course in historiography but was excused from it because of the seminar I had taken with Jack Ogelsby and Tony Emery at Victoria College. This left me free to take an elective, and I opted for Brown's course because I had enjoyed my courses in U.S. history and thought that a comparative Canadian–U.S. perspective would be useful.

What I would write my dissertation on I did not yet know, but serendipity took care of that. My essay for Brown examined attitudes to the United States in the *Canadian Forum* and *Saturday Night* during the 1930s. In this way I encountered the League for Social Reconstruction (LSR), a group of left-wing intellectuals who had controlled the *Forum* during the later Depression years and about whom no one had ever written. I learned that two privately held collections of papers were available in Toronto and borrowed them from their owners, G.M.A. Grube of the Trinity College classics department (the father of my English instructor in 1958–9), and a philosophy don, Jarvis McCurdy. What I saw in these collections suggested to me a topic tailor-made for a research paper in Cook's course. After reading my paper, Cook, whom by this time I was calling Ramsay, agreed to supervise a Ph.D. thesis on the LSR. I did not yet think of myself as a historian of Canada, but willy-nilly I seemed to be moving in that direction.

My essay for Jack McLeod had its origin in an event in 1964. At a press conference in March that year, Ontario's attorney general, Fred Cass, had inexplicably described a bill to amend the Police Act in these words: 'It's drastic and it's dangerous and it's new and it's terrible legislation in an English common law country.'* The resulting furore focused on a section of the bill that would have enabled the Ontario Police Commission to hear evidence in secret. The Opposition and the media united in damning the government's attempt to introduce 'Gestapo methods' into the province.

On 23 March I joined two political science students who lived at Massey, Stewart Goodings and Paul Pross, in the visitors' gallery at Queen's Park. The government wanted to refer Bill 99 to com-

* *Globe and Mail*, 20 March 1964.

mittee, hoping to amend or delete the offending section there, but the Liberals and NDP wanted the government to eat crow publicly. Because some of its own members were disaffected, the government resisted just long enough to save some face, then prudently caved in. An NDP amendment to delete the section passed unanimously. Cass's letter of resignation, read by Premier John Robarts, came as an anticlimax.

In the course of researching the subject, I decided that a mountain had been made of a molehill. The offending section had much to recommend it, and its equivalent was present in other statutes. Yet the press had been right to challenge the bill, I thought, given the way it had been presented to them. I wrote to Cass for his comments and got a brief reply: 'The incident you mention closed a chapter in my book of life which I am unwilling to re-open, nor do I desire to add either a post script or an addendum.' Fair enough: had I screwed up as spectacularly as he, I would have been equally reluctant to relive the episode.

More surprising was the attitude of two Southam Fellows I spoke with. Both had condemned the bill at the time, but neither had ever actually read it. Was this good journalism? 'Cass said the bill was terrible,' Alan Anderson of the Toronto *Telegram* answered me: '*That* was the story.' I asked the opinion of Leslie Millin, who was writing for the *Globe and Mail* in 1965–6. Reporters rarely had the time to do a thorough job, he explained: shortcuts were unavoidable. Was this not likely to lead to incompleteness and error? 'The rag's got to get out,' he said: 'Who cares what's in it twenty-four hours after it's been published?' Historians did, I ventured. 'In that case you're a pack of fools,' he snorted. I remember his comment every time I read a newspaper story on a subject about which I'm knowledgeable: it invariably contains errors.

For three years I wrote regularly in the weekly *Varsity Review*. Politics constituted my main subject. My first article discussed the provincial election in British Columbia, held in the early fall of 1963 and predictably won by W.A.C. Bennett's Socreds; but soon I turned to topics with broader appeal to a Toronto readership. Separatism was on the rise in Quebec; so was talk of constitutional change. The focus of the debate troubled me. 'Ontarians tend to assume that they ... speak for all of English Canada,' I wrote in my diary in November 1963: 'Had an argument with Jim Laxer [features editor of the *Varsity*] about this. He thinks Ontario & Quebec could always reach a settlement which would leave the rest of Canada out.'

This seemed to me unwise. 'Don't Forget the West' was the title of one article I wrote; in it I argued against making concessions to Quebec that would not be available to the western provinces. 'I'm glad I came to Eastern Canada ...' I confided to my diary: 'The concern here is with things quite different from those which excite B.C. There I think biculturalism is pretty well an academic issue which really interests only a few people. Here it has become more than academic.'

Multiculturalism and the related issue of becoming Canadian were the subject of another article. Some thought there were more ways of being Canadian than by conforming to English- or French-Canadian norms, I wrote, and a few asserted that Canada should be a cultural mosaic. I disagreed with them. Having at Hart House heard Senator Paul Yuzyk, 'self-proclaimed champion of Canada's ethnic groups,' preach the multicultural gospel, I rejected his proposed policy, instead counselling assimilation. This was 'not a negative thing ...' I wrote, 'the loss of personal or group identity ... [but] something positive, the process of coming to terms with a new environment while one is shaped by it. This is and should be the experience of people who have consciously changed their allegiance from one country to another.'

Easy to say, harder to make true, and a view far from shared by all. In 1966 I lunched at the home of another Masseyite, Stan Kirschbaum. His parents, proud of their Slovak heritage, must have assumed that ethnic origin meant to others what it did to them. In any case, Stan's mother greeted her various guests as 'the brilliant Australian/Dutch/Japanese/Swiss student Stan has been telling us about.' The others had no reason, other than modesty, to quarrel with this description, but *I* said I was Canadian. 'But you were born in Holland?' 'Yes, I was.' 'Well, then you are Dutch!' she said triumphantly.

At some point I interviewed the first Soviet exchange student to live at the college. Vitaly Korsun was a physicist from Dnepropetrovsk whose sense of humour I signally failed to capture in what I wrote. Just before dinner one day he came striding into the quad carrying two shopping bags from Honest Ed's, the discount emporium at Bloor and Bathurst. 'How's life under capitalism, Vitaly?' someone shouted from a Common Room window. Looking over his shoulder, he grinned broadly, raised his shopping bags, and yelled back: 'It is great, if you have capital!'

In 1964 I tackled the subject of tuition fees. 'Forcing students to take up the slack in university operating budgets created by niggardly governments can in no way be interpreted as providing an incentive to enter university,' I opined. However, I took a different line in a Hart House debate in 1965. Having done some research, I noted that in low-fee countries the participation rate was actually lower than in the United States and Canada, where fees were moderate or high. (I ignored the social causes of this.) Fairness might well require higher tuition fees, I argued, for low fees mainly benefited the children of the better-off. Neither low fees nor ample loan funds, in fact, were likely to attract the offspring of the poor in large numbers. If universities were to be made truly accessible, poor families must be compensated for the loss of the contribution to family income that their children might have made. This line was less than popular: my partner and I lost handily.

My first letter to a Toronto newspaper – it was not to be my last – was prompted by a column in the *Toronto Daily Star*. Ron Haggart had pointed out that the Ontario legislature had permitted a company to foul the Spanish River in perpetuity after the Supreme Court of Canada had ordered it to desist. 'That the entire episode made it permissible for a paper mill to continue to dump its waste into a river must be distressing to all citizens worried by water and air pollution,' I wrote.

Of course, expecting corporations to protect the environment voluntarily is like expecting cuckoos and cowbirds not to lay their eggs in other birds' nests. It is government's job to safeguard the public interest. Unfortunately, governments often ignore this responsibility. Like the people they represent, they worship 'getting and spending' as the epitome of the good. This is a deadlier threat to human survival than thermonuclear war. Still, the self-destruction of our species, should we accomplish it, will not be a total or an unqualified disaster. The planet's flora and fauna (other than ourselves) will surely benefit.

All North Americans then alive are said to remember where they were when they heard of the assassination of President John F. Kennedy on 22 November 1963. I was at my desk. An American student who had the room next to mine pounded on my door and asked whether I had heard the news: the president had been shot! 'Bissell?' I asked incredulously, 'Why would anybody want to shoot Claude Bissell?' 'Not *him*,' my neighbour said in obvious exasperation: 'President *Kennedy*!' (When I recounted this story to Dr Bissell many years later he said that, like me, his wife had misunderstood the news when their gardener had burst in to share it with her.)

Writing in my diary, I worried about the effect the assassination would have on U.S. politics: 'My fear is that this will give the rightwingers additional impetus & that Goldwater will be elected president next year as a result. Moreover, Johnson is a Texan and not nearly as likely as Kennedy to pursue a policy of integration.' Still, Johnson was preferable to Barry Goldwater, whose economic conservatism served the interests of the social class he so ably represented and no one else. I recall a cartoon that appeared in the course of the 1964 campaign: Goldwater, talking to a woman and child on a stoop, both dressed in rags, says: 'Why don't you show some initiative and inherit yourself a department store?' Goldwater's political career owed much to his good fortune in being born into a family of substance.

In early 1964 I was in Hart House to debate for the ayes the question: 'Would this house support Lyndon B. Johnson as the next president of the United States?' My partner and I argued that, with Goldwater bound to be the Republican candidate, there was no choice but to support Johnson. We won without difficulty. When in turn Johnson won the election in November I was pleased. I despised Goldwater's policies, and was as yet uncritical of U.S. involvement in Vietnam, which Johnson was expanding.

I liked Canadian conservatism little better than American.

George Grant's *Lament for a Nation*, which I read soon after it appeared in the late autumn of 1965, didn't change my mind. Without exonerating the Conservative party, Grant argued that Canadian Liberals, starting in the time of William Lyon Mackenzie King, had combined with the country's capitalists and much of the media to subvert the country's essential conservatism and with it Canada's independence. The country's eventual absorption by the United States, Grant argued, had become unavoidable: 'The impossibility of conservatism in our era is the impossibility of Canada.'*

There was much in the book with which I agreed, yet much, too, that struck me as exaggerated and even wrong-headed. Grant's sympathetic portrayal of Diefenbaker's attitude to nuclear warheads for the Canadian armed forces was one example. I did not think that the Conservative prime minister was in principle opposed to nuclear weapons, but rather that he was confused about the agreements his government had made. After all, the Bomarcs made no sense unless they were armed with nuclear warheads!

Then there were Grant's confusions with respect to Canadian commercial policy: his apparent inability to recognize that the Liberal policies he deplored had their origins in the so-called 'National Policy' introduced by John A. Macdonald's Conservatives in 1879. I filled the book with annotations, not a few of them reading: 'Is this true?'

In early 1966, CBC Radio asked Rick Clippingdale, a fellow Masseyite, and me to discuss Grant's book with him. He turned out to be a large, untidy man who smoked heavily and gestured expansively. Cigarette ash littered the front of his cardigan. When I controverted some point he had made he took up my challenge with delight. Later he autographed his book 'in thanks for an interesting broadcast.' I didn't care for some of his ideas, but I liked him.

I liked also Walter Gordon, whom I met at about the same time. An election in November 1965 had failed to give the Liberals the majority they sought. Gordon, the minister of finance, had resigned from the cabinet because he had advised Prime Minister Pearson

---

* George Grant, *Lament for a Nation: The Defeat of Canadian Nationalism* (Toronto 1965), 68.

badly in urging him to ask for the dissolution that made the election necessary. Gordon was at Massey College for lunch a few months later as the guest of Bill Dobson, who had written to me with a request to put together an 'impromptu little group' that would meet Gordon over coffee after lunch.

We listened respectfully as he talked about his experiences as a cabinet minister and as a government backbencher ('a very nearly useless form of life'). Intelligent and witty, he seemed free of that blend of guile and gutlessness that marks the born politician. I welcomed his commitment to social welfare but was less enthusiastic about his economic nationalism. Still, he struck me as an example of Canadian Liberalism at its most attractive, though not its most effective.

I was no longer a Christian, having lost my faith while in Europe, but I still attended church from time to time. On Christmas Eve, 1963, I accompanied Jennifer and Rosamond Davies to the midnight service at St Thomas's Church on Huron Street. Nothing in my background had prepared me for a High Church service with all the stops pulled out. Incense I associated with Roman Catholicism, yet here was incense in great, suffocating clouds! At first it put me off. However, the music was excellent and the elaborate ritual pleased the senses. After a while I began to enjoy myself. A year later I joined my friend Sheila Wolfson, an art history student, at the midnight mass at St Michael's Cathedral. She claimed that on Christmas Eve it was the best theatre in town. She was wrong: St Thomas's put on a better show.

I saw a few professional theatre performances. In the fall of 1963 I joined the Davies family in seeing *Dylan* at the O'Keefe Centre: 'Not a very good play, but it was saved by Alec Guinness.' Later, also at the O'Keefe, I saw Richard Burton in *Hamlet*. Strange to say, this was the first time in my life I had seen Shakespeare professionally produced and performed! I knew the play, of course; his works had been well-represented in my studies. 'An interpretation which made Hamlet a more decisive figure than I thought was warranted,' I wrote in my diary: 'Polonius, played by Hume Cronyn, was very fine.' I was less impressed by Burton.

Most of the theatre I saw in those days was of the amateur variety, but no less enjoyable for that. The Intimate Stage folded after the summer of 1962, I believe, but at the Gordon Head campus of the University of Victoria, Carl Hare took over where Tony Nicholson had left off. I recall performances of *The Alchemist*, Ionesco's chilling *The Lesson*, and above all John Mortimer's tragicomic short play *The Dock Brief*. It starred two friends of mine, John Gilliland and Horace Mayea, who took the parts of the aging barrister who has never had a case and his equally gormless client, accused of murdering his abusive wife. The play was both funny and sad. Since seeing it I have become an admirer of its author's Rumpole stories, and of his novels.

In 1966, having enjoyed the songs of Michael Flanders and Donald Swann since first hearing them on record half a dozen years earlier, I went to the O'Keefe for a performance of *At the Drop of Another Hat*. The show was pleasing, but the performers were almost lost in the vastness of the hall. I should have brought binoculars! Now that I go to the O'Keefe regularly to see and hear opera, I do exactly that.

In spite of its size, Toronto did not have an opera house. (It still doesn't, though the Princess of Wales Theatre would do nicely were it not largely devoted to presumably profitable schlock.) The Canadian Opera Company performed several works annually at the O'Keefe Centre, in spite of the building's unsuitability for that art form. For more than a decade I attended few performances, however: I couldn't afford good seats, and even bad seats were expensive. Not until the mid-1970s did I get a subscription. Even now my attitude resembles that of the gambler who, about to enter a gaming house, is warned that it is crooked. 'I know,' he replies, 'but it's the only game in town.' In recent years I've enjoyed the COC performances at the Elgin Theatre: not an opera house either, but easily superior to the O'Keefe.

Having joined David Trott's TV consortium, I watched most of the World Series in 1963, the first time in my life I had been able to do so. The outcome was gratifying: the Dodgers beat the Yankees in four, with the great Sandy Koufax winning the first and fourth games. Aside from the occasional sports event, I watched the news at eleven and current affairs programs such as *This Hour Has Seven Days*. We all enjoyed an irreverent late-evening variety show called *Nightcap* and once went to the CBC's Yonge Street studio to watch it being taped. With millions of other North Americans, we saw the Beatles perform on the *Ed Sullivan Show*. Although I did not think much of their singing I liked the group's enthusiasm and some of their songs. Among the films I saw in the mid-1960s I recall their first, *A Hard Day's Night*, with pleasure. Others that stand out are *Tom Jones*, Tony Richardson's energetic if uneven homage to Henry Fielding, and that blackest of black comedies, Stanley Kubrick's *Dr. Strangelove*. To be able to laugh at the coming of the thermonuclear end: that took panache!

My favourite pastime continued to be reading. My diary for 1963 and 1964 mentions novels by more than twenty authors, among them Amis, Beerbohm, Bellow, Malcolm Bradbury, Greene, Isherwood, Malamud, Orwell, and Evelyn Waugh. In 1965 I read *The Apprenticeship of Duddy Kravitz*; soon I was also reading Davies and MacLennan. As well, I discovered the American novelist Peter De Vries. His celebration of the comic possibilities of language delighted me, and his 'guarded pessimism' – his term – struck a chord.

Aside from *Lament for a Nation*, two other works of non-fiction that I read in the mid-1960s stick in my mind: *The Feminine Mystique* and *The Vertical Mosaic*. Betty Friedan convinced me that I didn't want a conventional wife, while John Porter's description of a Canada whose élites were dominated by Anglo-Canadians reinforced my belief that assimilation into the mainstream was the best policy for those who could manage it. All I had to do was look around the history department: professors not of Anglo-Canadian, British, or American stock were rare.

Porter's book also gave me insight into a class system of which I had become conscious since my arrival in Toronto. My friendship with Jennifer played a significant part in this. She had attended Bishop Strachan School, and many of her friends were graduates either of that institution or of the private boys' school near it, Upper

Canada College. As her escort I found myself going to parties in Forest Hill, Rosedale, and, on New Year's Eve of 1963, at a house set in a large estate on Leslie south of highway 401.

Many of the people I met on these occasions believed, with some justification, that the world was *their* oyster, and not someone else's. At a cocktail party on Old Forest Hill Road I was introduced to a young man who had spent a year or two at Royal Roads Military College. Hearing that I was from Victoria, he asked whether I had attended Shawnigan Lake Boys' School. This was the most expensive private school on Vancouver Island; I answered in the negative. 'St George's?' he continued, mentioning a private school in Vancouver. 'No,' I said again. 'University School, perhaps?' he ventured, referring to a Victoria institution that, though estimable, lacked the cachet of the other two. When I demurred once more he asked: 'But *where* then? Is there some place out there I haven't heard about?' I had attended Victoria High, I replied. 'But,' he said in evident confusion, 'isn't that a *public* school?' I confessed my shameful secret. He considerately changed the subject and soon afterwards moved off.

It was my first exposure to an attitude which I hadn't noticed in Victoria but was to encounter more than once in Toronto: that private schools are superior to public schools, not so much for what their pupils learn as for the people they rub shoulders with and the advantages this gives them in later life. At Massey College, a junior fellow who had attended Trinity College School told me in 1964 or 1965 that people like himself were, by virtue of having attended an exclusive private school, pre-eminently qualified to run the country's corporations and governments. As near as I could judge, the bases of his school's exclusiveness were sex (no girls) and money (no people whose parents were of modest means, except for a few scholarship winners). But I knew that he had made a point worth taking seriously when I read Porter. He indicated the importance that these schools had in Canada and the role they played in maintaining the country's class system, none the less real for being largely unrecognized.

I found the attitude my acquaintance expressed disturbing, but in a rather strange way. Not having attended a private school in Canada, I resented his attitude. Yet I sensed that, had we stayed in

Holland, I would probably have held a similar attitude where my own schools were concerned. Only exceptional human beings take issue with systems that are rigged in their favour, and in that sense, at least, I was not exceptional.

Upon returning to Victoria in 1965 I bought a new Austin 1100, my 1949 Dodge sedan having given up the ghost. In September I took my car to Toronto with Martin Petter, who was on his way to Oxford and joined me for five days of hard driving. That winter I stored the vehicle in a parking garage on St George Street, putting a mere 700 miles on the odometer between mid-September and May. Then I found some use for the car at last. Having been accepted by the graduate school of Yale University, Jack wanted to check out New Haven before he took a flight to Europe. Eager for a holiday, no matter how short, I took a week off to drive with him into New England.

After spending a few days in Amherst and Northampton – Sheila Wolfson was studying at Smith College – we drove on to New Haven, where we were the guests of Keith and Rachel Wilson. I had met them at Tante Phiet's place when they were travelling through western Europe with the Yale band in 1962. Yale, though spectacular, was located in a neighbourhood that seemed little better than a slum. The decay that was hollowing out so many U.S. cities and towns had not spared New Haven, and like many Yale faculty Keith had moved his family to the suburb of Hamden years earlier. Jack was pleased to find a room near the university at very modest cost, however, saying that the area was still better than Chicago's South Side, where he had worked in 1960.

A bonus was a day-long visit to New York City. The Wilsons' oldest daughter studied at Barnard College and sang in its choir; we were going to hear a choral concert near Columbia University. In the afternoon Keith drove us around Manhattan. The architecture was overwhelming even to someone used to Toronto; I spent much of the time looking up. I promised myself I would try to return to visit the many art galleries, for which we had no time on this occasion.

Not long after our return to Toronto, Jack left for Holland and I faced the chore of driving west to Victoria alone. This turned out to be a mind-numbing grind. The car radio being my only companion, some of the pop hits of the time are still engraved on my memory: 'Red Rubber Ball,' 'Paint It Black,' 'Paperback Writer,' 'Strangers in the Night,' and Simon and Garfunkel's haunting 'I Am a Rock'. American AM radio provided a choice only between pop and country and western. For me that was no choice at all, since I've never enjoyed country music.

Driving south of Lake Michigan, I took the opportunity to visit my cousin Henk Reitsma, who was working on a Ph.D. in geography at the University of Wisconsin. He had married the daughter of a Madison dentist, and I was taken to meet her family. They greeted us warmly but did not turn off the TV set. *I Spy* was apparently too important a cultural event to miss. A commercial break: Smokey the Bear urged us to prevent forest fires. I said I hoped God was watching, since more than half such fires were caused by lightning. The atmosphere around the set cooled noticeably. Henk later told me that his in-laws, evangelical Christians, found my remark sacrilegious.

I drove on to Minneapolis, where I stayed with Jan and Ruth Broek for two days. Jan had been at the University of Minnesota ever since leaving Utrecht in 1948, and liked the area (I could see why: the Twin Cities are attractive and, much like Toronto, clean). For a geographer, Minnesota was more interesting than California, he explained over dinner. Berkeley, where he had taught from the mid-1930s until he went to Holland in 1946, was beautiful, but it lacked a real winter, which Minneapolis emphatically did not! (Eighteen months later I dined with them again, this time in Berkeley. He was spending a sabbatical there and told me they had bought a house on Southampton Avenue in anticipation of his retirement. What of the Minnesota winter and its interest for the geographer? I asked. Jan regarded me pensively for a few seconds, then smiled: 'The retired geographer does not intend to shovel snow.')

On to Carman, Manitoba, home to a Southam Fellow I had met at Massey College, and from there into Saskatchewan along a secondary road that was so badly potholed I could literally *feel* why virtually no one else was using it. When I stopped to stretch my legs I was almost overcome by the openness of the landscape and the sky. There was not another car or human being in sight: I was alone with the land and a few birds. The best way to experience Canada's huge size would be to walk or cycle across it, but driving without a passenger is a passable second best.

After spending a night in a Swift Current motel, where I heard the startling news that the Union Nationale had defeated the Quebec Liberals, I continued into Alberta and the B.C. mountain ranges, stopping one night with friends in Field, a pretty hamlet surrounded by mountains. A day later I reached Victoria. Since early in 1965 Mother and Father had lived on Piedmont Drive in Saanich, ten kilometres north of the Victoria downtown core, in a large house that Father had designed. Cedar predominated throughout, and an open fireplace, Father's architectural signature, dominated the living-room. It was the most attractive house he and Mother lived in during their years in Canada.

A few weeks later I hit the road again, this time accompanied by Father. We drove east through the B.C. interior, following the Trans-Canada Highway. Our objective was Calgary, where I had been engaged to teach the survey course in Canadian history in the university summer school. The weather that Dominion Day weekend was miserable, however, and the clouds hung so low that Father saw virtually no mountains until his train ride back to the coast.

My first-ever students were fifty-two in number, almost all of them teachers completing their degrees or, in the case of several immigrants from the United States, taking Canadian history as a precondition for receiving a permanent teaching certificate. It occurred to me that perhaps the reason the Canadian school year was so short was that many teachers had to devote six or seven weeks of the summer to finishing their education. As they also had to do end-of-term work and have some time for holidays, school necessarily ended in mid-June.

There were two other visiting teachers in the department. I played tennis with a U.S. historian from Ithaca College in New York state, but I saw more of Marc Ferro, an expert in Russian history from Paris. Like me he had a room in residence, and as his tennis was roughly at my level we spent several hours a week together on the courts. Marc was a shrewd observer of his surroundings. The dominant values of France were secular, he once said to me, but if Calgary were typical, Canada's were not: 'You have freedom of religion here, but not freedom *from* religion.'

Having been given two tickets to the Stampede by an oil-company executive, the father of a Victoria College friend, I asked Marc along. The roping events and chuck-wagon races seemed to thrill him: *this* was the Canada of his imagination! I found the Stampede to be a bit hokey, but as a tourist attraction it was unquestionably effective.

I had little time for such outings, though I did attend the cinema club, which introduced me for the first time to the Bogart films of the early 1940s, saw a performance, by students of the Banff School of Fine Arts, of Farquhar's *The Beaux' Stratagem*, and accompanied a colleague to a Canadian Football League game between Calgary and Saskatchewan. Most of the time I was hard at work, however. Two hours a day I lectured, followed by half an hour meeting my students. Except for Saturdays, I spent six to eight hours daily at my desk, reading books and writing lectures.

The weeks were an exhausting grind, and I was happy to greet the end of classes. My students had already submitted their essays; their exam was on 16 August. After handing in my grades a few days later and packing my belongings I drove west with a huge sense of release. The university was all right, its staff helpful, and some of my students stimulating, but I was ready for a rest. Besides, I had come to dislike the city, finding it crude, self-satisfied, and so provincial it made even Victoria seem cosmopolitan. I once told my students at Glendon College, in a slip of the tongue, that I spent seven years in Calgary one summer. It almost felt that way at the time.

Within two days I was taking part in a seminar at UBC on 'regional views of Confederation in 1867 and today.' Sponsored by the Canadian Historical Association and the Association of Universities and Colleges of Canada, its stated purpose was 'to give a group of the most promising young historians from all over Canada an opportunity to discuss a major national problem in close and informal association with senior members of the profession.' There was also a financial lure: full expenses and a small honorarium. Jack Saywell, dean of arts at York University, chaired the seminar in a manner I came to recognize as characteristically sardonic; Michel Brunet, Marc LaTerreur, and Donald Smiley were among those who presented papers. The 'young historians' included my friend Rick Clippingdale as well as Jack Granatstein, Jacques Monet, Peter Oliver, and Allan Smith. There were few women, although I seem to recall Marilyn Barber and, from UBC, Margaret Ormsby and Margaret Prang. In 1966 the historical profession was still very largely a male preserve.

At the end of the week I gave the LaTerreurs a ride into Victoria. When Marc, a large, likable man who was about to join the editorial staff of the *Dictionary of Canadian Biography*, saw the portraits of royalty around the lobby of the Empress Hotel he sighed contentedly: this was *le vrai du vrai*. One evening he and Monique dined at Piedmont Drive. Father, happily reminiscing about his artistic apprenticeship in Montgeron, near Paris, forty years earlier, became confused because neither of his guests seemed to know much about France. They spoke French, *n'est-ce pas?*

Having sold my car, I returned to Toronto by air, stopping off in Edmonton to interview King Gordon. He had for several years been active in the LSR and in the Fellowship for a Christian Social Order (FCSO), an organization of socialists mainly within the United Church in the 1930s and 1940s, and had told me that he had some papers I could examine. A tall man with a deliberate, even grave, manner, he patiently answered my questions about his intellectual development, his dismissal from Montreal's United Theological College, his travels for the LSR and FCSO, and his political campaigns (he ran for Parliament and lost three times within three years in Victoria, B.C., once in a by-election coming within a hundred votes of victory). Occasionally, he gave me a document that he said might interest me. His wife came in and asked whether we were ready for tea, and over several cups we chatted informally. He smiled more than he had earlier and urged me to talk with 'the two Franks,' Scott and Underhill, 'together the driving force behind the LSR.' I had every intention of doing so.

Back in Toronto, I moved into an apartment on Davenport Avenue near Dupont, a ten-minute walk from the campus. My flat-mates were Stuart Niermeier and Michael Daschtschuk, a German-born chemical engineer. The three of us got on well, partly because none of us spent much time in the apartment. I ate many of my meals at Massey College, where I was a non-resident fellow. I did not much like keeping house, in fact, and was happy to move back into the college the following May.

My comprehensive exams were in late September. I was on edge, probably unnecessarily so. Alix Henderson, a Victoria friend who was teaching high school in Toronto, thought I needed diversion and invited me to see *Twelfth Night* at the Stratford Festival on the weekend before I was writing. It was my first visit to Stratford, and I couldn't have asked for a better introduction: Leo Ciceri (Malvolio), Martha Henry (Olivia), Christopher Newton (Orsino), and Douglas Rain (Sir Toby Belch) in what to me is Shakespeare's most enjoyable play. Perhaps it inspired me: I got three firsts.

The history comps were far from being the traumatic test the English students had to undergo. If you got a C+ in just one of the five fields, you had to rewrite all five: a fearful prospect. At a sherry party in Bill Dean's rooms, Robertson Davies, who taught English drama, noted that many of the English faculty had themselves been graduate students at the University of Toronto (as he had not). Their attitude resembled that of the elders of an aboriginal tribe, he said. 'Young men facing initiation are told: "I was circumcised with the flaming stick; so also shall you be." ' (He did not speculate about what young women would be told.)

In November I spent a weekend in St Catharines with Rob Taylor and his wife, Anne. Rob had just started teaching at the recently founded Brock University. Academic jobs were easy to get, he said. He didn't expect to have his Ph.D. (from Stanford) until 1968, but this had not deterred Brock from appointing him to a tenure-track position. I learned soon afterwards that Beth Boyle, who had also worked at the Department of Education in Victoria, had landed a job teaching English at York University's Glendon College before she had finished her Queen's M.A.!

I, too, would benefit from the temporary shortage of fully qual-ified young academics, brought about by the baby boom, the desire for economic growth, the fears created by *Sputnik*, and the resulting pell-mell expansion of North American higher education in the 1960s. Out of the blue, Hilda Neatby, head of the University of Saskatchewan history department, offered me a job as assistant professor. Thinking I could get another fellowship for 1967–8, and hoping to complete my dissertation before I began to teach, I declined her offer. Besides, I had no wish to go to Saskatoon. (In the 1980s I visited the city more than once, mostly on business. Less agreeable than Winnipeg and Edmonton, Saskatoon seemed to be more so than Calgary and Regina. But I don't want to live in any of them.) When I *did* begin to teach, in 1968, I had not completed my dissertation and would not finish it until the following year.

It should have cheered me to realize that I need not worry about finding employment. Instead, however, I began to wonder whether I really wanted to teach history. I don't know what brought this on. Perhaps it was a rereading of *Lucky Jim*, with its negative depiction of history teaching. Perhaps Norbert Wiener's prophetic *The Human Use of Human Beings*, about cybernetics and human life, led me subconsciously to the view that I had been too much occupied with the past at the expense of the present and future. On the other hand, I may have been suffering from depression, an illness that in more serious form has affected more than one member of my immediate family. Whatever the reasons, in early January 1967 I wrote in my diary: 'A month of fitful soul searching is past, and my mind is made up (I think) that I won't stay in academe. "I gotta get out of this place" just about sums it up. I'm teaching again and am already wondering what the hell for and why history? and why Canadian history?'

In spite of my misgivings, and because I couldn't think of anything else to do – after all, I had a fellowship – I stuck to my research. The LSR was, in fact, an interesting topic, not only for its ideas but because its leading figures were fascinating to talk with. In a country that valued reticence and caution in its academics, they had been unusual in openly embracing controversial causes. Several of them had lost their teaching positions, allegedly as a result. Others had been threatened with dismissal. My research led me to take a greater interest in freedom of expression and more particularly in academic freedom.

Possibly the most fascinating member of the LSR was the one I would in the 1970s get to know better than any of the others. Frank Scott was a poet, law professor, constitutional lawyer, and civil libertarian, a patrician with a strong faith in ordinary people: altogether a complex and engaging person. Two weeks before Christmas I took an early morning train to Montreal and presented myself at the McGill Faculty of Law. Scott had left some files with his secretary and instructions to take me to a carrel in the library. An hour or so later he dropped by, a tall man in his mid-sixties, with a slight stoop, one glass eye, and an imperious manner (he reminded me of Tony Nicholson, my director in *The Ghost Sonata*). 'Be in my office at 4:30,' he said.

After he had poured me a cup of tea he reminisced at length about his intellectual development, about the LSR and its centralist constitutional position (largely shaped by Scott himself), and about his battles with Quebec's Premier Maurice Duplessis. His large office was decorated with the mementoes of more than forty years in academe and politics. Noticing my glances around the room he said a bit plaintively: 'I'll have to leave this office soon. Then what will I do with all these things?' At times his manner was just a bit *de haut en bas*, but he was courteous and pleasant. More important, he seemed to take my questions seriously and took time and care in answering them.

After finishing with Scott's papers I went on to Ottawa, but not before taking an opportunity to visit the site of Expo 67, then under construction. My friend Robin Green was working for Expo in connection with its arts program, while another friend, Prudence Emery, had a job in the public relations department. They arranged for me to join a group of British journalists who were getting a guided tour. The site was a mess, but the accounts and illustrations of what was to come were fascinating. Best of all I remember an illustrated lecture by Moshe Safdie, the designer of Habitat, an intense young man who spoke with conviction about the need to combine high density with privacy in urban architecture. Alas, in Canada, at least, his vision has been ignored.

My visit to Ottawa was my first to the capital. I liked the city in spite of the intense cold. Parliament Hill particularly impressed me: spacious (like Canada itself) and attractive. My first interview was with Eugene Forsey, then the research officer of the Canadian Labour Congress, in his office on Sparks Street. He warned me that his memory was unreliable, but he was soon regaling me in detail about events at McGill in the 1930s, going so far as to mimic voices. Listening to him was a delight. I liked less what I later saw of him in letters he had written at the time, marshalling point after picky point in order to prove someone else wrong. Years later Frank Scott said to me: 'Eugene's way of dealing with a weakness in an argument is to say "There's a fly on your forehead; let me kill it for you." Then he uses a sledgehammer.'

Joseph F. Parkinson was a courtly senior officer in the Department of Finance who, having left his radical days long behind, was perhaps excessively judicious in his comments. He expressed an interest in what I was going to be writing and offered to read it.

The MPs I met were less informative than the former academics. What Grace MacInnis told me about her father, J.S. Woodsworth, the CCF's first leader and honorary president of the LSR, I had already known from her biography of him. David Lewis leaned back and spoke expansively of his admiration for Woodsworth, Scott, and Angus MacInnis, Grace's late husband. He was not otherwise forthcoming, however, and I got a sense of a man who had learned not to say things that might come back to haunt him. Andrew Brewin pointed out that he had neither held an executive position in the LSR nor contributed to its publications, then looked at me as if to say: 'Do you *really* think I can help you?' I soon left his office.

None of these interviews lasted long. It was another story when I met Frank Underhill. We talked for several hours. Bright-eyed behind his glasses, the diminutive historian said he had no papers that he wanted me to see. (This, I suspected, was his way of keeping me from cluttering up his house, for I did not doubt that he must have many boxes of files in his study, or in his attic or basement. A few years later I was to find out that I had been right.) However, he invited me to test his memory. We discussed his schooling and his memories of the 1930s and early war years, including his near-dismissal from the University of Toronto in 1941.

I knew from his writings that he could be provocative and waspish (a term he objected to when I used it to describe him in my dissertation), but there was no sign of this in our conversation. He was mild-mannered and subdued, treating even my sillier questions with respect. My attention strayed once or twice to the periodicals rack. He subscribed to at least twenty current-affairs journals: Canadian, British, and American. I remembered Ken Windsor saying that Underhill was a political journalist more than a historian; certainly his reputation depended more on what he had said about current domestic and international affairs than on his scholarly output.

I paid two more visits to Ottawa that winter, staying with friends and working my way through volumes in the records of the Co-operative Commonwealth Federation and the papers of J.S. Woodsworth, both kept in the Public Archives. By coincidence I began my work in one location and completed it in another, as the Archives moved from their old quarters on Sussex Drive, now the War Museum, to a shiny new structure on Wellington Street. The latter had conveniences the former lacked, but the new building was remarkably ugly.

My Queen Elizabeth II Scholarship, large enough for my material needs, did not suffice for my travels. These I paid for out of the stipend I received for lecturing in a Canadian history survey course during the winter term (I taught it again in the summer of 1967). In March I went to London, Ontario, in order to talk with the classicist R.E.K. Pemberton and a few of his associates about the LSR branch in that city. I also renewed my acquaintance with Jack Ogelsby, who had left Victoria for the University of Western Ontario. We commiserated with each other about the length of the Ontario winter.

After the teaching term ended in April I visited New Haven, Princeton, and New York. Yale's Sterling Professor of Classics, Eric Havelock, had taught at Victoria College, Toronto, from 1928 to 1946; he paced the floor like a caged polar bear while reminiscing about his education, the trouble he had got into after criticizing Premier Mitchell Hepburn during the 1937 Oshawa Strike, his disagreement with Underhill over Canadian foreign policy, and many other things.

The two men with whom I lunched at the Princeton Inn a few

days later, R.B.Y. Scott and Gregory Vlastos, added little to what I knew. Both had been active in the LSR, Scott while teaching at United Theological College in Montreal and Vlastos at Queen's. Neither having kept his correspondence, however, each was speaking strictly from memory. This, as I already knew, was of limited value. On the whole, the interviews I carried out demonstrated the strength *and* weakness of oral history. People could often recall attitudes and feelings with clarity and vividness, but on facts they were usually weak. The documentary evidence was much better in that respect.

The slim return on my American journey did not trouble me, for it enabled me to visit Jack in New Haven and also to explore New York, including a visit to the headquarters of the United Nations. I stayed with Jack's friends Stephen and José Shriber. He was a medical student at New York University, she a ground hostess with KLM Royal Dutch Airlines. Strongly opposed to the Vietnam War, Stephen was thinking of emigrating to avoid the draft and asked me with interest about Canada. More out of courtesy than conviction, I joined him and José in a peace march on 15 April, though I did not stay the course: at some point I defected to do some shopping at Bloomingdale's.

Still sceptical about their cause, I was nevertheless impressed by the number of marchers – more than a hundred thousand, the media said. Over dinner that evening I listened with increased attention to Stephen's criticism of U.S. policy in Vietnam. As I recall his argument, he conceded that the Viet Cong were no lovers of freedom and democracy but said that the regime in South Vietnam was no better, and that the United States supported it only because it was anti-communist and because some people claimed that the fall of South Vietnam would lead to the triumph of communism in all the countries of Southeast Asia. This, of course, was the domino theory. Discredited today, it commanded wide belief throughout the 1960s. Stephen deprecated it, but said that even if it *were* valid, the United States had no business taking sides in the region and sacrificing American lives there. Asians should settle their own differences. I did not yet fully agree with him, but he had given me food for thought.

(When I saw them again, late in 1969, Stephen had renounced

his citizenship in protest against the war and had taken refuge in José's native Holland. He was continuing to prepare himself for the practice of psychiatry. His Dutch was shaky and heavily accented, but this didn't seem to faze him. New Yorkers had got used to analysts with Viennese accents, he said: the Dutch would get used to a psychiatrist with an accent made in New York!)

While in New York I saw Harold Pinter's perplexing but gripping play *The Homecoming* and visited the major galleries. I saw the Frick with Jack, who had come in from New Haven for the day. While I deplored Henry Clay Frick's labour practices, Jack thought they might have been justified to a degree by the magnificence of the collection they had made possible. This seemed harsh, but perhaps Jack's view was more realistic than mine. Human beings will probably exploit each other so long as the species survives; Frick's miners, at least, made an indirect contribution to human happiness. They, of course, would doubtless have preferred to earn a living wage.

Late in June I visited Expo 67, by now gloriously complete. I stayed with an easygoing Victoria acquaintance and financier-to-be, Tim Price, who asked only that I keep the fridge supplied with beer. Many a happy hour did I spend on the Expo site. The British and Czech pavilions struck me as the most effective of their kind, but the theme pavilions and the art gallery were admirable as well. I also liked the Ontario pavilion. The Stanley Cup was on display in it, the Toronto Maple Leafs having beaten the Montreal Canadiens that spring. I have no doubt that the cup was meant to remind Montreal visitors to the pavilion just who had won and lost. (Montrealers have had the last laugh and more, for the Maple Leafs have not won since 1967 whereas the Canadiens have won it several times.)

In the Expo library I met, by arrangement, another one of 'my' people. The UBC social scientist Leonard Marsh, best known as the author of the 1943 *Report on Social Security for Canada*, bubbled over with enthusiasm for both Expo ('a grand learning experience') and my work on the LSR, whose president he had been from 1937 to 1939 while working at McGill. He undertook to send me some scrapbooks from that period and also offered to read the chapters of my dissertation as I completed them. I liked him; in time he became a good friend.

On 24 June I joined Sheila Wolfson and an American friend of hers who had also become a friend of mine, Kate Pflaumer, in watching the Saint-Jean-Baptiste parade. In the 1960s the celebrations increasingly conjured up images of a separate country. The mood of the crowds lining the street was good-natured, but I was struck by the fervency with which younger people waved the Quebec flag. The absence of the maple leaf flag, too, was striking. Emotionally, these youngsters seemed already to have seceded from Canada.

Afterwards we joined Sheila's husband, a philosophy student named Louis Greenspan, at a party in Notre Dame de Grace. An argument was raging about Quebec separatism, pro and con. My views were ambivalent. I wanted Quebec to stay in Canada, but I opposed the decentralization of power that would probably be the price to be paid for keeping the province in. (It took time for me to come to the view that important concessions could be made to Quebec that should not be made to any of the other provinces.)

When I arrived in Toronto in 1963, I had favoured a shift of power towards the provinces on terms treating all of them as equals. Reading Scott and Underhill had changed my mind, however: only a strong Ottawa, I now believed, could deal with country-wide problems or combat corporate power. This view, I recognized, was not likely to appeal to Quebec or, indeed, to British Columbia. Nor did it find much favour in Ottawa, though I was slower to recognize this. The federal decision in 1966 to end direct subsidies to the universities and instead transfer the money to the provinces should have alerted me, for it signalled a retreat from the centralism that marked the early years of the Pearson government, a retreat that would continue, though slowly, under Pierre Trudeau. (Made without consulting the universities, the decision has in the long run turned out calamitously for them.)

What was Quebec's future likely to be, or Canada's? I couldn't guess. But it seemed to me, that evening of 24 June, that many French-speaking Quebeckers had a clearer idea of themselves and what they regarded as their country than did most other Canadians. What, beyond a geographical entity, was Canada anyway? What was a Canadian? Perhaps such questions were and are pointless – perhaps we should simply *be* – but in a country with two major cultures and languages, a country populated by recent immigrants and the descendants of immigrants, the questions are inescapable.

The celebration of Canada's centenary, and the magnificent success that was Expo 67, fostered great pride in Canada. Quite possibly that year was the high point in Canada's national history. Patriotic fervour obscured the reality, however, that many Canadians were unsure of what they and the country were. Could a Canadian identity exist and flourish that included everybody, even those living in Quebec and speaking French, even recent immigrants from other continents? We were no longer British: prefacing Toronto Symphony concerts with 'God Save the Queen,' as happened into the mid-1960s, was clearly an anachronism. But if we were Canadian without a British qualification, there was as yet no large measure of agreement as to what this meant.

Confusion over our identity had been manifest during the flag debate in 1964, when the Diefenbaker-led champions of the red ensign had tried to fight off those who wanted a flag less obviously symbolic of the country's British past. In Victoria the *Daily Colonist* had, for the duration of the parliamentary debate, added the old flag to its masthead together with the misleading slogan: 'Our Flag since 1892. Why Change It?'

The new maple leaf flag, officially adopted in 1965, was supposed to symbolize a Canada in which everyone would feel at home. The government's commitment to making a greater place for French had the same purpose. So far, however, many French Canadians seemed unimpressed. Perhaps they were aware that a good many English Canadians were unwilling to make concessions. In Victoria's Empress Hotel in the summer of 1964 I had attended a plenary session of the Royal Commission on Bilingualism and Biculturalism, appointed to explore the relations between the two founding peoples and make suggestions for their improvement. Someone in the audience asked permission to introduce a motion that English be Canada's sole official language. Accommodating the French had not worked, he claimed: it was time for a new course of action!

The popular choice in Montreal that June of 1967 was not the red-and-white maple leaf flag but Quebec's blue-and-white banner with its fleur-de-lis. In parts of English Canada, including Victoria, the red ensign still appeared. The British past was largely over and done with, but this had not brought clarity as to what Canada was in the present, or might become in the future.

Our ties to Britain having weakened, those to the United States acquired ever-greater significance. Was Canada just a subdued version of the United States? Were Canadians, at least those who were born here and had English as their first language, really little more than Americans *manqués*, un-American Americans? Was Canada, as I had speculated in 1963, fated in time to merge with the republic to the south? To such questions, too, I saw no easy answers in 1967.

That year there were many Canadians, of course, who had no doubt about their identity. They knew what they were celebrating. As a relative newcomer I was unsure, however, and I was not alone. Yet doubts seemed distant, even to me, on Dominion Day that year. It was the one-hundredth birthday of the Confederation settlement. The maple leaf flag waved over Varsity Stadium; older traditions found expression in the trooping of the colour by the 48th Highlanders of Canada. Memories of the summer of 1945 came vividly to mind as I listened to the pipers, and upon returning to my room in Massey College I wrote in my diary: 'I love bagpipe music.' The North Nova Scotia Highlanders still occupied a corner of my brain.

Near the end of that summer I visited Nova Scotia for the first time. Some months earlier, Ken Windsor had asked me whether I would take his place on the University of Toronto fishing team should his uncertain health keep him at home. Although my interest in fishing was slight at best, I agreed because I owed him a favour. When his physician advised him not to go I was on the spot: too late to back out. On 29 August I was on my way to Wedgeport, Nova Scotia, in order to participate in the Twelfth Annual Intercollegiate Game Fish Seminar and Fishing Match.

The five other team members were all from Massey College,

among them my neighbour and friend Doug Lavers, a quiet-spoken electrical engineer from Halifax. Their company made up for the 'sport,' which I found supremely boring. On the first day we spent several hours trying vainly to hook a tuna, then gave it up in order to jig for cod. This was productive but dull, the cod being altogether too obliging a fish. 'If it struggles it's kelp,' someone quipped. Actually it was dogfish, but because that animal was regarded as unfit for human consumption it didn't count in the match. The Acadian fishermen who operated our boat hated dogfish because they preyed on cod, and broke their snouts before throwing them back, so that they would starve to death.

The evenings were devoted to 'seminars' that gave the enterprise a pseudo-academic legitimacy. These were actually slide shows tedious enough to make the pursuit of cod seem thrilling. The match organizer, the athletic director at Yale University and a bore so monumental that I still think of him with a certain awe, droned on about the various species of fish unlucky enough to have attracted his lethal attention. It was hard to know whether to giggle or fall asleep. Our team captain, the physicist Manny Tward, warned me to do neither: the U of T team might not get invited back. Fortunately, the competition lasted only three days. Had it gone on longer I would surely have disgraced myself.

Sorry that I could not spend more time in Nova Scotia, I joined three of my fellow anglers in driving to Montreal via Bar Harbor, Maine, which we reached by ferry from Yarmouth. We arrived in Montreal during the late afternoon of 3 September, my twenty-eighth birthday. I celebrated it by dining with Joan Dixon, a friend who was doing her medical internship at the Montreal General Hospital. Then, once more taking advantage of Tim Price's hospitality, I spent three days at Expo, mostly in the company of Jan D. and his friend Jasper van Voorstvader. I also said goodbye to Mark Levene and his wife, Kathy, on their way to England where Mark would be researching the life and work of Arthur Koestler. They were going by ocean liner, then still the preferred method of travel for people who were not in a hurry. Air travel has speed to recommend it and not much else. Except for those who can afford to fly first or business class, spending six or seven hours on an aircraft is one of the least enjoyable experiences this side of the rack.

I returned to Toronto by train on 7 September and that evening joined Bill Dean and a few others at Maple Leaf Gardens to hear John Diefenbaker address the Progressive Conservative convention in a last attempt to retain his leadership. 'The Chief delivered a rambling, frequently incoherent and yet very stirring peroration,' I wrote in my diary. He attacked the 'two nations' resolution adopted at a recent Tory conference. Canada was one nation, he said: talk about two nations relegated those not of English or French stock to second-class citizenship and would divide the country.

Many delegates may have agreed with these sentiments, but they didn't let this interfere with the business at hand. They buried Diefenbaker on the first ballot, and he withdrew his name. It took four more ballots before Nova Scotia's Premier Robert Stanfield won the leadership. 'The Conservatives have a new leader with an unflappable "Mr. Cool" image,' I commented: 'He looks *simpático*, but he doesn't lead a very attractive party.'

In 1967–8 I had a Canada Council doctoral fellowship and travel grant. Having finished my research, I looked for a pleasant place in which to write my dissertation and chose Berkeley, California. Its mild winters and intellectual reputation drew me. As well, I wanted to assess what I had missed by not doing my graduate studies there.

I reached Berkeley in mid-September and stayed with Neil and Evelyn Sampson while I looked for a small apartment. Berkeley turned out to have a severe shortage of affordable housing, and I was thinking of going to Victoria when Evelyn came up with a solution. Their two oldest daughters having moved out, they had lots of room. I could stay with them, paying her whatever the university's International House charged for room and board. I accepted gratefully.

Although I spent most of my time writing, I talked a lot with Evelyn, who was home for much of the day. A teacher by vocation, she had moved from Alabama to California in the 1930s. There she had met Cornelius Sampson, an art student from Montana via Chicago. Upon their marriage, Neil had opened an industrial design studio in San Francisco, and when it began to thrive Evelyn had quit teaching to become a housewife and mother. In 1967 she was still at home, while Neil, around sixty years of age, was almost ready to retire and rest on his laurels. These were highly visible. Among the corporate logos he had designed were those of Safeway (the old one, based on the Chinese yin and yang), Chevron, Dymo, and Foremost.

Their sixteen-year-old daughter Debbie was concerned about what was 'in' but not excessively so. She was fun to have around, a substitute younger sister. I saw little of the two older Sampson daughters. Shelby lived in Berkeley but was busy with her husband and children; Ginny and her husband lived the hippie life near Monterey. During one of their visits to Berkeley I got my introduction to marijuana. 'Unlike getting drunk, getting high involves an expansion of one's senses,' I diarized. 'It's quite pleasant. But writing proved impossible. Too many possibilities opened up as I put a sentence on the page; too many ideas crowded my mind.' Instead I listened to the Beatles' *Sergeant Pepper* album. Its songs seemed to go on almost for ever.

I liked the high, but I was cautious by nature and marijuana's illegality made me wary. I wasn't tempted to become a regular user. Nor did the rumoured delights of San Francisco's Haight-Ashbury district – the 'summer of love' had just ended – draw me. I drove through it once or twice: its flower children seemed almost like a different species.

Never have I lived in a house with a more magnificent view than the Sampsons' at 1080 Grizzly Peak Boulevard, high above San Francisco Bay. From my study window I could see the Golden Gate Bridge; the living-room and kitchen windows opened to a panorama that extended from the Oakland Hills in the east to Mt Tamalpais in the west. It was impossible to tire of the view, or even get used to it. The sunsets were particularly splendid: I photographed them scores of times during my eight-month stay. It was a long hike to the university, but buses wound their way between Grizzly Peak Boulevard and Shattuck Avenue, on the western edge of the campus. Moreover, I could borrow Evelyn's Plymouth or Neil's Rover 2000TC – *there* was a car! – whenever they were not in use. I was in clover!

Berkeley, on the eastern shore of San Francisco Bay, is best known for the university locally known as Cal, founded in 1868, the oldest of the campuses of the University of California and an institution of world-wide cultural and scientific importance. Sproul Plaza, focus of the 1964 Free Speech movement, teemed with student life, as did nearby Telegraph Avenue. But I spent less time there than I would have liked, for I was at my desk most of the day. I stayed in shape by jogging in nearby Tilden Park, breathing in the unforgettable perfume of the eucalyptus trees that abounded in the hills.

Into November it was very warm, but December and January were cool, daytime highs rarely exceeding twelve to fifteen degrees, and early one morning it was cold enough for wet snowflakes to come tumbling down. They didn't stick, but newscasts made much of the inch or two of snow that had fallen overnight on Mt Tamalpais. By mid-February that snow was a distant memory. The lemon bushes in the Sampsons' garden bloomed, and I spent an hour most afternoons sunbathing and reading a scholarly work or sometimes a novel, by Peter De Vries or Kurt Vonnegut, Jr, whose humanism greatly appealed to me. Years later I found the perfect description of Berkeley's climate in David Lodge's *Changing Places*: 'There was no real winter in Euphoria – autumn joined hands with spring and summer, and together they danced a three-handed jig all year long, to the merry confusion of the vegetable world.'

The first, historical part of my dissertation took little time, but when I got around to dealing with the LSR's ideas I slowed down. I was trying to come to grips with difficult concepts: capitalism, liberalism, socialism, and nationalism. This required a good deal of reading, including Elie Kedourie's *Nationalism*, Robert Lekachman's *The Age of Keynes*, and Karl Polanyi's *The Great Transformation*, a superb analysis of nineteenth- and early-twentieth-century responses to market capitalism, showing how all social classes in Europe sought to modify and control its harsher effects.

Also slowing me down were the responses I got from LSR members who, along with Ramsay, were reading my chapters. Whereas Ramsay was sparing in his comments, they were not. Forsey, Gordon, Havelock, Marsh, Scott, Underhill, and Graham Spry all responded with minor and sometimes major suggestions for change. Marsh was the most commendatory, Spry the most critical. He also wrote the longest letters. I had met him in Toronto in the summer while he was taking a holiday from his position as agent general for Saskatchewan in England. Voluble and opinionated, he feared that I was giving too much space to the LSR's intellectuals at the cost of its 'men of action,' of whom as national secretary (for a year or two) he had been chief. The pages of detailed comment that he sent (not even Forsey, a careful reader who caught me in numerous minor inaccuracies, wrote letters half as long) were meant to set me straight. His argument did not sway me: as a quasi-political organization the LSR had amounted to little. It was for their ideas that its members had been noticed, not for their organizational work.

I worked too hard to take full advantage of the area's cultural opportunities. The San Francisco Opera and Candlestick Park were within easy reach by car, but I never went to either (today this astonishes me). I did see half a dozen NHL games in Oakland, where the Golden Seals were playing that season, and cheered the hockey greats of the era: Gordie Howe, Bobby Hull, and Bobby Orr. The only concerts I attended were by Buffy Sainte-Marie, one of Debbie's favourites, and Country Joe and the Fish. Joe McDonald was a local musician who had put together a high-energy band whose raucous 'Vietnam Rag' was a signature song for students opposed to the war. The music was loud and ragged, the auditorium redolent with the scent of burning cannabis. It was music best heard stoned.

A different kind of entertainment was on offer in San Francisco's Barbary Coast. I went there once with Neil and Evelyn. Through picture windows we admired the law office of Melvin Belli, the 'king of torts,' then ate an excellent Chinese meal. We ended up at the Condor Club, where Carol Doda had pioneered topless entertainment. She was still there, huge breasts defying belief.

I saw a fair number of films. One was *How to Murder Your Wife*, a frothy comedy to which I took Evelyn. She confessed over coffee afterwards that she had understood no more than half of what the film's co-star, Terry-Thomas, had said. Many inhabitants of the United Kingdom might have trouble with Evelyn's blend of Alabaman and Californian, I thought. Was it because I was from Canada that I could understand both her and Terry-Thomas without trouble? Or had my years in Victoria taught me to decipher English accents?

Then there was *The Graduate*, which, being set partly in Berkeley, had local interest. Its campus scenes had been filmed at the University of Southern California, however, which was disappointing. Moreover, there were hoots of derision from the local audience when its star, Dustin Hoffman, was seen to drive east on the upper deck of the Bay Bridge. In real life, eastbound cars use the lower deck.

I saw that film with Joe, he and I having just returned from two weeks' skiing at Badger Pass in Yosemite National Park. Neil and Evelyn owned a cottage at Wawona, just inside the park, and the opportunity had been too good to pass up. By the time we returned to Berkeley I was fitter and more relaxed than at any time since leaving Germany.

Other memories: a warm Sunday afternoon in autumn, when I helped Evelyn and Debbie pick walnuts and figs on an abandoned farm in Sonoma County that belonged to friends of the Sampsons. To that point I had eaten dried figs only; freshly picked, they were incomparably better. Yet another memorable outing was to San Jose, where I knew Joe Boudreau, a member of the history department at the state college. With Joe and his two children I drove to Santa Cruz, to wade in the Pacific and watch the sun being swallowed by the ocean. It was early November, yet the afternoon temperature was in the high twenties (or eighties, as the Americans will have it)!

It was cooler but still pleasant when I was at Pebble Beach in January. Neil and Evelyn having gone to spend the weekend with Ginny and her husband, it fell to me to chauffeur Evelyn's mother and her friend, both from Alabama, to the Del Monte Lodge, where they were staying before leaving on a Pacific cruise. My reward was a lunch at the lodge, overlooking the famous golf course and the ocean. There was no time to visit Point Lobos Park across the bay; instead I drove along Seventeen Mile Drive to Monterey. In spite of the beauty of the area, I found the signs of great wealth (these huge houses were mostly *holiday* homes) oppressive. Paradise was not perfect.

Of the peoples among whom I've lived, only the French come close to Americans in their self-absorption. Convinced that whatever directly affected the United States mattered more than anything else happening in the world, the local media ignored much of that world and especially Canada. The California scene, U.S. politics, the Vietnam War: these monopolized the news and the commentary on it.

I enjoyed the *San Francisco Chronicle*'s columnists, notably Art Hoppe, author of one of the funniest columns I have ever read in any language. Appearing early in 1968 under the title 'The Surprise Candidate,' it tracked the rise and fall of Jesus Christ as a candidate in that year's presidential election and concluded with the opinion, purportedly by a veteran political observer, that the image was all wrong. The robe, the long hair, the beard, the sandals: 'a man like that would simply be crucified!' The *Chronicle*'s news coverage was spotty, however, and within weeks of arriving in Berkeley I entered a subscription to the *Globe and Mail* in order to get Canadian news as well as a broader perspective than the Bay area newspapers provided. I was unable to listen to CBC Radio, alas.

The 1968 elections loomed ahead, and as California's Governor Ronald Reagan, the affable ex-actor, was thought to nurture presidential ambitions, this angle got a lot of play. But the Vietnam War overshadowed everything. Berkeley had been the scene of the first major outbreak of 1960s student protest in North America, the Free Speech movement, but in 1967–8 radical students had moved from an attempt to reform the university to an effort to close down the Army Induction Center in Oakland. It was the scene of many clashes.

As a foreigner I stayed clear of these, though even before leaving Toronto I had come to the view that the United States should get out of Vietnam. What gave the Americans the right to decide the form of government South Vietnam would have? 'Just over ten years ago you condemned the Russians for brutally crushing the Hungarian uprising,' I had written to the editor of *Time* in May, '[but] recently you accorded high praise to General Westmoreland, a man who holds a position directly analogous with that of the Russian Commander-in-Chief in Hungary in 1956.' Many people in Berkeley shared this view. I lunched once with one of the most persuasive of them, Peter Dale Scott, a professor of English at Cal who was the only child of Frank and Marian Scott. Even Neil, who said he had voted for Goldwater in 1964, had come to oppose the war.

Early in 1968, Senator Eugene McCarthy announced his decision to challenge Lyndon Johnson for the Democratic nomination. I joined thousands of students in the Greek Theater on campus to hear McCarthy's anti-war message. His manner seemed too didactic to be fully effective, I wrote in my diary, but 'he gave straight answers to questions.' I donated $25 to his campaign.

Faced with a fight he might have lost, Johnson on 2 April bowed out of the contest for the nomination. That was big news; even bigger came two days later with the assassination of the civil rights leader Martin Luther King. Berkeley High School, which Debbie was attending, was closed, and she came home to report that black students were beating up whites. There were stories of window smashing and looting on the Berkeley flats and in adjacent Oakland. That evening Neil and Evelyn worried about race riots in the Bay area. They needn't worry, I said: looters would lose their breath and energy for pillage long before they got up to Grizzly Peak Boulevard. The joke was lame. There were riots in more than a hundred American cities, and almost fifty people died. 'A sad event,' I wrote in my diary: 'America will be in trouble this summer, I imagine. I'll be glad to leave.'

I knew where I would be going: back to Toronto. Having decided to teach for a year to see whether it suited me, I had sent out applications to ten universities in September 1967. First to reply was the head of history at Glendon College of York University, Edgar McInnis, for whom I had done a bit of work as a research assistant the year before. (Nine years after his death in 1973 I added a chapter on 'The Trudeau Years' to the fourth edition of his text-book in Canadian history.) When I wrote to him I thought that he was still in charge of the York history department, only to discover that he had stayed at Glendon when the larger part of the department moved to the new campus at Keele and Steeles. In late October he offered me a position teaching Canadian history. 'I don't think it is really necessary for either of us to go to the expense of getting you here for an interview,' he wrote: 'I would be prepared to recommend to the Principal your appointment as lecturer at a salary of $8500, with promotion to assistant professor at $9100 when you have qualified for your doctorate.'

Very soon afterwards I got my second offer in two years from Hilda Neatby. She promised me an assistant professorship and $10,000 *without* the Ph.D. I still didn't want to go to Saskatoon, but the spread between the two offers seemed large. Ramsay was attending a conference in San Francisco at the time, and I asked his advice as I was driving him around the Bay area. Why not, he suggested, ask McInnis for $9000 without the Ph.D. and another $600 with it? I did so. Days later a telegram arrived: 'Terms basically acceptable subject to clearance with Dean.' A subsequent letter informed me that the dean had agreed, and that settled that. (My account must sound like pure fiction to graduate students looking for work today.)

I settled for my second choice. The job I really wanted went to someone else. The head of history at UBC, Margaret Ormsby, wrote that my interests were too close to those of someone already in the department (presumably Margaret Prang), and that 'in the interest of Canadian history generally we also thought it would be a good idea to bring someone from the East into this environment.' Viv Nelles, a fellow doctoral candidate at the U of T and an Ontarian, got the position. However, three years later he, too, was at York University.

My Berkeley sojourn ended in early May. I had enjoyed myself. The Sampsons had been fine hosts: they and their city, singularly blessed in its climate and scenery, had enabled me to be very productive. Whatever my misgivings might have been on the night of King's assassination, I came to look back on my time in Berkeley with great nostalgia. I used to say that if I were compelled to choose a place on earth from which I might not stray for more than fifty kilometres, Berkeley would be that place. I don't say it any more. I was lucky to live in Eldorado before the golden age came to an end. In the last two decades the state of California, Berkeley and its great university with it, has been in a downward slide.

What might have changed in my life had I gone to California for my graduate work? My thesis topic would have been different had I attended Cal (or Stanford, whose campus I liked when I visited it). Would I have tried to stay in the States? It is possible. And yet: by the time I left I had come to regard the country as one cursed by the legacy of slavery and racist to the core. The Berkeley Hills were an agreeable white enclave, but the flat lands between the downtown core and San Francisco Bay, with their large black population, harboured pressing social problems. Neil warned me against going there at night, even by car. Certain parts of Berkeley and Oakland were simply not safe.

Used to Toronto and Victoria, I found the racial realities of the Bay area unsettling. The Vietnam War made the United States appear even less agreeable. Canada was not as rich, but despite its own racism, directed especially against the Native peoples, and despite the mounting unrest in Quebec, Canada *was* more peaceful and civil. In 1963 I had written almost complacently about the union of the two countries. My stay in Berkeley began to cure me of complacency. Since then I have come to regard the prospect with growing dismay.

All the same, I sometimes regret not doing the work in German history I would very probably have done had I gone to California or Stanford for my graduate studies. In that way I might have made a name for myself in the international scholarly world. Whatever modest reputation I may have earned as a historian of Canada, I am, like others of my kind, all but invisible in that larger world.

Did I choose a Canadian subject because it was safer? Because living in Toronto gave me an interest in Canada that living in Victoria had not? Did I simply stumble across a likely dissertation topic, one thing then leading to another? Was I trying to prove I belonged, becoming a historian of Canada as a part of becoming Canadian? Or was something else at work?

In the spring of 1963, while Tony Emery and I were discussing bias in history and the selection of facts – I had read E.H. Carr's *What Is History?* – he suggested I take up the history of Canada. My perspective would be clearer than that of most people who were born here, he said, and I might make a contribution few others could. I had shrugged this off: it was the history of Nazi Germany that then attracted me. Perhaps his suggestion had taken root, however. Once at the University of Toronto, I had found the study of Canadian history increasingly fascinating. When I began to teach, it was as a historian not of Germany but of my adopted country.

6
A Place of Liberty

On the way back to Toronto I stopped for several days in Victoria. Father had retired from the B.C. Forest Service a few days before I turned up and was mostly happy about doing so. His work did not challenge him, and he had repeatedly been refused the promotion his qualifications warranted. The rank of architect was out of the question, his supervisor had finally said, because he wouldn't be doing anything that he wasn't doing already but would have to be paid more.

The explanation offended him. So did the process whereby his work was validated: an engineer put his seal of approval on it. It didn't help that the engineers with whom he worked did not impress him. 'Ze denken dat ze de wereld leiden' (They think they are leading the world), he said scornfully, 'maar Europa is ze vijftig jaren vooruit' (but Europe is fifty years ahead of them). He was unhappy also with his superiors, complaining that they invariably chose the option that was cheapest to build, for that reason alone. One example: charged with designing a building somewhere in the interior, Father noted that the area had heavy snowfall and designed something with a roof on the alpine model. His drawings came back with the comment that pitched roofs cost too much. Maintenance of a flat roof would soon exceed the higher initial cost of a pitched roof, Father countered. That was beside the point, he was told: maintenance was budgeted annually whereas construction had to be budgeted for one year. This dictated a flat roof. 'Ze bouwen niet voor de toekomst' (They don't build for the future), he grumbled: 'Alles is temporary.' It had symbolic *and* practical significance that the building on Superior Street in which he worked had been erected as temporary accommodation in the 1920s. (It is still in use today!)

Never notably democratic in his outlook, Father had over time acquired a low opinion of what he called *de doorsnee Canadees*, the average Canadian. Except for our trip to Calgary in 1966, he had never got more than a few kilometres east of Abbotsford, in the Fraser valley, where Karel and Hansje van Voorstvader had settled. But Father, like most people, was ready to generalize from limited experience.

The average Canadian, in his view, was barely capable of finding his way to a washroom if given a map and pointed in the right direction. Whatever seemed to call for criticism in his surroundings he easily turned into a dictum. 'De doorsnee Canadees is te dom om te begrijpen dat de zon de ramen niet mag bereiken' (The average Canadian is too stupid to understand that the sun should not reach the windows), he commented, on the failure of his neighbours to install awnings or shutters for summer use. 'De doorsnee Canadees weet schijnbaar niet dat water alleen maar heuvel af loopt' (The average Canadian apparently doesn't know that water runs downhill only) took care of a botched job by a road crew. 'Van de architectuur heeft de doorsnee Canadees eigenlijk geen flauw benul' (The average Canadian doesn't have a clue about architecture) explained the reluctance of Canadians to use the services of architects.

Father was reacting to the limited opportunities he had found in Canada. The contribution he might have made had not been welcomed, and he resented this. He was right in sensing that many Canadians rejected even reasonable suggestions when they came from outsiders, and he had remained an outsider. He continued to enjoy the climate and scenery of Victoria, but seemed to think they were wasted on many who were born there.

Though pleased to retire, Father worried about the financial aspects of doing so. He had been a public servant only since 1955, and his superannuation payment would be small. He could expect something from the Canada Pension Plan and the Guaranteed

Income Supplement Plan, but his income would drop by more than half. Although he was designing a few houses for clients, he didn't know whether he could count on this in the long run. He and Mother therefore asked me to take an interest in the property on Piedmont Avenue. I lacked the money to buy a share but undertook to make their mortgage payments.

On 10 May I was back in Toronto. Three days later I joined my friend John Evans and one of his friends to see Godard's *Breathless.* John was an economics graduate of Carleton University – he now teaches the subject at York – whom I had first met when he lived at Massey College while holding down a summer job with Imperial Oil in 1967. We hit it off well together, playing tennis, going to movies, and talking. A self-confident man, he had an incisive mind and a ready wit. Once, as I was railing against government waste, he said that my grasp of the problem was incomplete: 'Don't think of it just as *government* waste, Mike. Government is as wasteful as the private sector requires it to be.'

John's friend Sheila, whom I met for the first time that evening, had graduated in English literature from Carleton and was working as a flight attendant during the summer. I had a lingering interest in an art history student with whom I had gone out in the summer of 1967, but Peggy had become interested in someone else. Ready for someone new, I fell almost immediately in love with Sheila. She was less committed than I was but seemed happy in my company, and we saw each other as frequently as her irregular work schedule allowed.

One weekend we drove to Algonquin Park, where Sheila insisted that we rent a canoe. As we headed out into the lake she derided my crab-catching beginner's stroke: *real* Canadians knew how to paddle a canoe. (She may have been right, but since 1968 I have declined all invitations to go canoeing. When I want exercise I play squash, walk or swim; when I go on vacation there are many things I'd rather do than risk my life in an unstable craft.) I felt more comfortable accompanying her to the movies or the theatre, most memorably in Stratford for a performance of *Waiting for Godot* and at Toronto's Royal Alexandra Theatre for *The Misanthrope* in Richard Wilbur's verse translation. (This was the first time I saw Brian Bedford on stage, in the role of Acaste.)

When Sheila left Toronto in August I missed her badly. Early the next month I was in Ottawa to see some of my LSR people (Forsey, Gordon, and Spry for an evening at the Spry cottage on Lake Kingsmere: a splendid talkfest) and to celebrate birthdays with Sheila, hers being the day before mine. On one of these occasions I proposed marriage. She turned me down gently. She was leaving for Europe in October and knew neither when she would return nor how she would then feel about me. But she promised to keep in touch.

The Canada I returned to from Berkeley was in the grip of Trudeaumania. An election would take place in June; the Liberals seemed to be on the verge of winning the majority that had eluded them in 1963 and 1965. Upon reading of Pearson's resignation I had speculated in my diary about who might succeed him. After dismissing Paul Martin ('too old'), John Turner ('too young'), Jean Marchand ('too FC'), Paul Hellyer ('blotted his copybook over the armed forces unification business'), and Mitchell Sharp ('a choice between Stanfield and Sharp will be no choice at all'), I settled for Pierre Elliott Trudeau: 'an intellectual, an enlightened man, impeccably bilingual. He might tempt me to vote Liberal once more.'

On the final ballot at the leadership convention in April, Trudeau defeated a man I hadn't even considered as a candidate because he seemed too conservative to lead the party, Robert Winters. The outcome pleased me. In the course of the election campaign, however, I began to fear that Trudeau would be ineffective in the face of the country's economic problems. Voting Conservative was out of the question, so I voted for the NDP candidate in Toronto–St Paul's, Bob Fenn. I knew him distantly, as a political science instructor at the University of Toronto and as an eccentric who took into Toronto Symphony concerts the scores of the works being performed, reading them with the aid of a penlight. Bob would have had difficulty winning a safe NDP seat, but in one of those, of course, he would hardly have got the nomination.

My vote was quixotic. The NDP had no chance of winning, in St

Paul's or nationally. This was just as well, for I did not believe its policies could produce the results that NDPers expected from them. In late 1967 I had written to the Ottawa journalist Ron Grantham, once an LSR member: 'The traditional solutions proposed by social democrats are of little use, though probably they're better than nothing.' Today I'm not sure even of that. Social democrats are optimists and assume the existence of an utterly unrealistic potential level of goodwill and selflessness in the population. I see no persuasive grounds for such optimism.

At the same time, I can see no reason for the confident faith in the workings of 'the invisible hand' that is evident in classical British liberalism and more recently in neo-conservatism. It is an optimistic error to believe that capitalism can itself, without intervention, solve the problems it creates. A market economy calls forth great ingenuity and produces great wealth, more than any other economic system known to us. (Its commitment to growth at all costs may yet lead to the extinction of our species, but that's another story.) The system does not regulate itself, however, or does so over a period of time so long as to be intolerable to most mortals. Furthermore, unrestrained capitalism has other unwelcome effects. Unless governments intervene effectively (a tall order!), high unemployment may become the dismal rule, income and wealth will be ever more unequally distributed, public amenities will be starved for funds, and the environment will continue to deteriorate.

Capitalism must be controlled so that its constructive energies may be harnessed for the common good and its destructive tendencies checked. Governments must seek to modify the marketplace so as to ensure that socially valuable but financially unprofitable projects, such as the rearing of children, mass education, housing for low-income earners, high culture, public transportation, policing, environmental protection, and national defence, don't get skimped. As well, governments must seek to curb capitalism's tendency to concentrate wealth and power in the hands of relatively few. By and large, governments should not, however, bail out private industries that get into financial trouble, which usually involves throwing good money after bad.

As guides to the future, the Manchester School and Friedrich Hayek are no more helpful than Karl Marx or Eduard Bernstein. My preference is for the welfare capitalism championed by the likes of Gunnar Myrdal, John Maynard Keynes, and John Kenneth Galbraith, and pursued with varying degrees of vigour by European centrist politicians since the Second World War. Private property is not sacrosanct; sharing some of the wealth is essential.

These are unpopular ideas nowadays, especially in the English-speaking countries, and I am not optimistic about the ability of national governments to tame the capitalist beast, even if they were willing to try. International action is required to control international enterprise but is unlikely to be forthcoming. The very rich and their proxies are now increasingly unchecked in the economic warfare they are waging on much of the rest of humanity. This is one more reason for thinking that the globe will become a much nastier place during the next few decades.

An economic system that impoverishes a growing number of people sooner or later requires the exercise of force in its defence, at the expense of political democracy if necessary. Of course, the rich have always been perfectly at ease with repressive regimes. These are mostly controlled by wealth, and even when they are not, the rich and business people generally manage to maintain their privileges. The exceptions to this are unpalatable, being dominated by people – Lenin, Stalin, Mao – who are often even more ruthless and vicious than those they have displaced. Knowing that my views are out of favour with the powerful, I can only scan the future with apprehension, fearful of worse to come.

In the 1970s and 1980s the Liberal party spoke to some of my concerns but not to others. I once joined it in order to help a friend get a nomination, and over the years I have voted Liberal rather more than half of the time. The other times I voted NDP. The latter I now see as evidence of irresponsibility more than anything else. I lived in constituencies where the NDP did not have a shadow of a chance, so that voting for it was a safe way of expressing dissatisfaction with the choices available to me. It was not, however, a particularly constructive thing to do.

When my vote for the NDP in the 1990 provincial election found me in support of a victorious candidate and party, my surprise was great. I suspected that I had made a mistake, and I knew it when the government withdrew financial support, pledged by the previous administration, for the construction of a ballet-opera house. The NDP did some good things: parts of their labour legislation, such as prohibiting the use of strikebreakers, was enlightened and long overdue (and now gone, courtesy of a new government that is anything but enlightened). But they proved to be less effective in office than they had been in opposition. The incompetence of the party in Ontario has, I think, permanently cured me of voting for it. Henceforth, when and if I vote, I shall probably vote Liberal, though I may have to hold my nose while doing so.

I have never voted Progressive Conservative and don't imagine I ever shall. I know that decent, thoughtful people adhere to the party: Dalton Camp, David Crombie, and Robert Stanfield come easily to mind. And I do not oppose conservatism in all senses: in financial and social matters I am more conservative than anything else. But today's Tories seem committed less to preserving what is good in our institutions than to fattening the wallets of the wealthy at the expense of everyone else. Theirs is the party of business and the propertied seeking to maintain and expand their privileges, of Bounderbys preaching the virtues of self-help to the poor, of parvenus eager to increase the distance between themselves and those they have left behind, and, not least important, of die-hards clinging to an ill-understood past. It is the home, too, of ideologues whose idea of the good society seems to be the England excoriated by Charles Dickens. Until Reform came along, the Progressive Conservative party was the main preserve of Canadians at their most obscurantist and least generous.

Disbelief grips me when I learn that someone I like and respect admits to voting Conservative. (This doesn't happen often enough to force me to reconsider my prejudice.) Lunching with an old friend in the Snug a decade or so ago, I cited John Stuart Mill in describing the Tories as 'the stupid party.' 'Mike, you *do* know I'm a Tory,' he said crustily. 'My apologies, Stewart: I had no idea!' I exclaimed: 'You've always seemed so sensible I assumed you must be a Grit.' He did not seem much mollified.

The Liberals won a majority in 1968. 'Not convinced that Trudeau will do much about important issues such as housing, taxation and inflation, but we'll see,' I wrote in my diary. In any case, Canadian politics were much less depressing than American. On 5 June, Senator Robert Kennedy was assassinated as he stood poised to win the Democratic nomination. I had not been one of his fans, but his murder, two months after King's, appalled me. A pervasive stench clung to U.S. politics that year: another outrage was the attack by the Chicago police on students protesting against the Vietnam War during the Democratic convention. Richard Nixon's victory over Hubert Humphrey in November was to me an anticlimax. Neither deserved to win. It *does* seem unlikely, however, that Humphrey would have disgraced the office as egregiously as Nixon did.

Political events in the United States paled alongside those in Europe in 1968. I had no strong views about the student riots in Paris during the spring or the way they were put down, but the crushing of the reform government in Czechoslovakia was another matter. In August the socialist reformers, who sought to introduce a measure of popular participation in government and loosen the country's ties to the Soviet Union, were ruthlessly crushed by the forces of the Warsaw Pact, and the 'Prague Spring' came to a sudden end. I felt rage as I listened to radio news reports. Would the powerful always stomp on the faces of the weak?

Glendon College is located above the west branch of the Don River near the Bayview Avenue viaduct. The estate's first owners, the financier E.R. Wood and his wife, were keen horticulturalists; as a result the campus resembles a botanical garden. Alterations have compromised the original elegance of the villa, Glendon Hall, but it is easily the most attractive building on campus. Of those constructed in the 1960s none rises above mediocrity.

The Woods willed the property to the University of Toronto in 1950. A decade later that institution transferred it to York University. When the board of governors decided that the university must become larger than the Glendon site permitted, a sometime farm in distant Downsview became the main campus. Glendon College was then founded as a liberal arts institution, initially with departments only of English, French, economics, history, philosophy, political science, and sociology, as well as multidisciplinary studies.

Offering full programs in the natural sciences would have been too costly, but in retrospect it seems regrettable that anthropology, art history, geography, mathematics, psychology, classics, and languages other than English and French were excluded. The plan was to add geography, mathematics, psychology, and modern languages in due course, and some of them *have* been added since 1970, but the straitened financial circumstances of the last quarter-century have made it impossible to fund them adequately.

The bilingual program for which Glendon College is best known was the brainchild of its first principal. Escott Reid was a recently retired diplomat, an intimidating yet kindly man: steady of gaze, bluntly direct of speech, and full of enthusiasm. Soon after his appointment he informed the York senate that he wanted the college to be 'a small, residential, undergraduate, co-educational, liberal arts college of high academic standards where there would be a special emphasis on public affairs and on the acquisition of skill in the use of and appreciation of the English and French languages.'* He spoke no French himself and regretted this: educated Canadians ought to be able to get along in both English and French.

He underestimated the difficulties anglophone students would have in becoming bilingual in a predominantly English setting. Even more than the limited course offerings, the bilingual program, which required students to take at least two years of French, undercut enrolment in the early years. As well, the resources Glendon College could draw on from York were insufficient for what Escott hoped to accomplish. By 1968 he was eager to secure additional money, and that fall he solicited my help with a document he was drafting for a fund-raising campaign. (He chose me because I had interviewed him about his membership in the LSR and had borrowed some of his files: one favour deserved another, he said.)

In its final form the document made a case for an additional

* Escott Reid, *Radical Mandarin: The Memoirs of Escott Reid* (Toronto 1989), 344.

$850,000 annually for five years. This would have more than doubled the 1968–9 budget and was intended to permit the hiring of bilingual teachers, the awarding of scholarships, and the reduction of class sizes in first-year courses. Escott had begun to approach foundations for money when the board of governors found out what he was doing. They instructed him to stop: fund-raising was *their* concern. I am not aware that they have ever raised a nickel specifically for Glendon.

The college was unable to recruit more than a handful of bilingual professors in subject areas other than French language and literature. Fully bilingual faculty were in even shorter supply in the late 1960s than university teachers generally. Some department heads saw no need to look for them at all. Edgar McInnis did not so much as mention the word 'bilingual' to me when I was hired. My colleague Irving Abella, who joined the college when I did, confirms that this was also his experience.

The college also found it hard to attract students, although many of those who did come in the early years were impressive, and some – Ruth Cawker, Greg Gatenby, Adèle Hurley, M.T. Kelly, Michael Perley, and Helen Sinclair, for example – have become well known. The limited number of departments and the French requirement were partly responsible for our low enrolment. So, too, was York's image. The new university played second fiddle to the University of Toronto, even though several departments were soon as good as those at the senior institution. Some U of T professors changed allegiance. The dean of arts, Jack Saywell, had been recruited from Toronto; Ramsay moved north in 1969. (Fortunately, he was allowed to continue supervising his Toronto Ph.D. students.) A York degree was often perceived as inferior to one from Toronto, however, and that hurt Glendon, too.

Lagging enrolment made Glendon abjectly dependent on the university's goodwill and fed fears that the board of governors might find another use for the estate. The feeling of embattlement has survived into the present, but around 1969 it bordered on paranoia. By and large, I managed to ignore it. I didn't want to go to Downsview – the campus was bleak and the routes to it passed through one of the ugliest cityscapes in Canada – but didn't think it a fate worse than death. As traffic in North York has grown heavier, however, the prospect has become steadily less pleasing.

Having accepted a position as don in the Wood residence, I moved in on the Dominion Day weekend. Among the students I got to know that summer was Trish (now Kate) Nelligan, who was hoping to make a career in acting. That winter I saw her in *Hamlet* (as Gertrude) and was impressed. She did not return to the college in 1969; when I next saw her on stage, in 1983, she was on Broadway in David Hare's *Plenty*. Another new acquaintance was Bill Powell, a future social worker who had entered college in his late twenties after a serious traffic accident had left him nearly blind. Five years later, in 1973, I was his best man; in 1993 I delivered a eulogy at his too-early funeral. A third was Rick Schultz, an argumentative political science graduate and a devoted fan of *Beyond the Fringe*. He went to England for further study but returned to the college in 1969 as an instructor and secretary of the faculty council.

Among the ten other dons, one I knew already. Doug McTavish I had met several times when he shared an apartment on Bernard Avenue with my Victoria friend Bruce Warburton and a law student from western Ontario, David Peterson. Doug was taking the bar admission course; another don to be doing so was Paul Cantor, who introduced me to the game of squash. I am still grateful to him, because it has become my favourite form of exercise.

Presiding over us was the dean of students, Brian Bixley, an English-born economist with a quirky sense of humour. Once, trying during a conversation in the Senior Common Room to explain the falling birth rate in Canada, he referred to children as 'an inferior consumer good.' Michael Gregory, head of the English department and the father of four, objected, and Brian withdrew the remark. His manner suggested, however, that he had not changed his mind. (He had a point, of course. Children are expensive to raise, and Canadian society offers little help.)

In exchange for acting as a supervisor and older sibling, dons got a one-bedroom apartment rent free and meals during the academic session. The job took as much time as we were prepared to give it. When I wanted to work I stayed in my office; when I was in my apartment students would drop in to listen to music, to watch TV (sports, the news, *Monty Python's Flying Circus*), to play chess, bridge, or Diplomacy, or just to talk. A few personal problems came my way, and once in a while I was roused from my bed in order to drive someone to the emergency ward at nearby Sunnybrook Hospital, usually because of a bad trip brought on by LSD. Dropping acid was less common than smoking marijuana, however, while alcohol was the drug of choice. As a result, the noise level in the residences was often high, especially on weekends.

The job's chief drawback was the lack of privacy. Anne Fawcett, a cheerful high school teacher from New Brunswick, once said that she never knew what to do on a weekend until she heard on the grapevine what she was supposed to have done the weekend just past. Then she went out and did that. I avoided behaviour likely to raise eyebrows, such as using illicit drugs while students were around. I did permit myself marijuana off campus or with other dons. But my use of the drug, never frequent, effectively ended after I stopped smoking in 1970. (I had begun in Germany, had quit in 1965, but had fallen off the wagon two years later.) Knowing how addictive tobacco was, I feared that smoking marijuana would lead me back to the evil weed.

When classes began I had already met all my colleagues. Edgar had retired in June but kept an office until 1972 (he died the following year). I explained to him, somewhat sheepishly, that I hadn't completed my dissertation as I had in October 1967 confidently predicted I would. 'Don't worry about it,' he said. 'I never for a moment expected you to finish it on time. These things always take longer than you think.' He was, of course, quite right.

Edgar's successor, Albert Tucker, was a native Torontonian who taught British history. John Brückmann, our medievalist, was an original. Alsatian by birth, he cultivated a deliberate manner and told anecdotes in an accent that was an inimitable blend of German, French, and American English. I liked best one that dated from late 1944, when the Allied armies were approaching the borders of the Reich. Fourteen years old at the time and living in Strasbourg, John had been drafted into the *Volkssturm*, a citizen army made up of young teenagers and old men beyond the age of military service. They received some rudimentary training, John said, happily recalling an hour spent in aircraft recognition that ended when the sergeant instructing them said: 'Well, never mind all that, lads. If you hear a plane head for the ditch: nineteen times out of twenty it will be one of theirs.'

Bill Echard was a U.S.-born expert on Napoleon III and his diplomacy. Walter Beringer, a classicist of German origin, educated at Tübingen, was the department's contrarian, embracing lost causes with enthusiasm. Our historian of Russia and eastern Europe, Bob Augustine, was a refugee from a Wall Street law firm. Wise-cracking Don Pilgrim, originally from Hamilton, Ontario, specialized in seventeenth-century French history and twentieth-century French vintages. As he was only six months older than I was – he had joined the college in 1967 – we saw each other socially as well as professionally.

Irving Abella I already knew as a classmate at the University of Toronto. Witty, able, and ambitious, he was the person I would be working with most closely, since he had been engaged to teach two courses in Canadian as well as one in American history. In those early years I saw a good deal of him and his wife. He married in December 1968 someone who was his match in every way. Rosalie Silberman was charm personified. She seemed to like everyone she met and was never at a loss socially. During that first year she, Irv, and I were invited for an evening at the home of Walter and Mary Beringer. Having learned that I had studied in Freiburg and that Rosie had been born near Stuttgart (in a refugee camp), Walter invited us to gather around the piano for a medley of German student songs. Irv paled and hung back, but Rosie sang along *con brio*.

The departmental secretary was Esther Rousselle, ever-smiling and uncommonly well informed. (She had been Escott's secretary and kept her lines of communication intact.) Anyone who wanted to know what was happening in the college would ask her. If she thought her interlocutor could be told she would lean over her desk and begin conspiratorially if ungrammatically: 'Well, just between you and I ...'

I had responsibility for two courses: a third-year course on the history of Ontario and western Canada with three discussion groups (there was one hour a week for a lecture, but I used it only to show the occasional film), and a fourth-year seminar on Canada since the First World War. I also had three tutorial groups in Irv's survey of Canadian history. This gave me eleven hours a week in class and almost a hundred students: a heavy load by the standards of the college. I managed to make my load lighter than it might have been, however, thanks to 'Liber-Action,' Glendon's bow to the student movement of the 1960s. Claiming the courses to be insufficiently 'relevant' (a popular buzz-word of the time), some students announced in early September that they would launch 'people-generated courses,' spontaneous experiments in learning. Meanwhile, existing courses would be 'liberated' by the students in them, their instructors becoming 'resource persons.'*

There were calls, too, for the abolition of the faculty council and its committees and the creation of a 'more democratic' form of college government, and for an end to 'symbols of oppression' such as the High Table in the dining-hall and separate student washrooms. Escott promptly abolished both. (In the case of High Table this saved many hundreds of dollars, or so the senior administrator of the college, Vic Berg, claimed with a pleased smile.) To the three student members of faculty council nine more were soon added; the council remained otherwise intact.

Few if any of the people-generated courses ever amounted to much or survived for long. As the academic dean, the philosopher H.S. Harris, repeatedly reminded everyone who cared to listen and even those who did not, new courses as well as major changes in existing ones had to be approved not only by the faculty council but also by the senate. His carefully enunciated 'I do not think Senate will care for that' became something of a standing joke. But the words had the desired effect.

In the meantime, reformist zeal came to focus on courses, among them mine, in which the keener liberators had registered. Jim Park,

---

* See Tim and Julyan Reid, eds, *Student Power and the Canadian Campus* (Toronto 1969), 78–87.

a feisty student journalist, led the attack in my fourth-year course, with Glen Williams, a political science major, in close support. Course outlines imposed too much structure, they said: the students ought to decide each week what should be discussed the next week, and I could suggest appropriate readings. Exams were intolerable. Grades, tolerated only because the York senate still required them, should depend solely on class participation and essays.

I gratefully accepted suggestions likely to have the effect of saving me time. Besides, I was not unsympathetic to some of the aims of Liber-Action. Having done too well on exams to value them highly as a means of determining what students knew, I announced to my upper-year courses that there would be none. Furthermore, I undertook to discuss with all students individually their final grades. Sometimes these meetings were difficult. 'Of course in the end you'll just give me what *you* think my work is worth,' one young woman said resentfully. I was not totally inflexible, but she was very nearly right. Why then all the wrangling? Deciding they were mostly a waste of time, I ended the meetings in the early 1970s. Soon afterwards I introduced exams in my third-year course. I had begun to prepare course outlines before the end of 1968 after several students, in thrall to unliberated educational ideas, had asked me to supply them.

As I think back, I am reluctantly forced to conclude that the course I adopted in 1968 was largely opportunistic. I was seeking to mollify the more radical of my students while reducing the amount of grading I had to do. I liked to be thought something of a radical, moreover, because I knew that many radicals, influenced by Herbert Marcuse's notion of 'repressive tolerance,' regarded liberals (like me?) as the real – the most dangerous – enemy. I argued for increased student participation in faculty council and its committees, privately telling sceptical colleagues that it would make no real difference to the way the college was run (in which I turned out to be right). I invited the Marxist historian Stanley Ryerson to speak on campus, taking care to check first with Al Tucker and Edgar McInnis. 'Radical' enough to suit most of my students, I was not so radical as to want to offend my elders.

At bottom I had little sympathy with the social goals of the student movement or with its low regard for due process in trying to achieve them. Universities are at the same time conservative and radical: conservative as the guardians of the cultural past and the transmitters of knowledge and tradition to the present and the future, radical as the constant destroyers of much of that knowledge, replacing it with new information and hypotheses. That is why philosophical liberals feel at home in the university, for they believe in the free exchange of ideas and are, or ought to be, able to cope with both conservation and change. I suggested to one or two activists whom I got to know that the attempt to use the university as a lever for social change was bound to fail in its purpose, and might undermine what universities *could* do. My success in arguing this point was not impressive, and I did not push it.

Adopting a stance of sympathy with student demands was the path of least resistance and made my life easier. Besides, the young woman I was escorting by December saw herself as a student radical. Jan hailed from the same part of Ottawa as Sheila, knew her slightly, and accepted that my affections were engaged. That she was my student did not trouble me. The standards of the late 1960s were permissive: I was not the only faculty member to transgress. What a few years earlier would surely have drawn a warning from my department head raised few eyebrows in 1968. And I believe that neither of us exploited the situation, in any case not consciously. Jan would not have allowed me to pull rank, and I did not try to; she did not expect me to assess her work more favourably because of our friendship, and I don't think I did.

One of Jan's many endearing qualities was her ability to get along with people, and she got on well with my brother Steven and his housemates. He was taking a degree in library science at the University of Toronto in 1968–9 and lived in something like a commune on Lonsdale Road near Yonge Street. I write 'something like' advisedly: the organizer was Michael Clark, with whom I had worked in the Department of Education for two summers. A thoughtful economics major who had become a good friend, he was articling with a large firm of chartered accountants and ran the finances of the house in a thoroughly businesslike fashion. He and Steven were joined by another recent UVic graduate, Michael de Rosenroll, and two other men. The five threw many parties, and at these bashes Jan and I were regulars, helping to make the house shake to the music of the Rolling Stones, the Chambers Brothers, and the Doors, 'Light My Fire' being a particular favourite.

Liber-Action or no, the tutorial groups and seminars proved to be demanding work. Lecturing is easy compared to leading a group: a lecturer is in control, whereas a seminar leader is not, or not to the same extent. Small groups are unpredictable. When a seminar goes badly, almost any other form of work may seem more attractive than teaching. But not for long.

During that first session at Glendon College I lost my misgivings about teaching, enjoying it more than I had before, perhaps because I was closer to my students than I had been in Calgary or at the U of T, perhaps because it now engaged me fully. In Calgary a student had asked me why I taught history; I had replied flippantly that it allowed me to pursue my interests and kept me off the streets. In the course of 1968–9 I decided that there was much more to it than that. Not only did I enjoy helping students try to make sense of Canada's past, I thought it was important they do so and do it within a university, the last institution left on earth where knowledge is sought disinterestedly and not mainly for the income that it may produce for the seekers or their employers.

I still love teaching. Many of my students have been a pleasure to teach; some have become and remained friends. As well, I appreciate the opportunity to do research and write that university teaching gives me, and the security of tenure that has allowed me, for example, to undertake my work on the history of academic freedom. Begun in 1985, it isn't finished yet: not exactly a quick pay-off! With J.T. McLaughlin in Jack MacLeod's *Zinger and Me*, I can say: 'If I were a rich man, I'd cheerfully pay for the privilege of being a professor.'

How long will that remain true? The mood in universities is changing. Not only are they under financial pressure, with budget cuts and rising tuition fees the order of the day, but there is growing pressure to make them conform more closely to a business model.

There have been demands that universities confine themselves to practical subjects of instruction and research. Some people, resenting that a particular group of employees should enjoy a degree of security and freedom not available to the rest, are calling for the end of tenure and, effectively, of the academic freedom that has come to depend on it.

At the same time and little less menacingly, academic freedom is under attack from within. Freedom of expression, essentially safe in Canadian universities since 1960, is again in danger. The notion that something should not be said or written if it may offend someone or other has gained support during the last few years. It is not yet dominant, but warning bells are ringing.

I remember that first year of full-time teaching partly because of several conferences that I attended. Early in the fall, a student group, the Glendon Forum, held a symposium on Canada's Aboriginal peoples. The event brought many visitors to the campus and provided a lively two days. The best session followed the closing dinner, when Harold Cardinal, a young Cree from Alberta, locked horns with the deputy minister of Indian affairs. The conference led me to take a more sympathetic view of what are now called the First Nations. I not only took Indian land claims more seriously but incorporated more material on the Amerindians into my courses.

In late November I was at McGill University, where a conference of the Canadian Association of American Studies compared the 1930s in Canada and the United States. It was a judicious blend of the personal and the scholarly. Among those who offered reminiscences were my LSR acquaintances Frank Scott and Graham Spry, the novelist Hugh MacLennan, and Hazen Sise, an architect who had served with Dr Norman Bethune's blood transfusion unit during the Spanish Civil War. Especially MacLennan's talk was fascinating, as he described the feelings of a generation of young people with few opportunities to get ahead. 'The essence of being in your twenties in the Thirties,' he said, comparing young people to aircraft ready to take off, 'was that no matter how well tuned up you were, you stayed on the ground. Many of us stayed on the ground, or just above it, for ten years.'* (This sounds dismally familiar today.)

A reception at the U.S. Consulate was followed by a dinner at the McGill Faculty Club, to which I caught a ride with Scott. Years later, when I edited his last book, *A New Endeavour*, for him, we got to know each other well, but in 1968 I was still just one face among the many he had seen in the course of his life. He mistook it for that of the poet George Bowering – there is a slight resemblance, at least when I wear my glasses – and wondered what I was doing at *this* conference. I reintroduced myself. He paused, then chuckled: 'Oh yes, you're the man who's been writing all those nasty things about the LSR.' Not knowing quite how to respond, I mumbled something noncommittal. He changed the subject: 'You're brave to come with me. No one else thinks I can see enough to find my way to the faculty club, especially when I've had a drink or two. But they're wrong, you know. I could find the club blindfolded.'

Upon our arrival he ordered chilled gin and an olive, then reached into his pocket for a small bottle. Adding a measure of liquid to the gin, he explained that a strike at the *Régie des alcools* had caused the club to run out of dry vermouth and forced him to supply his own. 'Should you be in Montreal again soon, do bring along a bottle of vermouth,' he said mock-plaintively: 'I'm nearly out, and while I don't like breaking strikes I must have my martini.'

In March 1969, Bill Powell in tow, I attended a conference of the University League for Social Reform at the Ontario Institure for Studies in Education on Bloor Street West. The subject was the Americanization of Canada. The absent hero was Walter Gordon, known for his concern about the extent of U.S. ownership of Canadian industry. In attendance was the University of Toronto economist Mel Watkins, who had given his name to a 1968 report arguing that Gordon was right and that a concerted effort was necessary to counter the American threat. There was a lot of talk about the evils of the American empire, to which I contributed my

* Hugh MacLennan, 'What It Was Like to Be in Your Twenties in the Thirties,' in Victor Hoar, ed., *The Great Depression* (Toronto 1969), 145.

two cents' worth. I was no longer as complacent about Canada–U.S. relations as I had been when talking with George Grant in 1966.

At the same time, I was not convinced that U.S. investment in Canada was the menace that some ULSR members perceived. Nor was I sure what Canadians could do about it even if the threat were real. I agreed to write something for a book that Ian Lumsden, a political scientist at York University's Atkinson College, was editing for the ULSR (it appeared in 1970 under the title *Close the 49th Parallel Etc.*). My task was to compare LSR attitudes towards the United States with those of the ULSR three decades later. The LSR had been much friendlier to the United States than Watkins and company, however, and I could not decide how to square the two viewpoints. My essay was badly focused, and Ian's criticism, had I heeded it, would have pushed me farther along the path of economic nationalism than I found congenial. Instead of trying to rewrite the piece I begged off.

The 1969 Learned Societies met at York University in May and June. I remember the meetings mainly for a paper by Donald Creighton and for P.B. Waite's presidential address to the Canadian Historical Association. Speaking about the decline of the empire of the St Lawrence, Creighton was mordantly witty, his paper part scholarship, part tirade, part elegy. He deplored the harm done to Canadian autonomy by U.S. imperialists, Quebec nationalists, and Liberal politicians, and predicted that internal division and the steady weakening of the central government would sap Canada's will to resist the United States.

I feared he might be right but thought that he understated the role played by the business community, and that he too easily absolved the Conservatives of complicity. (What would he have made of Brian Mulroney, our branch-plant prime minister, of the 1988 Free Trade Agreement with the United States, of NAFTA, of the Meech Lake and Charlottetown accords?)

Unlike Creighton, Peter Waite had no axe to grind. He talked, simply and lucidly, about the writing of history. Some in the audience had been boisterous during dinner, but he soon had everyone's attention. When he ended there was silence for a moment;

then the applause began, loud and insistent. I have heard several presidential addresses since and have read more. None has come close to Waite's.

Having for several years had little time for holidays, my brief forays into New England and Nova Scotia and my two weeks' skiing in Yosemite excepted, between November 1968 and January 1970 I took no fewer than four. The days before Christmas 1968 saw me in London, my first visit to that city, where I stayed with Mark and Kathy Levene. I saw the major churches and galleries as well as the Houses of Parliament, and made a detour to Oxford to see a number of friends, among them Martin Petter and Manny Tward, who was there on a postdoctoral fellowship.

After spending Christmas day in Amsterdam with Tante Phiet, Flora, and Jack, I went on to Geneva on the twenty-sixth. My ultimate destination was Leysin, east of Lake Geneva, where John Evans and I had arranged to meet for a week of skiing. A dollar still bought four Swiss francs – what a fool's paradise we inhabited then! – so the price was more than right, especially because we stayed at the ultra-cheap Club Vagabond. The scenery was marvellous, moreover, the weather fine, and the *pistes* challenging without being impossibly hard: who could ask for more?

John and I were roughly at the same level in skill, and much of the time we were on the slopes together. In the evenings we palled around with Jim Lindsey, a young mathematician from Mono Road northwest of Toronto, and three female students from the University of Utrecht. We dined, danced, and drank with our newfound friends and enjoyed ourselves immensely.

(A few years later I got a telephone call from one of the Dutch students, Corinne Elias: she and her husband, a radiologist named Wilfred Müller, were visiting friends in Toronto. From the mid-1970s into the mid-1980s, when they separated, I stayed with them regularly in Overveen, a small town west of Haarlem. Among the people I was delighted to meet at their house was my friend from grade school, Louise Hasseley Kirchner, a baroness by marriage but, in the way she smiled and giggled, still the girl I had played with a quarter-century earlier. She lived in nearby Bloemendaal, which also happened to be the location of the first large house Father had ever designed. Now a home for handicapped children, Schaepe Duyne is a huge brick edifice, but the manner in which the sections of the house have been placed at angles to each other makes it look cosy in spite of its size. The young architect had known what he was doing.)

My 1969 summer vacation again began in London. After a few days there and in Oxford, I went on to Amsterdam for a couple of days. Jack had heard that the headmaster of the NBS, Meneer van Dijk, and our grade one teacher, Juffrouw du Burck, were retiring, and a reception had been laid on for them. On impulse we drove to Baarn. We waited in a long queue, clapping politely as Queen Juliana was ushered in ahead of us. Once inside the gymnasium I paid my respects to the retirees, chatted with Juffrouw Muis, herself nearing retirement, and looked in vain for former classmates. If any were there, they and I had changed too much to allow recognition. But the visit was worth it for enabling me to talk with former teachers and look around the school. How large it had seemed once; how almost lilliputian it now appeared. Had it really been so difficult to get over that ancient pommel horse? Now it would be easy, but now it no longer mattered. I felt a certain melancholy: 'To think that two and two are four; / And neither five nor three, / The heart of man has long been sore, / and long 'tis like to be.'

The next day I took a flight to Athens, where I spent a couple of days exploring the historic sites and antiquities before continuing to Xania, in the western part of Crete. Sheila was teaching English in a girls' school there: three hours in the morning and three more in the early evening. During the hot afternoon people stayed home, but we demonstrated our foreignness by swimming after lunch, in the Mediterranean Sea or in the local pool.

Xania attracted few tourists in those days, so we stood out. One evening we were dining with three New Zealanders, among them Sheila's roommate, Maggie, when the restaurant owner came to our table. An article that he wanted us to read, from an old *Globe and Mail* magazine, informed us that he had been the stand-in for Anthony Quinn in the dancing scene of the film *Zorba the Greek*.

I'm not sure what impressed me more: the information contained in the article – I had seen the film and liked the dancing – or the man's possession of a piece of paper printed in Toronto.

So that we could leave Xania more quickly after the end of term, I helped Sheila mark the year-end essays and exams. A striking number of them expressed a wish to move to Athens and enjoy a freer life. Cretan mores were very conservative, Sheila said. Unmarried women were closely guarded, something most clearly evident on Saturday in the early evening, when the Xanians ventured out *en famille*, strolling along the harbour. The young women stuck close to parents and older brothers; from other, passing grouplets young men regarded the young women speculatively. None would be allowed into the company of a woman before an engagement had been contracted. Breaking an engagement was said still to be the occasion for blood feuds in remote parts of Crete, as male relatives of the 'dishonoured' woman sought to kill the man who had 'shamed' her and her family.

According to Sheila, foreign women were held to be fair game unless they 'belonged' to a man, so she wore an engagement ring when we set out on our travels. First we walked down the Samaria gorge, the longest in Europe, to the south coast and took a small boat to Sphakia. There we drank retsina with the police chief. He was not allowed to fraternize with the locals, so he was constantly on the lookout for likely tourists to drink with. Along with a teacher from New Zealand named George, we were stuck with the garrulous chief until the small hours. As he spoke no English and very little German my exchanges with him were minimal, but George and Sheila made up for that. The chief not only paid for our drinks but also authorized our registration in a hotel, even though Sheila and I did not have our passports. In the Greece of the colonels, we had learned earlier that evening, one should not leave home without it.

The next day we visited Iraklion and the ruins at Knossos. A vast, sunbaked labyrinth, it vividly evoked the myth of Ariadne, Theseus, and the dreadful Minotaur. We rented a car and drove east along Crete's main highway, in most places little more than one lane wide, in order to visit a former Venetian fortress, more recently a leper colony, on the island of Spinolonga, deserted and more than a little eerie. Two days later I said a reluctant goodbye to Sheila and returned to Canada via Amsterdam and London.

Soon after getting back to Toronto I dined with David Trott and his wife Ildiko. It was Sunday, 20 July. As we ate the chicken paprikash that Ildiko had prepared we watched the ghostly images of Neil Armstrong's first steps on the moon. In twelve years we had gone from peering at *Sputnik*s to witnessing this 'giant leap for mankind.' In spite of the evidence of our eyes it seemed unreal. Over the telephone that evening Father recalled the first airplane he had seen, around 1910. It was almost a fantasy that people had now reached the moon. Marvelling at the achievement, he also wondered about the cost (a typically Dutch concern?). Did I think the money had been well spent? I couldn't decide. Since then I have become more sceptical, however. So far, the moon landing has led the human race nowhere.

This might have been expected. When the Soviets took an early lead in the space race with the launching of *Sputnik*s I and II, many of us in the West had worried about the military implications of Russian technological superiority. In order to reassure the American people and their allies, the U.S. government had had to make it clear that 'we' could do better than the Soviets. The undertaking to put a man on the moon was a key part of this. That famous Yankee know-how was equal to the challenge, and in July 1969 the Americans had a stunning success to celebrate. But twenty-seven years later the enterprise seems to have been, more than anything else, a huge, spectacular WOMBAT (waste of money, brains and time).

I visited Father and Mother in August, just before the new academic session began. Mother, facing a lung operation to remove a fungus, had asked her sons to rally round, and Steven (who had flown in from his librarian's job in Ottawa) and I had responded. Peter, who lived in Montreal, was saving money for his marriage later that year, Jack was in Holland, doing research on the sixteenth-century artist Jan Vermeyen, and Jan D., who had dropped out of the University of Victoria, was travelling somewhere in the United States or Mexico. Joe lived in Victoria at the time.

The operation was a success: within two days Mother was out of intensive care. In the meantime Joe, Steven, and I spent a lot of time together, sailing off Oak Bay in Joe's Shark-class boat, drinking a beer or two in the Snug afterwards, talking at Joe's place in the evening. The weather was sunny and dry, and we enjoyed ourselves thoroughly.

One day we drove to Shawnigan Lake to visit Hilda Parkinson at her cottage. She waxed enthusiastic over us: hadn't we done well since arriving that June day in 1952? and weren't we making a wonderful contribution to Canada? She seemed inclined to take some of the credit for this. And who knows: as our immigration officer perhaps she was entitled to. I had not seen her for several years, but she was as welcoming as ever and her cookies were just as good.

My fourth holiday within a year took me to Amsterdam in December 1969. I was staying with Jack and Flora, who had married in October and moved into a flat on the Cliostraat, not far from where Tante Phiet lived. (Father had attended the wedding and returned unhappy about what cars had done to the city of his birth. Amsterdam had undergone two disasters in this century, he said. One was the destruction of Dutch Jewry; the triumph of the automobile was the other.) On the day of my arrival I succumbed to jet lag, falling asleep during a performance by the Concertgebouw Orchestra. After the intermission a brilliant and appropriately noisy rendition of *Pictures at an Exhibition* made staying awake easier.

The next day Sheila flew in from Geneva. She was attending university in Grenoble, a city she described with such enthusiasm that a dozen years later I would spend part of a sabbatical there. She hit it off well with Jack and Flora, and during the two weeks that followed we had an excellent time.

One evening a few days before Christmas we joined Tante Phiet at a high school symphony concert in Haarlem. The young conductor, Ed Spanjaard, and the cello soloist, his brother Lodewijk, were sons of old Reitsma family friends. Jaap and Ima Spanjaard were Holocaust survivors, but whereas Ima had been in a concentration camp, Jaap, a psychiatrist, had managed to evade detention throughout the war. What I remember was not the concert but a joke that Jaap told during a reception at the Spanjaard home afterwards. Featuring two staple figures of Dutch Jewish humour, *Sampie en Mosie*, Sam and Moshe, it is that rarity, a joke about income tax.

Sam gets a letter one day that puts him in a cold sweat. He phones his friend: 'Moshe, I'm in trouble. A tax inspector wants to see me on Tuesday.' The two talk for a while and decide that Moshe will come along. He stays in the anteroom while Sam goes in to face the inspector, who is already rubbing his hands in anticipation of unmasking a tax evader. He trots out the evidence – the expensive house, the cottage, the cars – and concludes: 'The way we figure it, meneer, your income over the last five years must have been several times higher than what you have declared.'

'That's right,' nods Sam: 'I make lots of money from wagers, and that is tax-free.' The rubbing stops. 'Meneer, we're talking hundreds of thousands. Do you mean to say you make that much money from *wagers*?' 'Just so.' 'Frankly, I don't believe you.'

Sam leans over. 'I'll demonstrate, meneer: I'll bet you ten guilders I can put my left eye between my teeth.' The inspector regards Sam closely and says dubiously: 'Okay.' Sam removes a well-made false eye and puts it in his mouth.

Collecting his ten, he continues: 'Now I'll bet you twenty-five I can put my *right* eye between my teeth.' The inspector smiles: 'You're on!' Sam removes his false teeth and places them around his right eye.

While the inspector is extracting a twenty-five guilder note from his wallet Sam says: 'Meneer, wait a moment! I'll bet you a hundred you've got a boil on your rear end.'

The inspector laughs: 'You say you make money this way? Pay up, my friend!' 'Not so fast,' says Sam, 'I need proof.' 'But surely you'll accept my word as a gentleman that I don't have a boil there?' Sam shakes his head: 'Oh, *now* we're gentlemen, are we? A minute ago you all but accused me of lying. No, meneer, if you want your money, you'll have to show me.'

Thinking of the money he has lost and the money he will win, the inspector sighs, gets up, turns to the wall, undoes his belt, drops his pants, and is pulling down his shorts when Sam makes a dash for the door, throws it open, and yells: 'Moshe, come on in and look! You owe me a hundred grand!'

On Christmas Eve Sheila and I drove to Baarn with Jack and Flora in order to drink tea with the Schoutes and dine with the Cazants. Upon our return to Amsterdam late that evening we stopped at Tante Phiet's flat. She was out of town, but a young man who roomed with her that year, Kees Bakels, welcomed us warmly. His fiancée was in the United States and he felt a bit abandoned. Kees studied conducting – he is now principal conductor of the Netherlands Radio Symphony Orchestra – and, using records and tapes, he demonstrated his craft until well after 3:00 a.m. At one point he announced 'the most beautiful opera music ever composed' and put on the trio from the last act of *Der Rosenkavalier*. As I listened to the voices of the two sopranos soaring over that of the mezzo-soprano, I thought that he might be right.

(At the time I was unfamiliar with the opera; since then I've seen it several times, in Munich and New York as well as in Toronto. Father Owen Lee has written, in his fine book *First Intermissions*: 'Some thoughts lie too deep for words, but not for music. The transcendent trio of *Der Rosenkavalier*, the song of three people caught up in the most important moment of their lives, assures us that this is what makes us human: we alone among creatures have a consciousness that reaches beyond the present moment. We are able to conceive, beyond time, some notion of an eternal and immutable. The still point of the turning world.'* I can't possibly say it better myself.)

A few days later, the four of us accompanied Kees to a performance in the Concertgebouw by the second orchestra in the city, the Amsterdam Philharmonic. Herman Krebbers was the soloist in a performance of Brahms's Violin Concerto, my favourite work for the instrument. We had podium seats alongside the orchestra, which gave us ample opportunity to study the conductor, Anton Kersjes, as he led the orchestra. Kees was understudying Kersjes

---

* M. Owen Lee, *First Intermissions* (New York 1995), 218.

at the time, and after the concert he introduced us to conductor and soloist.

On New Year's Eve, Tante Phiet, Flora, Sheila, Jack, and I were guests at the home of Jan and Erna van der Vlis in Blaricum, north of Hilversum. I had met Jan several times: he owned the cottage on the island of Texel where I had spent the 1962 Easter weekend. A former schoolteacher, more recently a businessman, he was also a published historian and altogether an engaging human being.

Those of the guests who had not come by automobile were planning to spend the night in Blaricum. Public transportation ended at 9:00 p.m. and would not resume until twelve hours later. New Year's Eve being pre-eminently a family festival, it was thought unfair to force workers in public transportation to be away from home!

Among the other guests were Stephen and José Shriber, who had left the United States in protest against the Vietnam War. It seemed hard to have to leave one's country the way Stephen had, especially because it was unclear whether he would ever be able to return. Yet I envied him just a bit. While showing Sheila around I looked at my native country with a more careful, even a proprietary eye. I liked much of what I saw. Holland lacked the grandeur of Canada, but it had been shaped more intelligently.

One day we went by train to The Hague. Sheila noted with surprise the existence of farms between Amsterdam and Haarlem, Haarlem and Leiden, Leiden and The Hague, even though by Canadian standards the distances between these cities were minuscule. Nowhere in evidence were the tracts of detached single dwellings that ring Canadian towns. In Holland a free market in land exists only in a limited way, land being too precious to leave its development to the private sector. Given their circumstances, it may be no great credit to the Dutch that they have avoided wrecking their country with shopping plazas, highway strip developments, and suburban sprawl. But avoid it they did. Well, almost: the Bijlmer, a high-rise development southeast of Amsterdam, ranks with the worst built in North America.

Canada, where land seems plentiful, has become an architectural garbage dump. Driving into almost any Canadian town makes me want to curse or weep. I don't know what is worst: the unrelieved ugliness of the buildings that line the approaches to Canadian cities and towns, the waste of land represented by these strips and the low-density suburbs behind them, or the uncaring way in which many attractive older buildings are destroyed to make way for the meretriciously new. Having spent three years on the North York Local Architectural Conservancy Advisory Committee, I know that the wish for unearned increment in land is deeply engrained in the Canadian soul. Many people value highly the opportunity to make a buck from the ownership of real estate. The dismal results are plain to see.

A visit to the Mauritshuis may have been my first to what has become my favourite gallery in Holland and one of my favourites anywhere. It is manageable in size and has the canvas I would rather own than any other: Vermeer's *View of Delft*. The cityscape is redolent of the here and now, but the clouds above it hint at the infinite.

Another gallery I visited for the first time was the Kröller-Müller Museum at Otterlo, in the Hoge Veluwe National Park northwest of Arnhem. The Kröller-Müller is best known for its collection of paintings by van Gogh, but it has many other fine Impressionist, Expressionist, and abstract canvases and sculptures as well. Sheila and I visited it on a crisp day very early in January: a thin layer of snow on the ground, above us a thin layer of cloud not quite obscuring the sun. In the distance we saw deer foraging. I was in excellent spirits.

We dined that evening with Tante Pieta, who had moved from Doorwerth to a flat in Velp, northeast of Arnhem. Staying with her while convalescing from a hip operation was my cousin Thera. She had married a Frenchman and lived near Paris, but she needed around-the-clock care that her husband was unable and her mother was glad to provide. We carried on a trilingual conversation: Sheila and I spoke English with each other, she French with Thera and Tante Pieta, they Dutch with me and among themselves.

Thera offered a comment on the Dutch that has stuck with me. As a people they were more *bemoeizuchtig* (eager to interfere) than the French, but also more willing to help neighbours and even strangers. The Dutch were not at bottom more accepting or under-standing of foreigners and their mores than other peoples, she thought, but they were significantly more willing to put up with them. Perhaps living in a small country, cheek by jowl with fifteen million other human beings, has taught the Dutch the necessity of getting along with people they may dislike.

Sheila and I returned to Amsterdam that evening through one of the thickest fogs in which I've ever had to drive. It had lifted by the morning, however, and we went our different ways from Schip-hol airport, she flying to Geneva in order to catch the train to Grenoble, I to Montreal and Toronto. The holiday was to be my last for well over a year.

The first draft of my dissertation was complete by August 1968, but I gave little thought to the LSR during the session. In May 1969 I got a note from Ramsay, who had been at Harvard that winter. He was puzzled to have heard nothing since August: 'It then seemed to me that a couple of weekends' work would have seen you through your thesis. What's up?' What had been up, I wrote to him, was that I had had other things to do. As well, it would take time to assess and incorporate the comments I had received from Forsey, Scott, Spry, and company. And, eight months having passed since I had stopped writing, there were things that I wanted to change.

'A couple of weekends' became three months, with time out for holidays, but by August Ramsay had approved all revisions. My defence took place on 21 October 1969. The dissertation was ac-cepted without changes, and I got the degree at the November convocation. I did not go in person to receive it: it was enough to know that I had got the doctorate and, with it, my promotion to the rank of assistant professor.

Some people loathe their doctoral theses by the time they finish, but I wasn't one of them. My research had been enjoyable and had introduced me to some fascinating and highly estimable people. It had also forced me to take seriously ideas with which I had so far felt no real affinity. Although I did not become a social democrat, I had come to see some merit in the socialist position. As well, I had learned a lot about Canada and, not least important, I had gained a heightened concern for freedom of expression in general and academic freedom in particular.

(This subject has continued to interest me. In the 1980s I served for six years on the Academic Freedom and Tenure Committee of the Canadian Association of University Teachers. At that time I began to expand my research on academic freedom into archives from Halifax to Victoria, and I am now writing the first history of academic freedom in Canada.)

On Ramsay's advice I took the typescript to R.I.K. (Rik) Davidson, a wiry, chain-smoking Scot who was an editor with the University of Toronto Press. He liked what I had written; in time he sent me two reader's reports. Both suggested changes. I filed these for future use, having already begun another book.

This project had its origins in that conference I had attended in Vancouver in 1966. Among its participants was Jack Granatstein, a junior member of the York University history department. He telephoned me soon upon my return to Toronto in 1968 and asked me out for lunch. Over a plate of excellent pasta – we were at La Scala on Bay Street – he asked me whether I would prepare a book of readings on the Depression for Copp Clark's Issues in Canadian History series, of which he had recently become general editor. I eagerly seized the opportunity he offered me. By August 1969, my dissertation finished, I was searching through the Public Archives in Ottawa for documents and articles dealing with the social and economic history of the 1930s.

Well before my first book, *The Dirty Thirties: Canadians in the Great Depression*, appeared in print, I decided it would carry the name *Michiel* Horn. At the time of the Learned Societies meetings at York I was completing a book review for the *Canadian Historical Review*. In student publications I had signed my articles and reviews 'Mike Horn,' but that seemed too informal for a scholarly journal. I could have used my initials, as I did when working for the Bank of Montreal, or 'Michael,' which then as now most people assumed to be the correct spelling of my name (they also like to add an 'e' to Horn). Upon reflection, however, and after asking the opinions of Rob Taylor and Ken Windsor, I signed myself 'Michiel.'

I wasn't consciously asserting my ethnic origin. It seemed time to use the name I had been given at birth. If it had the effect of drawing attention to my non-Canadian origin: no matter. I knew that I belonged here.

In 1970 I spent several weeks at the Public Archives. My main sources were the papers of R.B. Bennett, prime minister from 1930 to 1935, of his minister of trade and commerce, H.H. Stevens, of the Liberal leader, William Lyon Mackenzie King, and of the CCF. Having learned that the longtime CCF leader, M.J. Coldwell, was living in the city, I paid him a visit. He had been a school principal before running for political office in the early 1930s, but didn't regret the career change. His life in politics had brought many satisfactions, he said, and he had learned much that would have been hidden from him had he stayed in Regina.

He offered an example. After giving a speech in the drought area, he had been engaged in conversation by a farmer who said he was not a socialist but would vote for the CCF because the capitalist system had killed his daughter. The girl had become ill, but the hospital required a nominal payment in advance for the use of its operating theatre, and precious time was lost while the farmer borrowed the sum from his neighbours by dollars and quarters. Appendicitis became peritonitis, usually fatal in that age before antibiotics. The surgeon emerged from the operating room to tell the parents that their daughter had died.

The anecdote explained something of the passion that men like Coldwell and T.C. Douglas brought to the fight for public health care. Into the 1960s many Canadians faced illness unprotected by insurance. The misery that this caused can easily be appreciated by looking at the United States today. The steps taken to bring universal health insurance to Canada in the 1960s, first by the governments of Douglas and Woodrow Lloyd in Saskatchewan and later by the Pearson government in Ottawa, were of profound importance. Our present health insurance system is incomplete, and it is possible to think of publicly sponsored schemes that would have served Canada better. However, it is hard to think of any legislation in the last half-century that has done more for more people. Only the blindest reactionaries now oppose the principle, even if the practice may be in need of change.

My interpretation of the Depression was strongly shaped by the economist A.E. Safarian, whose book *The Canadian Economy in the Great Depression* stressed the domestic causes of the slump. Other books that influenced me included *The Great Crash*, by John Kenneth Galbraith, and Broadus Mitchell's *Depression Decade*, which I used to sketch the international background. What I have written about the Depression during the last twenty years, however, notably a booklet published by the Canadian Historical Association and a book intended for use by high school students, shows the influence of C.P. Kindleberger's *The World in Depression 1929–1939*, which appeared in 1973 and continues to be the standard by which other economic histories of the period must be judged.

Although I made no claim to originality, *The Dirty Thirties* did make a contribution in pulling together disparate sources testifying to the impact of the Depression on Canadian business, society, and politics, and to the different responses of Canadians to the crisis. The book has been out of print for well over a decade, but students still use it.

Helped by a Glendon sociology major (and still a friend), Elizabeth McRae, who acted as my editorial assistant in the summer of 1970, I completed a first draft in September. Jack Granatstein suggested revisions; these I made in the spring and summer of 1971. By the fall I was reading proofs. *The Dirty Thirties* appeared in February 1972, a fat book (of more than 700 pages) with a striking cover: two men and a woman, blank-faced and dishevelled.

What should have been a moment of triumph – my first book! – found me unhappy. I feared that the price ($9.95 for the hardcover, $5.95 for the paperback) was too high. Errors that I had caught while reading proofs had not been corrected, the most egregious being a description of Eugene Forsey as a Christian Scientist (Christian socialist had been intended). More annoying still was Copp Clark's failure to secure a key review. Diana Crosbie, a friend who worked for *Time Canada*, called me late in 1971: a review was planned of a book on the Depression, and mine would be reviewed with it if page proofs were available. I telephoned my editor at Copp Clark but nothing happened, and the review dealt only with *The Wretched of Canada*, a selection of letters to R.B. Bennett edited by my friends Michael Bliss and Linda Grayson. My chagrin found voice in a letter to Diana a few weeks later: 'Did you get a copy of the book? Copp Clark say they've sent one, but they've messed up so many things already that I'm reluctant to take their word for anything these days.'

The reviews were generally gratifying. Bob Fulford invited me to join him on his radio show; this and his subsequent review of the book in the pages of the *Toronto Star* and Ottawa *Citizen* no doubt increased my sales, even though he said that I had given too much weight to economics and not enough to literature. That I felt compelled to correct him in letters to the editor reflected greenness on my part rather than ingratitude. I should, of course, have ignored the criticism and thanked him for drawing attention to my book.

No review pleased me more than one that appeared in the *Victoria Daily Times*. R.H. Roy asserted that my book would be 'a "must" for anyone interested in Canada's social history.' It was delightful to be reminded of one of my former professors in this way.

Once *The Dirty Thirties* was finished, I began the process of turning my dissertation into a book. Upon Frank Underhill's death in late 1971 his personal papers had gone to the Public Archives (I was right to have surmised that he had many boxes of files). Eager to sift through them, I spent a lot of time in Ottawa in the summer of 1972.

I found much that expanded my knowledge of the LSR and its ideas, but by far and away the shiniest nugget that I unearthed was Underhill's first draft of the Regina Manifesto, adopted by the CCF at its 1933 founding convention. He later wrote: 'I cannot find a copy of the original draft anywhere, and my friends cannot supply me with one.'* In fact, he had simply misfiled it. Around 9:00 p.m. on 22 August I found it in a file marked Writings 1934, one year out. As I realized what I was holding in my hands, I began to shake with excitement. 'Then felt I like some watcher of the skies / When a new planet swims into his ken ...' Feeling too overwrought to

* Frank H. Underhill, *In Search of Canadian Liberalism* (Toronto 1960), xii.

continue working, I locked the box away and left to have a cele-bratory drink with Steven and our friend Jan Armstrong.

The next morning I had coffee with Craig Brown. I asked whether the document should be reproduced in the *Canadian Historical Review*, of which he was then editor. He liked the idea. A documentary article appeared in December 1973, consisting of an introduction and the draft manifesto, two related documents I had also found in Underhill's files, as well as a textually clean version of the manifesto in its final form.

While working in Ottawa I usually stayed with old friends from Victoria, Rob and Alayne (Waller) Hamilton, but the evening of 30 August 1972 found me at Steven's apartment in Sandy Hill. The British Columbia provincial election results would be broadcast on the CBC starting shortly after 11:00, and we wanted to listen. To our amazement we heard that Social Credit was going down to defeat. Faced not only by the NDP but by revived Conservative and Liberal parties, Wacky had met his Waterloo at last!

The NDP would be in power for rather more than three years. During that time, strange to tell, Father and Mother became sup-porters of the party. Until then they had voted Progressive Con-servative or Social Credit, but NDP legislation protecting agricul-tural land appealed to them because it prevented their neighbour, a Dutch-born dairy farmer, from turning his property into a sub-division. Self-interest proved stronger than political loyalty. Of course, European Conservatives are readier to sanction interfer-ence in the market than their North American counterparts.

In the summer of 1973 I completed my research for what became *The League for Social Reconstruction: Intellectual Origins of the Demo-cratic Left in Canada 1930–1942*. (A dull title, to be sure, but I aban-doned my first choice, 'Left in the Cold: The League for Social Reconstruction,' after Frank Scott and Rick Schultz, with whom and whose family Frank and I were dining at the time, objected to its 'flippancy.' Academics weren't ready for puns in titles, Rik Davidson said later. Peter Waite, in a review for *Choice*, would write that the title was just about the only dull line in the book.) I wrote a draft during my first sabbatical, in 1974–5, then put the manuscript aside for two years while serving as treasurer and

chairman of the Ontario Confederation of University Faculty Associations. Only after leaving office was I able to return to the book,
which finally appeared in 1980.

In 1969–70 I taught a survey of Canadian history in Atkinson College, York's extension faculty. Ordinarily this course would have
been taught by Harry Crowe, but having become dean of the college he no longer had time for it. His name rang a bell: it had
featured prominently in the pages of the *United Church Observer* in
1958 after he was fired from United College, Winnipeg, for reasons
allegedly linked to his religious scepticism. Harry did not seem
dangerous or controversial. Rather he was avuncular and eager to
help me, providing me with a teaching assistant when I complained that a tutorial group with sixty students made no sense.

   During the next few years I got to know him better, particularly
during the crisis that wracked York in the fall of 1972 (see below).
My favourite memory of him, however, is of his enunciation in
1974 of the 'Vyshinsky corollary' (Andrei Vyshinsky had been
prosecutor in Stalin's show trials of the 1930s): 'It is important not
only that justice be done but that it be seen to be done, especially
when it is *not* being done.' Made at the time that Harry received
the CAUT's Milner Award for services to the cause of academic
freedom, the quip has many applications.

   Teaching in the evening was tiring, but my students suffered
more than I did. Most of them had already worked a full day,
whereas I needed to do nothing more strenuous than look over my
lecture notes and sit in on a seminar on Quebec history and society.
In this course I was one of three instructors. The other two were
the head of the sociology department, Jean Burnet, and Ron Sabourin, a young sociologist recently arrived from the University of
Montreal, with whom I would later co-edit a book of readings in
Canadian social history. The result of having three teachers in the
classroom was predictable: we hogged the discussion while our
students listened.

   One example may suffice. A student presenting a report cited
the absence of 'the Protestant ethic' as the cause of Quebec's alleged
economic backwardness. Having that summer read the Swedish

economic historian Kurt Samuelsson's *Religion and Economic Action*, I challenged her: what *was* this ethic? She looked confused and began to stammer. Jean stepped in: surely I knew the seminal work of Max Weber? Surely she was aware of Samuelsson's damaging critique of that work? I countered. A spirited debate ensued that ended only when Jean and I agreed to disagree. No student contributed a single word; most looked politely bored.

(Afterwards I went to the library to read what sociological journals had made of Samuelsson's book when it appeared. The consensus was that it would force a reassessment of Weber's work. A decade later that reassessment was apparently incomplete, however: at least one senior sociologist still preferred Weber's theory, however flawed, to the historian's contrarian facts.)

That second year of teaching lacked the turmoil of Liber-Action, but an echo sounded in the Glendon Forum conference. 'The Year of the Barricade' was a celebration of student protest. I remember little of the weekend, but one session lingers in memory, a panel on radicalism and the university. Among the participants was C.B. Macpherson, a political theorist with impressive left-wing credentials. They were not enough to save him from attack, however. A graduate student from Simon Fraser University, which had recently witnessed a student strike as well as the resulting suspension of several professors, accused Macpherson of being, *au fond*, an apologist for capitalist and reactionary social forces. Escott, sitting next to me, whispered: 'Michiel, please pinch me. I want to make sure that I'm not dreaming.' He had a point: if Macpherson was a reactionary, who was left on the left?

Escott retired at the end of the year. Al Tucker succeeded him as principal while also remaining as the head of history, until I assumed the chair in 1973. If there was a committee to find a new principal it must have acted very discreetly, for I can't remember one. Perhaps there was none. In 1969 it was still possible for a president to appoint a dean without consulting an advisory body.

Among my more agreeable memories of the year, Frank Underhill's eightieth birthday dinner, held in Ottawa's Rideau Club on 26 November, ranks high. The evening was a tribute to a provocative historian and thinker; it was also a good party. The speakers were all historians: Ramsay, Hilda Neatby, Lester Pearson, and, of course, Frank himself, who spoke at length but entertainingly throughout.

Donald Creighton later described the dinner as 'very much a Liberal establishment affair.'* There was some truth in this but also a leaven of malice. As he had made clear in his address to the CHA the previous June, Creighton loathed Liberals, and among them he counted his former colleague Underhill. It needed only Pearson's participation for Creighton to brand the dinner as a Liberal love-fest. I belonged to no Liberal establishment, however, nor did Ken McNaught, and I did not get the feeling that we and others like us were there on sufferance. But perhaps I was insensitive.

In 1969 the history department had a new member. Ian Gentles was a historian of Stuart Britain whom I knew from Massey College days as an activist in the cause of disarmament. By the time he reached Glendon he had changed his allegiance to the campaign against abortion. Although I didn't much like abortion I didn't think it my business to tell women what they should or shouldn't do. I avoided the subject when Ian was around, however, and I enjoyed working with him in the department and in Wood Residence after he became dean of students in 1971. More than twenty years later he became our son Patrick's godfather.

Two more historians joined us before hiring suddenly stopped in 1972. Arthur Silver was our French Canada specialist until he moved to the University of Toronto in 1975. (We appointed Gail Cuthbert Brandt to replace him, but eventually she, too, left us.) Bill Irvine, tall and opinionated, arrived in 1971 to teach European and U.S. history. A graduate of UBC and Princeton, Bill became my best friend in the college. I also liked his wife, Marion Lane, also from British Columbia, who had as many opinions as her husband and by no means all the same.

Before Bill's arrival my closest friends on the faculty were Rick Schultz, Roger Gannon, and Orest Kruhlak. Back from England, and a don-in-residence as well as an instructor in political science, Rick was always good company, disputatious and amusing. Much

---

* Donald Creighton, 'The Ogdensburg Agreement and F.H. Underhill,' *The Passionate Observer: Selected Writings* (Toronto 1980), 143.

of our conversation was in the form of banter, occasionally with a bit of an edge. 'Historians are political scientists who are unable to conceptualize,' he once said. I rejoined that 'political scientists are historians who are unable to get the facts straight.' Both of us had a point, I think. Some years later he took a position at McGill, which was a real loss to Glendon College.

Also a don in Wood Residence, Roger was an English-born, Cambridge-educated linguist with a languid manner and a passion for jazz that he tried vainly to impart to me. There were at least two clubs downtown where jazz was a staple, and he invited me more than once. Usually I enjoyed the music, but it made no lasting impression on me. His great ambition was to own land, and after renting a farm in the Orangeville area for a couple of summers he bought his own, near Hanover in western Ontario. Thereafter, he spent as little time in Toronto as he could. But, unlike Rick and Orest, he still teaches at Glendon College.

Orest, an Alberta-born political scientist whose athletic prowess made him quarterback of the faculty flag football team, liked to describe himself as 'a Uke and proud of it.' He had a lively interest in the politics of ethnicity. I knew, of course, that early in the century Ukrainians had experienced serious discrimination in Canada. But that was in the past: their descendants, like Orest himself, were well established. Why, then, did he continue to nurture a Ukrainian-Canadian identity? Although I was more Dutch than he was Ukrainian, I saw no point in asserting for myself a Dutch-Canadian identity, whatever that might be, or in seeking out organizations for people of Dutch background.

Orest tried to explain to me his feelings and motives, without, I fear, a great deal of success. I didn't understand the facts of ethnic life in Canada, he said, but he didn't seem to hold this against me. After the federal government adopted a policy of multiculturalism in 1971 he went to Ottawa to join the department formed to administer it. I occasionally saw him in Ottawa during the next few years and listened sceptically to his accounts of the initiatives undertaken by his department.

Sheila returned to Canada in the early spring of 1970. Although we got together from time to time while I was in Ottawa, researching my book on the Depression, I had at last come to accept that there was no hope of a lasting attachment. (In 1971 she married Marinus Wins, a Dutch-born chartered accountant; she became a lawyer. We are still friends.)

Emotionally at loose ends in the summer of 1970, I fell in love with a recent sociology graduate of Glendon College. Kathleen and I shared interests in music, reading, and theatre, but as she was an evangelical Christian our outlooks differed markedly. Aware that I would need to show an interest in religion, I joined her in attending Little Trinity Church on King Street. Although I liked Tom Harpur's thoughtful sermons, they did not revive the faith I had lost a decade earlier. I reread C.S. Lewis, but there was no spark this time. I turned to other fare: Albert Schweitzer's *Quest of the Historical Jesus*, William James's *Varieties of Religious Experience*; George Moore's novel *The Brook Kerith*, with its stunning confrontation between Jesus and Paul. This was good stuff, but not designed to turn me into a Christian.

As great a difficulty was my lack of enthusiasm for parenthood. We quarrelled with growing frequency about our differences until Kathie called it quits in 1972. The end of the affair left me feeling unhappy and depressed. At the rational level it was impossible to fault her assessment that we were unsuited to each other, but I found this hard to accept emotionally. For the first and only time in my life I had trouble sleeping.

In this mood I rediscovered Albert Camus. In the mid-1960s I had read his novels; this time I read several of his philosophical works. *The Myth of Sisyphus* especially impressed me: a bleak vision but not without appeal. I decided I was willing to forego trying to answer the big religious questions. And for the second time in my life I resolved to avoid serious romantic involvement for a while. It would turn out to be eleven years.

The year 1970–1 I remember mainly for a course, a political crisis, a dinner, a conference, and a visit that Father and Mother made to central Canada.

The course was not mine but someone else's, for I was back in the classroom as a student. William Dray, then at Trent University, was teaching a course at Glendon College in the philosophy of history. I had scratched at this subject with Tony Emery back in 1963 and wanted to do more. Dray's presence offered too good an opportunity to miss, so I obtained permission to audit his course. I'm glad I did. He was an extremely conscientious teacher, endowed with a penetrating intellect and the ability to communicate his insights to students. When 1 later came across a letter in the Underhill papers describing Dray as perhaps the best student Underhill had ever taught, I was not surprised.

Not only was the professor great, but there were several excellent graduate students in the course who added significantly to its value. Among them I remember Michael Behiels, Douglas Francis, who became Underhill's biographer, and the late Howard Palmer. We read and discussed the works of a number of historians and philosophers of history, among them Collingwood, Hempel, Toynbee, and Dray himself, as well as a fascinating book by two legal scholars, H.L.A. Hart and A.M. Honoré, *Causation in the Law*. In the process I became persuaded that Hempel is wrong and that history can never be a science. As well, metahistorians like Toynbee are mistaken in positing an underlying pattern to the course of history. The craft of the historian is like detective work more than anything else. It is a lot of fun to try to puzzle out what happened, but it has no cosmic meaning.

The crisis was one that hit Quebec and Canada in October 1970. The kidnapping of the British diplomat James Cross and the Quebec minister of labour, Pierre Laporte (later found murdered), by members of the *Front de libération du Québec* (FLQ), was followed by Ottawa's use of the War Measures Act, ostensibly to prevent something like armed insurrection. These alarming events challenged my view of Canada as essentially a country that valued compromise. True: for some years bombs had been exploding in Montreal, the FLQ claiming responsibility, but I had never taken the group seriously. If Quebec's separatism ever came to pass, I thought, it would not be under the leadership of a terrorist and socially radical organization.

Not believing that the crisis warranted a response so extreme, I was critical of the Trudeau government's use of the War Measures

Act. That, as I recall, was also the view of most of my friends and colleagues. There were other voices, however. The poet Eli Mandel, whose wife, Ann, taught in the Glendon English department, brought his friend Irving Layton to the Senior Common Room one day. Layton offered a full-throated defence of Trudeau's invocation of the act, comparing those who questioned it with German liberal intellectuals who failed in the late 1920s and early 1930s to recognize the danger represented by the Nazis. This struck me as far-fetched: the FLQ was not a political party with substantial support but a small gang of terrorists out of touch, as I saw it, with most of Quebec opinion.

When, later in the decade, I worked with Frank Scott on his last book, *A New Endeavour*, I found to my surprise that he, too, had supported the use of the War Measures Act. I challenged him. 'Oh, so you're another one of those Toronto intellectuals who, from the safety of Ontario, knew exactly how to assess the extent of the troubles here in Montreal,' he said with some asperity. 'I agree with you,' his wife, Marian, said to me, smiling. Evidently she and Frank had had this argument more than once. 'Well, you're both wrong,' he said with finality.

We talked about the events of October 1970 several times in the years that followed, and in time I gained some sympathy for his point of view. The events were bound to look scarier to those who lived in Montreal than to people like myself, and there was something to his assessment that the use of the act had ended the FLQ's terrorist activity. More important, however, was that the great majority of Quebeckers felt revulsion for terrorism, a feeling intensified by Laporte's murder. Separatism is very much alive in Quebec, but the FLQ is now no more than a dark memory.

The dinner marked the seventieth birthday of Graham Spry. It took place in the West Block on Parliament Hill in February 1971 and drew even more people than the Underhill dinner in 1969. Spry had been a founder of the Canadian Radio League, which had agitated for public broadcasting in the 1930s, and he was still active in that field. Many who attended were veterans of radio and television, people I did not know. I was happy to encounter Escott, who introduced me to several of the other guests. One of them I had met before, at a Canadian Political Science Association reception in Ottawa in 1967, but I was not surprised that Mike Pearson did not remember me.

The next day I went to an 'at home' at the Spry home in Rockcliffe Park. Here I met Graham's wife, Irene, for the first time. She was a gracious woman who as a young economist at the University of Toronto had belonged to the LSR and contributed to its book, *Social Planning for Canada*. I enjoyed talking with her and decided that I liked this self-effacing scholar better than her somewhat self-important husband.

The conference took place in St John's, Newfoundland, in the early summer of 1971. The program committee of the Canadian Historical Association having accepted my proposal to present a paper on the LSR, it was in a mood of high anticipation that I took a flight east. The event also offered a welcome opportunity to get together with David Alexander, who had joined Memorial University's history department some years earlier. Deeply immersed in research into the economic history of Newfoundland, he was critical of the tendency of the island's politicians to claim that it would sustain a typical North American standard of living if only its people could find the key to prosperity. Time and again this led the government into ill-advised investment projects. The course of wisdom was to make do with less. This, David thought, had wider implications for Canada.

My session was in the late afternoon, and I got carried away by the desire to keep my audience awake. I realized that my paper had not hit altogether the right note when the commentator, Carl Berger, prefaced his remarks by saying that he was not a drama critic. 'You gave them a good show,' Irv consoled me, and Al Tucker said he didn't think that I had done my reputation lasting damage. Nevertheless, for years afterwards I kept hearing a throw-away line I'd used, to the effect that I would permit people to read my dissertation, on file in the U of T Library, for a small fee of $100 or so. I meant it as a joke, but historians can be quite as literal-minded as anybody else.

I was not the only one to ham it up at the meetings. At one session, Newfoundland's Premier Joey Smallwood and J.W. Pickersgill, a former federal cabinet minister, crowed about their roles in the entry of the colony into Canada in 1949. Both played the crowd unashamedly, but Pickersgill was particularly animated, mugging, tossing off one-liners, flapping his forearms in a manner suggestive of a hyperactive penguin.

I enjoyed their act but was puzzled by their evident conviction that, by itself alone, the physical expansion of Canada justified the event. Do countries become better as they grow bigger? Was it the Netherlander in me who thought this puerile? Another question occurred to me: had it made economic sense, for Newfoundland *or* for the rest of Canada, to incorporate the colony? From being a ward of Great Britain it had become one of Canada, without apparent prospect of change.

Father and Mother arrived in Toronto from the West Coast the same day I returned from the east. It was their first visit to central Canada, and they planned also to see Steven in Ottawa, and Peter, his wife, Raquel, and their infant son, Daniel, in Montreal. I took them to the usual tourist spots in and around Toronto, and to Stratford for a performance of *Macbeth*. The production was less than gripping to people who didn't know the play, and I couldn't blame Father for nodding off. He enjoyed far more George C. Scott's star turn in *Patton*.

On the notice-board in my study I have a memento of their visit, a photo taken at the guard-rail above Niagara Falls. Mother has a combative mien and seems to be lecturing Father; he looks down indulgently. It is among my favourite pictures of them.

Refreshed from a late-summer holiday spent in Holland, Belgium, Germany, and Austria with Jack and Annètje Huibregtse, the woman who would in 1972 become his second wife, I returned to Toronto soon after Labour Day in 1971. In the session that followed, for the first time in three years I did all my teaching in Glendon College. I took two tutorial groups in Irv's introductory survey and taught my third- and fourth-year courses. Never have I had a more rewarding group of upper-year students. The best were Gary

O'Brien, who went on to take a Ph.D. in political science, and Roger Riendeau, who took a Ph.D. in history, but several others were also excellent. Of twenty-six students in my third-year course one earned an A+ while seven got As, and of eight students in my fourth-year seminar no fewer than three received an A! Normally no more than 10 per cent of my students merit a grade of A or higher.

In addition to my regular courses I lectured in a course in Canadian studies intended for students in the new unilingual stream. It had become plain that an insufficient number of students were willing to take two years of French as a second language (FSL). Into 1970 we maintained our enrolment by admitting first-year students for whom there was no room in the Faculty of Arts. In 1970–1, however, this overflow ended. Our low enrolment meant not only that the college earned less revenue than we were supposed to, but also that York University lost entitlement to physical plant which it needed if students on the main campus were to be adequately accommodated. Under the formula being administered by the Committee on University Affairs, the body advising the government, the classroom space at the Glendon campus was deemed to be available to York University as a whole, even though the two campuses were twenty kilometres apart!

Few were sad to see the arts overflow end. From the outset it had been an unsatisfactory makeshift arrangement. Most of the students were with us for the first year only, our limited offerings and the French requirement both undermining any wish to stay. Not that the latter was notably demanding, but by 1970 second-language requirements had almost everywhere fallen victim to student dislike of required courses in general and language courses in particular. We were rowing against the stream.

In the course of 1970–1 the Glendon faculty council reluctantly accepted the need for a unilingual stream if our enrolment were to grow, and the first students in this stream entered in the fall of 1971. In order to ensure that they had at least an appreciation of the French-Canadian presence in Canada, the faculty council mandated a course that would focus on the history and society of Quebec. Ron Sabourin was course director, but I gave half the lectures in the first term. Fortunately, I was not responsible for any of the grading.

The course was a mistake. Many regarded it as a punishment for not taking French: not an ideal frame of mind in which to acquire an understanding of Quebec. Offering the course was also a problem in that no department wanted to take continuing responsibility for it. Within two years students were allowed to satisfy the 'unilingual requirement' by taking one of a range of courses, and by writing their essays about French Canada. The perceived element of punishment remained.

Observers soon spotted a tendency of students in the bilingual stream to take an introductory course in French and then switch into the unilingual stream. Most did so because they thought French too hard, a few because they feared their grades in that subject would drag down their grade point averages. Either way, their strategy seemed to make a mockery of the bilingual program.

Had this program always been too ambitious? I remember Edgar McInnis, during a reception in late 1970, rasping to me in his pipe-tobacco voice: 'I *told* Escott that Toronto is the wrong place to teach college students French. If they want to learn French they should go where it's spoken, to Quebec or to France. But he wouldn't listen.' Edgar was commenting on the discussions aimed at introducing a unilingual stream. His remark had more general application, however. Few English-Canadian students in the bilingual stream who were not bilingual when they entered the college became so before graduating, and the exceptions had usually spent a year at a French-language university.

(This continues to be true. With a growing pool of students willing to take French, the unilingual stream was cancelled in 1986. All the same, not a few of my students seem to have trouble understanding even simple sentences in French, and few of them speak it with ease. Still, over time not a few *francophone* students have significantly improved their *English* while at Glendon College: a modest accomplishment, perhaps, but not unworthy.)

In April 1972 I became chairman of the York University Faculty Association (YUFA). I had served on the executive as Glendon's representative since 1969, but when someone asked me to run for the top job I declined. Ramsay telephoned, asking me to reconsider. I wasn't tenured yet, I objected, and I needed time to turn my dissertation into a book. *The Dirty Thirties* should be enough for tenure, he said (he was right: I got it in 1973), and I need not worry that my lack of tenure would make me vulnerable. York's tenure document, in force since the fall of 1968, would protect me from arbitrary dismissal even if I were to offend important people.

Still I demurred. Then I got a call from Sidney Eisen, head of history in the Faculty of Arts. Promising to arrange to have money transferred to Glendon so that Al Tucker could replace me in one course, he urged me to become a candidate.

Feeling flattered, I allowed my name to stand. ('I knew I could rely on your Protestant sense of duty,' Ramsay said to me many years later.) The job was not exactly in demand, since I won by acclamation. Within weeks of assuming office, I was at McMaster University for a meeting of the provincial council of the Ontario Confederation of University Faculty Associations (OCUFA). The mood was gloomy. In 1971 the minister of colleges and universities had announced that the government's objective would be to get 'more scholar for the dollar.' More recently an Ontario royal commission on postsecondary education had issued a draft report which assumed that faculty-student ratios would increase. This raised the spectre of redundancies.

The prospect seemed sufficiently menacing that I prepared a short paper on 'redundancy and transferability of university professors' for discussion at the annual meeting of the national council of the Canadian Association of University Teachers (CAUT). The mood at this gathering, held in Vancouver in May, was also sombre, for the constraints that faced Ontario universities existed elsewhere in Canada as well. All the same, the worst fears of that time have not been realized – at least not yet. Since 1971 universities have responded to cutbacks by increasing class sizes and raising tuition fees, holding the line on salaries so that these have fallen in constant dollars, and relying increasingly on part-time teachers, less costly than full-timers and more easily released. In Ontario, however, we seem in 1996 to have reached the end of that road, and dismissals of full-time faculty are almost certainly at hand.

There were other problems as well. I listened with interest to Archie Malloch, a professor of English at McGill who headed CAUT's Academic Freedom and Tenure Committee. He reported that attacks on academic freedom now came from colleagues, rather than from administrators or governing boards as in the past. Right-wing faculty members harassed those on the left and vice versa: an unedifying spectacle!

While I was in Vancouver I looked up Leonard Marsh, as I would do often in the last decade of his life (he died in 1982). The books he wrote as director of social research at McGill are essential to an understanding of Canada in the 1930s; his 1943 *Report on Social Security for Canada* is a landmark in the history of welfare policy. If his contributions have not received the recognition that they deserve, this owed something to his personality. His enthusiasm seemed boyish and a bit naïve. Moreover, he utterly lacked that capacity for self-promotion which few who aspire to fame can do without. I found it difficult to share his *élan*: he was an optimist about the human future, whereas I tend to pessimism. But his eagerness was often infectious, and his ability and decency were unmistakable. I'm glad that I successfully nominated him for a York University LL.D. degree *honoris causa* in 1977.

After the CAUT meeting I visited Mother and Father in the retirement cottage they had built in 1970 on Kilmalu Road, Mill Bay, at the northern end of the Malahat highway forty kilometres from Victoria. The living-room focused on the large fireplace that was Father's hallmark; I loved the view across the valley to the range that forms the spine of Vancouver Island. 'We zitten hier voor een dubbeltje op de eerste rang' (We're paying a dime to sit in the best seats), Father said. But he admitted that, with just one bedroom, the house was too small. The next year I paid for an addition that did double duty as his studio and a guest bedroom. Some years before his death in 1990 he noted with a hint of surprise that he had now lived longer in this house than in any other in his life.

The YUFA job involved very little work until September. I had ample time for a month-long holiday in the Low Countries, France, and Spain, and for several weeks of research in Ottawa. Soon after classes resumed, however, life became very hectic. In September 1972, York registered fewer students than the year before, yet more than a hundred faculty members had been added to cope with an anticipated enrolment increase that did not materialize. In those days university income was still directly linked to enrolment. How large would the deficit be? And how would the university cope with it?

At a senate meeting in late September we heard that the shortfall would be between three and four million dollars. This left everybody in a state of suspense that was ended when, at a special meeting on 25 October, President David Slater told the senate that the board of governors had passed a resolution instructing the university to cut the academic budget for 1973–4 by $2.7 million, or approximately 10 per cent. I did a quick calculation. My own salary was $14,500; with benefits I cost York about $16,000 annually. It would take more than 150 salaries like mine to reach the target!

Slater expressed unhappiness with the board resolution, saying he believed that York University faced 'serious' problems, but that their 'precise size and nature ... and the remedial courses open to York, remain to be determined.' This confused senators, me included: was the cut to be $2.7 million or some other amount? Upon being pressed, he 'stated that the specific figure ... was not his, and that others must take the responsibility for it, although the figure is not outlandish, since it is [possible], by a combination of pessimistic approaches, to approximate a figure of $2.7 million as a potential deficit for 1973–74.'*

Slater assigned responsibility for setting the specific amount of the budget cut to the board of governors, and he seemed to imply that the board had taken the initiative in the matter. It was difficult to be sure that he actually meant to say this: even at the best of times he tended to ramble when he spoke, and this was not the best of times. A member of the board, Bertrand Gerstein, must have believed that the president was trying to evade his respon-

* York University, Senate, Minutes of special meeting, 25 October 1972.

sibility, however. I remember him as saying that 'the board knew its place' and would not have passed such a resolution without a recommendation from the president. The minutes do not contain this phrase, but they do quote or paraphrase Gerstein as saying that the board had passed the resolution on the basis of estimates 'presumably' developed by the president and his advisers.

Slater, in turn, insisted that he had presented no budget for 1973–4 to the executive and finance committees of the board, 'and answered Mr. Gerstein's question as to where the figure of $2.7 million had come from with the reply that other persons than himself had generated the figure on the basis of a series of pessimistic hypotheses as to 1973–74 enrolment.' If he identified these persons I don't remember their names, and the senate minutes do not mention any.

Gerstein said more emphatically than before that the board's action had been taken on the basis of a budget presented by the president. This, I think, fatally weakened Slater's authority. Some senate members thought that he had tried to deceive them. Others, prominent among them Harry Crowe and Ramsay, deplored the confusion that seemed to reign and questioned the budgetary information on which the board had based its resolution, whether supplied by Slater or not. Clearly unhappy, senators voted by a two-to-one majority not to accept the board's communication. As if to emphasize the gap that had opened between us and the board, we then unanimously passed a motion, originally introduced by Crowe and a member of the Atkinson College faculty, Pinayur Rajagopal, 'that no notice of non-renewal of a probationary or tenured appointment shall be given to a faculty member on grounds of budget necessity until procedures for non-renewal or termination ... have been adopted by Senate.'

The day after this special meeting, the senate met for its regular monthly meeting and created an ad hoc Joint Committee on Alternatives (JCOA), consisting of the president, the vice-presidents, and the deans, as well as the chairman of senate (who presided over the committee's meetings), three other professors, and one lonely student. This committee was charged with exploring ways out of the crisis.

As chairman of YUFA I was named in the motion establishing the committee, but I declined to join. The YUFA executive believed that, as many of our members would have to walk the plank if a large budget cut were made, we should be free to oppose the JCOA should it counsel such a cut. My membership on the committee might reduce our freedom to do so. We decided that we should observe JCOA meetings, however, and most of the time I was the observer. Usually, too, I was permitted to speak whenever I wanted.

The next two months were the busiest of my life. I worked twelve-hour days and seven-day weeks, only once in a while taking time out to see a movie, schmooze with colleagues, or go to Guelph, where Jack had taken a university teaching position in 1972.

(One occasion for getting together with friends was the federal election on 30 October. I watched it at Irv and Rosie Abella's place, Bill Irvine and Marion Lane also being there. The Liberals and Conservatives were neck and neck all evening, allowing scope for much instant political analysis. I find myself thinking sometimes that Canada might have been better served by a Tory minority government led by Robert Stanfield than by Trudeau's minority administration from 1972 to 1974. The Liberals proved too ready to kowtow to Conservative supporters in reducing taxes while they retained NDP support in the House of Commons by not cutting program spending to match the tax cuts. This sowed the seeds of major fiscal and budgetary problems whose bitter fruits we are now harvesting. The Conservatives might have been more consistent in their policies.)

Most of the time I was hard at work. It was a good thing I was single! I taught two courses and coordinated the newly founded program in Canadian studies, and I was also still a don. The JCOA met once a week, as for a time did the YUFA executive. There were many meetings of the senate, faculty council, and YUFA. As well, I served on the YUFA grievance committee, edited the *YUFA Newsletter*, and wrote much of it.

Finally, there was CAUT's committee on student relations. I joined Alwyn Berland, a former executive secretary of CAUT, and Don Theall, a professor of English at McGill, in trying to frame a policy on student rights. Two meetings failed to produce a coherent report, mainly, I think, because the older men were unwilling to concede something to students that I was prepared to, i.e., representation on tenure committees. But our failure mattered little. The committee owed its existence to student unrest in the late 1960s, and by the time we were trying to draft our report that unrest was very largely a thing of the past.

This was certainly the case at York, where faculty and not student unrest was evident that autumn. Several schemes to cut costs and increase income were in the air; most of the cost-cutting schemes threatened teaching jobs. From the beginning the budgetary drama had an important subplot, moreover. Many of the faculty blamed David Slater and his alleged administrative inexperience for York's troubles and for the resultant threat to jobs.

As a relative newcomer to York, Slater lacked the allies or the administrative savvy he needed to carry into effect a policy that was bound to hurt many people. On other grounds, too, he was ill-positioned to meet the storm that faced him and the university. He was affable and open, and most people seemed to like him personally, but few had forgotten that his choice as President Murray Ross's successor in 1970 had been an unhappy compromise. Ross says in his memoirs, *The Way Must Be Tried*, that many faculty members wanted the dean of arts, Jack Saywell, while the board wished to appoint the dean of administrative studies, Jim Gillies. Gillies had some faculty in his corner, but fewer than Saywell: the result was a messy conflict resulting in deadlock.

Either would have been a good president, Ross believes, but neither got the job. Slater, the man who did, not only lacked obvious qualification for the job, but was in the unenviable spot of having been the first choice of very few. An economist at Queen's, he was dean of graduate studies there at the time of his appointment to the York presidency. Two years after assuming his duties with us he still seemed to be on probation.

Chief among his opponents was Harry Crowe. He liked Slater personally, I believe. (Two decades later, in the course of my research into the history of academic freedom, I found that Slater had been part of a small group at Queen's who advised Harry after he got into hot water at United College, Winnipeg, in 1958.) But Harry believed that Slater wasn't up to the job of president. 'At Queen's he was a paper dean,' Harry would snort, alluding to the fact that as dean of graduate studies Slater's administrative and budgetary responsibilities had not been great. Some thought that Harry saw himself as a successor to David. This is possible, for he had been a candidate for the presidency in 1970 (and would be a candidate again). More important, however, was that he saw Slater as a threat to his faculty and to York University.

Harry was no negligible enemy. After the senate meetings of late October 1972 he was determined to keep Slater from resuming full presidential power, and he worked assiduously to that end. He was a resourceful conspirator, but his efforts and intentions were hardly a secret. Slater knew what was happening and must have resented it.

On the morning of Sunday, 10 December, at a meeting held in the Glendon College Principal's Dining Room, Slater informed the JCOA that he wanted to recover the powers that had effectively been in abeyance since late October, but that he needed the support of all the vice-presidents and deans. He was satisfied that all but one would be on his side, he continued, then turned to Harry and gave him a choice: state your loyalty or resign. Harry got up and left the room without saying a word, whereupon the chairman of the committee, Howard Robertson of Glendon's French department, announced a brief adjournment. (As this part of the meeting was held in camera I was not an eyewitness, but several committee members described the confrontation to me before the meeting continued later that morning.)

Slater's action did not surprise me. Two days earlier, on Friday afternoon, he had invited four senior academics and myself to a meeting in the Glendon Hall office he occasionally used, and asked us whether he would have faculty support if he sought to regain his presidential power. Our response was cautiously guarded, but I had the sense that what we said mattered little. He already knew what he wanted to do.

(While I was writing this memoir I heard from one of Slater's friends, the economist David McQueen, chairman of the Glendon economics department at the time and later principal, that on the same Friday he and Howard Robertson, who was chairman of the senate as well as the JCOA, had informed Slater that he no longer enjoyed the confidence of the deans. They did so on the instigation of Harry Crowe and Jack Saywell, but only after they were satisfied that the other deans were in accord. However, Slater either didn't believe David and Howard or thought that, if his main opponent vacated the battlefield, the other deans would come to terms.)

Harry returned to the JCOA meeting upon its resumption; Slater did not. The committee, no longer in camera, carried on without him all day and well into the evening. I have forgotten most of what was said, but I do remember that by the late morning the Glendon College Junior Common Room was crowded with Atkinson College faculty. Having expected trouble, Harry and his department heads had put into place that highly efficient communications system known as a telephone tree. Upon leaving the meeting, Harry called his associate dean, Henry Best. Henry phoned two prearranged people, each of them phoned two more, and so on, until within fifteen or twenty minutes virtually all faculty members knew that their dean was in peril. Most of them immediately rallied to his support.

The ultimatum failed to bring Harry to heel. Slater should probably have anticipated this: after all, he had been able to observe Harry when, fourteen years earlier, he was defying the principal and board of United College. My own observations of Harry in action, in the fall of 1972 and later, and my research into the United College affair of 1958, have convinced me that it was all but impossible to intimidate him. Having won the Military Cross in battle against the German army, he was not likely to be scared of Slater or any other university president in Canada.

Not only did Slater's ultimatum fail in its purpose, it probably led members of the JCOA to conclude, if they had not already done so, that he should *not* be permitted to resume his power. At their last meeting, held in the board-senate chamber at Glendon College on the evening of Monday, 11 December, they passed a motion (in Slater's absence) recommending to the board of governors that he be maintained as York's titular head, but that effective power be exercised by a troika of senior administrators. It remained to be seen whether he would swallow this humiliation or, no less important, whether the board would agree to this highly unusual arrangement.

The Christmas break was at hand, and the university went into suspended animation until the second week of January. I spent Christmas in Mill Bay with Father and Mother, savouring the peace and quiet of rural Vancouver Island as I marked the essays of my students. New Year's Eve I celebrated with Bill Irvine and Marion Lane at the house of Bill's parents in West Vancouver.

The next day I took the bus to Alta Lake, where Joe was working on the lifts at Whistler Mountain. The job gave him lots of time to ski, and he didn't mind the pay, much lower than he used to earn as a driller and blaster. His wife, Carole, was still working in Victoria but joined him in Alta Lake before the next time I visited Whistler, at the start of 1974.

Today Whistler is a luxurious resort; two decades ago it was very much a no-frills place. People braved the hazardous road from Vancouver for the skiing, not the *après*-ski; most got on the slopes early in the morning and stayed on them all day. And what slopes they were: a wide variety from easy to impossibly hard, a vertical drop of well over a kilometre, and a run into the valley that was ten kilometres long! The weather was cold and clear; I had a marvellously relaxing time. With considerable reluctance I returned to York University and its troubles.

Soon after the winter term began it became known that Slater had refused to accept the JCOA proposal. The board of governors then induced him to resign and appointed the historian Dick Storr as acting president. Dick resigned a day later, however, reportedly on medical grounds. (I have a rarity in my files: a letter signed by him as acting president.) The presidency passed to the philosopher John Yolton, while administrative control passed into the hands of Bill Farr, to this point the secretary of the senate and the board, who now became vice-president and Lord High Everything Else. Highly competent, with a puckish sense of humour and an ability to cut swiftly through bafflegab, Bill was an inspired choice.

One question remains with me to this day: did Slater get a raw deal? At the time I thought not. I felt no animosity towards him – he was always kind and courteous to me – but on 25 October 1972 I had lost confidence in his ability to manage the university. The scheme proposed by the JCOA in December suited me: provided Slater did not have the power to do anything impulsive, I did not object to his remaining president. But I shed no tears when he resigned.

In time I came to adopt a somewhat different perspective. Marion Boyd, who had been Slater's secretary until his resignation, later became secretary of YUFA (in the early 1990s she was to become attorney general of Ontario). At some point in the later 1970s we had a conversation about the events of 1972. She believed that her boss had been made a scapegoat. As I remember her remarks, she conceded that he had made mistakes but argued that he would have been able to overcome them had he received the support he was entitled to. She assigned special blame to Harry Crowe, who, she said, had done his best to bring down a president he had never accepted. Slater's biggest mistake, she concluded, was that he had been too nice.

Working closely with Slater during his presidency, Marion was no doubt biased, but in 1972 my bias against him was probably no less strong than hers in his favour. It does seem to me now that he was not solely or even primarily to blame for the mess in which the university, almost alone among the universities in Ontario, found itself that fall. Deans and department heads had been keen to hire in order to cope with the anticipated jump in enrolment in 1972–3, and the board of governors had not intervened. By the time it became known that enrolment would decline instead, it was too late to undo the hiring.

Whether Slater recommended to the board that the academic budget be cut by $2.7 million cannot be known until the board's minutes are opened to view. It is possible that the board turned a general assessment of the 1973–4 budget into a specific resolution. Tellingly, for it demonstrates the low trust that Slater inspired, most senators seemed to believe Gerstein rather than Slater when the two men offered their conflicting accounts of what had happened at the board meeting. Perhaps the reason Slater was not believed is that the senate, or at least the professors in it, wanted to blame *someone* for the budgetary crisis, and he was the most likely candidate. Perhaps, however, David McQueen is right in surmising that his friend's failure to express himself clearly at that fateful meeting caused people to think of him as evasive and untrustworthy.

Under more favourable circumstances, Slater might have been a very serviceable president. The times were unfavourable, however. Moreover, he was not well served by his vice-president (finance), who never did seem to get the numbers straight, by his vice-president (academic), who seemed a bit too eager to shrink the academic staff, and by the chairman of the senate's Academic Policy and Planning Committee, who seemed to be of a like mind. It was partly due to their advice that Slater came to be seen by many faculty members as deceitful, inept, or both. These judgments were unfair. His handling of the crisis was open to criticism, but it was wrong to question his decency and good faith. And he was a very able economist: upon leaving York he had a distinguished career in Ottawa, first in the Department of Finance and later as chairman of the Economic Council of Canada.

Slater's replacement was effective because he never forgot that he was acting president only. By way of illustration: in late May, George Eaton, head of our negotiating committee, and I were asked to meet John Yolton and the board chairman, Robert MacIntosh, in order to conclude salary negotiations. When we entered MacIntosh's office, we saw not only him and Yolton but also Hal Jackman, a prominent financier and the most powerful member of the board. Was this fair? George and I decided to risk it.

It turned out to be two on two after all, with Yolton acting as umpire. The board was raising its offer from 4 to 4.25 per cent, MacIntosh said, and would allow YUFA to divide up the money. (The board had tried to insist that a portion of the money be awarded differentially on the basis of 'merit.' Although not against merit in principle, YUFA held that rewarding it was inappropriate in the absence of an adequate across-the-board increase.) He admitted that the offer was low, but even this would add to the cumulative deficit. That might be true, we replied, but the offer didn't cover the rate of inflation, then around 7 per cent annually, and our members might reject it. Neither MacIntosh nor Jackman seemed worried. 'They can take it or leave it,' one of them said: 'If they leave it we can use it to reduce the debt.' Yolton turned to us: 'He's got a point there.' And so he did.

At the ratification meeting some members griped about the niggardliness of the offer – two decades would pass before we got a lower settlement – while others criticized us for insisting on a raise at all. How many jobs would it cost in the long run? I got impatient: the university would not be a tranquil place to work in for many years to come, I said, because governments were bound to restrain their spending further. Those who couldn't stand the heat should get out.

The board's offer passed narrowly: had the executive and negotiating committees not voted in favour, it would have been defeated. Would the board have frozen our salaries in that case? Would we have called for a strike vote? Would it have passed? Would we have struck? Would that have accomplished anything? I'll never know. I do know that I gratefully passed the presidency on to my successor, the mathematician Denis Russell.

I also know, although this did not become fully clear for some time, that we did manage to save jobs but at the expense of salary increases. It had become clear that early estimates of the 1972–3 and 1973–4 deficits had been too high, so that talk of a budget cut of $2.7 million had been premature. In the end, no academic positions were lost at all, other than that of the vice-president for academic affairs, Walter Tarnopolsky. He resigned in the late fall and was not replaced for several years (the loss in administrative efficiency was not conspicuous). It took longer to eliminate the debt; the cost was borne by everybody who worked at the university. In my view the price was not too high to pay.

Time-consuming and stressful as the YUFA presidency was, and even though hardly anybody thanked me for my work, the job had compensations. I learned a lot about York, enjoyed working with the other members of the executive, and got to know many people I otherwise might not have met, or not for years. One of them was Bill Farr, who for many years served York with distinction. Another was Pinayur Rajagopal, 'Raja' as he called himself and as almost everybody else called him. An unassuming professor of computer science and mathematics in Atkinson College, he was the senate's best budgetary critic that fall and winter of 1972–3, and for me a source of unfailingly good advice. A couple of years later I served with him on the senate committee on the budget, of which he was chair. I still treasure the line he used whenever someone said that such-or-such information might be useful to have: 'Don't tell me what you want to know, tell me why you want to know it.'

Yet another was the psychologist Esther Greenglass, to whom I owe a valuable insight into the conformity imposed in a liberal profession. We had been invited to have a drink with her brother, a lawyer, and his wife. As we parked in front of their house, I counted three Cadillac sedans. There were no other makes or models. This was no coincidence, Esther said: her brother drove the same sort of car. Something cheaper would be a tacit admission of failure; something more costly would be seen as showing off. Academics, happily, are subject to no such social discipline.

For reasons that are unclear to me now, I didn't renew my symphony subscription after I returned to the city in 1968, and I went to the opera no more often than before. I dimly recall COC performances of *Don Giovanni*, *Madama Butterfly* and *La Traviata*, but none was as memorable as two works I saw abroad in mid-decade, Verdi's *Macbeth* in Florence in 1975, with Riccardo Muti conducting and Gwyneth Jones as a convincingly evil Lady Macbeth, and a sparkling *Così fan tutte* at the Glyndebourne Festival in 1976. It was also in 1976, in part because of a shine I had taken to an attractive mezzo-soprano, that I began to attend COC productions regularly. By that time, I was once again a Toronto Symphony subscriber.

An increased interest in popular music in the late 1960s may be inferred from my seeing the rock musical *Hair* not once but twice, in London during the 1968 Christmas break and in Toronto a year later. This exuberant work, a few of whose songs I can still sing or hum, captured the youth culture of the time. Yet *Hair* was too much tied to the period to survive it, whereas *Joseph and the Amazing Technicolor Dreamcoat*, which is of the same vintage and has a musical score no less trivial, is still performed. Of course, Andrew Lloyd Webber did have the better book!

Massey Hall saw me only rarely between 1968 and 1975, but I do recall a concert conducted late in 1971 by Karel Ancerl, the Czech expatriate who was for five years the music director of the TSO. (When I visited Prague in 1978 I found that more than one Czech had heard of Toronto because of Ancerl's work with the TSO.) The Dutch soprano Elly Ameling sang Mozart arias and songs by Ravel; after the intermission the orchestra gave a performance of Bartók's *Concerto for Orchestra* so stirring that upon its conclusion I rose to my feet, shouting my approval. My neighbours looked at me with astonishment, even dismay. I had forgotten: this was Toronto and uninhibited displays of approval were frowned upon. That has changed since.

An increased interest in the theatre owed something to the existence of the Glendon College dramatic arts program. Its guiding light was Michael Gregory, a professor of linguistics who knew how to get the most from his student actors. His chief assistant was Beth (Boyle) Hopkins, an instructor in the English department who had worked with me at the Department of Education in the early 1960s. They collaborated on spirited productions of *Hamlet, Oedipus Rex, The Country Wife*, and *A Midsummer Night's Dream*.

Beginning in the 1970s, too, I saw more professional theatre than at any time since I left Germany in 1962. Among the more memorable productions were Peter Brook's electrifying *Midsummer Night's Dream* (with Ben Kingsley, later an Academy Award winner, as Demetrius), *The School for Scandal*, with Helen Hayes, and Tom Stoppard's witty *Rosencrantz and Guildenstern Are Dead*. After Jack and Annètje settled in Guelph in 1972, the three of us regularly attended the Stratford and Shaw festivals. Productions I recall with great pleasure include *She Stoops to Conquer*, with Pat Galloway and Alan Scarfe, *The Importance of Being Earnest*, starring William Hutt as a matchless Lady Bracknell, and *The Collected Works of Billy the Kid*, written by my Glendon colleague Michael Ondaatje. In the audience the day we saw it was Dustin Hoffman. This led us to speculate that he might star in an American production of the play, but Michael later told me that such speculation was groundless.

At Niagara-on-the-Lake, Alan Scarfe was a splendid Richard Dudgeon in *The Devil's Disciple*. Like Brian Bedford and Maggie Smith, who both came to the Stratford Festival in the mid-1970s, Scarfe added lustre to any play in which he appeared.

Perhaps my top theatrical memory of all time dates from the 1977 Shaw Festival. As John Tanner in the unabridged *Man and Superman*, Ian Richardson gave a performance for which superlatives are inadequate. 'One of the most absorbing plays I've ever witnessed,' I jotted on my program: 'More like an opera than a play. Richardson is fantastic with words!' His work in Act III, the 'Don Juan in Hell' scene, may be the greatest piece of acting I have ever witnessed.

I saw a good many movies, most of them on television. Few do I remember with any clarity; among the exceptions are *The Wild Bunch*, a blood-drenched adventure film that a saw the evening before my doctoral defence, *M*A*S*H*, which I liked for its wise-cracking nihilism, and *Lovers and Other Strangers*, a comedy of manners with a cast and dialogue almost worthy of Preston Sturges. At the time I was still ignorant of Sturges's work, but one evening I saw *Hail, the Conquering Hero* on TV, was immediately hooked, and did not rest until I had seen other films by him. For a few years in the 1940s Sturges wrote, directed, and produced a series of fast-paced comedies, among them *The Palm Beach Story*, *Christmas in July*, and *The Miracle of Morgan's Creek*, that are as good as anything else ever produced in Hollywood. Fortunately, Elwy Yost, the host of TVOntario's *Saturday Night at the Movies*, seems to be at least as fond of them as I am.

My favourite Sturges film is *Sullivan's Travels*, a Depression tragi-comedy that expresses his attitude to art and life, and captures something of my attitude as well. Its final words are by its protagonist, a movie director played by Joel McCrae: 'There's a lot to be said for making people laugh. Did you know that's all some people have? It isn't much, but it's better than nothing in this cockeyed caravan.'

In the spring of 1973 the provincial council of OCUFA made me one of its representatives on the governing board of CAUT. Attending my first board meeting, at Estérel, Quebec, in June, I was elected to the CAUT executive committee as a member-at-large. This committee, which comprised the president, past president, vice-president, treasurer, executive secretary, and three members-at-large, met ten times a year, usually in Ottawa, occasionally in Montreal or Toronto, and once in Vancouver. I served on it for two years.

Three memories of those years stand out. The first has to do with faculty unionization. In the fall of 1973 some professors at St Mary's University in Halifax invited the Canadian Union of Public Employees (CUPE) to conduct a campaign for certification, saying that CAUT had no experience in this field and 'lacked clout.' Don Savage, a jovial historian who served as executive secretary, and Dick Spencer, an austere civil engineer from UBC who was vice-president that year, argued that we must fight CUPE with all available weapons. Dick predicted that if the St Mary's faculty chose CUPE and signed a good first contract, faculty associations everywhere would follow St Mary's out of CAUT.

I agreed with the majority that we must respond energetically. The CUPE challenge failed, perhaps less because of the effectiveness of our efforts than because St Mary's professors who disliked unions cast their votes for the CAUT-linked faculty association. We seemed less like a union than CUPE!

Established first in the francophone universities of Quebec, faculty unions were spreading to English Canada: the University of Manitoba, Notre Dame University in British Columbia, and of course St Mary's. Carleton, first in Ontario to unionize, did so after its president had warned of dismissals on budgetary grounds. At York University, too, talk of dismissals in 1972 had frightened many faculty members. As well, the course of salary negotiations in 1973 (and earlier) served to demonstrate the limited value of a voluntary association. In early 1974 another member of the YUFA executive and I spoke with two labour lawyers to see whether unionization could help us. It was the first step to certification, completed in 1976. It has been no panacea, but the protection of the Ontario Labour Relations Act is reassuring, particularly in the current budgetary crunch.

My second memory arises out of an event that took place thousands of kilometres away. In September 1973 the Chilean armed forces overthrew the government of Salvador Allende. In the aftermath of this coup, the military unleashed a reign of terror against his leftist supporters. Soon CAUT was getting requests for help on behalf of Chilean professors who were seeking entry into Canada. Immigration officials were dragging their heels, it seemed to us, so we asked to meet the secretary of state for external affairs, Mitchell Sharp.

On 22 October, Don and I joined Evelyn Moore, the University of Calgary education professor who was CAUT president in 1973–4, in a meeting with Sharp in his office in the Centre Block. He was attended by an assistant deputy minister of Manpower and Immigration and by the External Affairs officer in charge of the Latin American desk, each with an assistant. From my diary:

Sharp started speaking. He was pleased to see us and to find that we were concerned about Chile. Initial reports that had reached his office had been confused, but his information was that the situation was now normalizing itself. It must be understood that the vigorous action of the army against the government was prompted by the discovery of large caches of arms and ammunition which led to grave apprehension on the part of the generals. Their actions could not be justified, but could be understood because they were in danger of their lives.

It was hard not to laugh, but no one did. We all spoke our pieces, with Sharp demurring at Evelyn's suggestion that professors were being jailed. That was not in line with his information. I offered the testimony of Mrs. Duràn [wife of Claudio Duràn, a philosopher who later joined York]. Charpentier [the External Affairs officer] said she was simply wrong, exaggerating hopelessly.

Nobody was buying the argument that Czechoslovakians and Chileans were similar cases and presented similar problems. Sharp said that the Czechs [the refugees of 1968] had no option but to leave the country; this was not the case with Chileans. And Chile needed all its freedom-loving people to be there, not in a foreign country like Canada.

Sharp added, however, that additional immigration officers had been assigned to Chile. Applicants without criminal records who had useful skills and were not security risks were eligible for entry.

This was not reassuring. I was aware of the difficulty York had experienced in appointing a Hungarian-born philosopher, Istvan Mészáros, and an American historian, Gabriel Kolko. The immigration department refused to say why they were inadmissible, and direct approaches to the Prime Minister's Office had been necessary to get them in.

As we emerged into bright autumn sunlight, Don said: 'Well, that was rather an unproductive hour.' In the months that followed it became clear that what we had heard was basically the American view of Chile. But the hour had not been a total waste: some Chilean academics were later admitted into Canada.

A third issue was the 'Canadianization' of the universities. Robin Mathews and Jim Steele, professors of English at Carleton University, had charged in their book *The Struggle for Canadian Universities* that many foreign academics were being appointed who knew little about Canada and lacked respect for its culture, and that qualified Canadians were often overlooked. These charges found echoes elsewhere; with them came demands that universities monitor the process of making appointments more carefully than they had been in the habit of doing. CAUT responded by forming a committee to gather information and formulate a new policy on Canadianizing the universities. CAUT's existing policy, although adopted as recently as 1969, failed to deal with many of the issues raised by Mathews, Steele, and others.

The committee moved at the pace of Pecksniff's horse because no agreement existed among the country's fifty-plus faculty associations as to what, if anything, ought to be done. At the beginning of 1974 there was still no final report. At that time Evelyn Moore asked me to replace her as chair of the committee. She was Australian by birth and education, and in order not unduly to provoke Mathews and his supporters a Canadian was needed. But I was also born abroad, I objected: might this not be held against me? Don thought not. All my degrees were from Canadian universities, he said: 'If you don't tell them, they'll never guess you weren't born here.' Apparently my assimilation was complete!

I had scant relish for the task, feeling as ambivalent about cultural nationalism as about the economic kind. Reading the committee's files convinced me, however, that a policy giving Canadians and landed immigrants a first crack at academic jobs had some merit. A quasi-colonial belief in the superiority of the top U.S. graduate schools, even schools of the second rank, was everywhere evident; this tended to give American applicants an edge and to discriminate against people with Canadian doctorates.

Don had drafted a statement which addressed these concerns, and I did no more than edit it a bit. Our main recommendation was that universities establish hiring review committees to ensure fair play. The report reached its first hurdle at the CAUT board meeting in March 1974, held at Ottawa's National Arts Centre. Robin Mathews asked to be allowed to address us. Although this was unusual, we granted his request, giving him a late-morning slot so that he couldn't tie up the meeting for any length of time even if he wanted to.

At the appointed time Robin strode in, gave everyone a statement that denounced CAUT for refusing to take the issue seriously, and left without saying a word. Perhaps thinking that if Robin didn't like it the report must be all right, the board approved it. It ran into heavy weather at the national council meeting in May, however. Most of the representatives of the local associations, opposing interference with freedom of hiring, rejected the report. Not until 1977 did a diluted version pass. Even so, almost all universities resisted our suggestions, and eventually the federal government acted to ensure fair treatment for Canadian citizens and permanent residents. On balance I think this was a good thing.

In August 1973 I drove into the interior of British Columbia with Father and Mother. The air-conditioning in the car I had rented turned out to be unnecessary: even in the Okanagan valley it was no more than pleasantly warm, and in the mountains it was decidedly chilly. After leaving the Fraser valley we took the Hope-Princeton Highway through Manning Park, headed north via Lakes Okanagan and Kalamalka to Shuswap Lake, then east to Revelstoke and over the Rogers Pass to Banff. The high point of the trip was the mountainous Banff-Jasper Highway. We stopped at the Columbia Icefields, where Mother and I ventured briefly onto the ice. Father declined to join us. If he wanted to break a leg, he said, he would try to do it in a warmer spot.

After spending a couple of days in and around Jasper, we returned to the coast via the Thompson and Trans-Canada highways. The weather had to that point been mostly sunny though cool, but in Lytton, in the arid sagebrush country east of the Coast range, we woke up one morning to rain. At breakfast, which we ate in a small diner, we overheard two old-timers trying to recall when it had last rained in August. They agreed that it had been five years at the very least.

Travelling with my parents was not free of friction. I had with me Jacob Presser's *Ondergang*, his history of the persecution of Dutch Jewry during the war. Reading this deeply affecting book led me to ask Father why he had made the Aryan declaration, affirming that there were no Jews among his grandparents. Because he would have lost his position as a civil servant if he hadn't done so, he replied. Would that have been so awful? 'Hoe denk je dat er eten op tafel was gekomen als ik werkeloos was geweest?' (How do you think I would have put food on the table if I had been unemployed?). It was thinking of that kind that had helped to isolate the Jews and paved the way to their destruction, I countered. If *no one* had made the declaration that might have been true, he said, but a handful of protests would have made no difference to the Germans. And besides, what did I know about the pressure that people were under at the time?

Father was right, of course, but so in his way was Presser, and I was not prepared to concede the point. We ended up shouting at each other to no good purpose, and the quarrel cooled relations for a day or two. It did not diminish our admiration of the scenery, however. Father had seen a little of the interior in 1966, but Mother had never been east of Hope. And although I had driven along the Trans-Canada Highway four times, I had never done so at a leisurely pace.

A few images stand out in my memory of that trip: standing high above Lake Kalamalka, the view from the CPR hotel across

Lake Louise, Mt Robson, crossing Hell's Gate in the Fraser Canyon by cable car. This was mountain scenery at its most impressive. Each of us said at least once that the region reminded us of Switzerland. This trip almost reconciled him to having left Europe, Father said. But he added that the towns and villages quite lacked the charm of their Swiss counterparts. Moreover, almost all the restaurants in which we ate were forgettable at best and often worse than that. During nine days of travel we had only one good meal, in a restaurant in Penticton. Its chef was Swiss-born!

Canada had many wide-open spaces, and they *were* splendid. As yet, however, the country had little to punctuate those spaces with. 'Nou ja,' Mother said indulgently, 'het is nog een jong land. Dat komt alles wel' (It's still a young country; all that will come). I said I hoped it would come soon.

7

What's Past Is Prologue

More than twenty years have passed since that holiday in 1973. It doesn't seem that long. 'Twintig worden duurt een eeuw,' the saying goes: 'Zestig wordt men in een handomdraai' (To reach the age of twenty takes a century. Turning sixty takes only a moment). And yet much has happened, the most important events being marriage, parenthood, and the death of my parents.

After Kathie and I parted company in 1972 I went out with a number of women, but only one tempted me even briefly to end a bachelorhood in which I felt steadily more comfortable. Yet I didn't think of myself as a confirmed bachelor. I wasn't looking to get married, but *if* a suitable person should cross my path ...

In November 1981 I attended a meeting in Massey College, held to launch a fund-raising campaign for the Robertson Davies Library. There I met an attractive lawyer in her late twenties who said that she had read some things I had written for the *Canadian Forum*. Feeling mildly flattered, I talked with her over lunch. Her name was Cornelia Schuh; she had been one of the first group of women to be admitted to the college in 1974. She seemed well-informed about music, theatre, literature, politics: at our wedding three years later I reported truthfully that I had felt 'instant mild interest.' It was no more than that, however. We met only once more, for dinner and a symphony concert, before I left the country in early March to spend the remainder of a sabbatical year in Grenoble, improving my French and reading about the history of taxation.

Not long after I returned to Toronto in August 1982 I received a change-of-address notice from her. Somewhat at loose ends at the time, and remembering the enjoyable conversation we had had, I gave her a call. A few months later we started seeing each other regularly, and as I got to know her better I fell in love. 'Find me a lawyer who can cook,' I had once said flippantly when a friend asked me what it would take to get me married. I had found such a treasure by myself. And, marvellous to say, she was in love with me.

Perhaps two people named Schuh and Horn were fated to link their lives together. More pertinent was that our intellectual and cultural interests were similar. Her undergraduate degree at Trinity College, Toronto, was in history and French, and she had taken an M.A. in history before going to law school. As well, we had at least some part of our backgrounds in common. Her parents were physicians who had arrived in Canada from Germany early in 1953, making much the same economic miscalculation my parents had made. After living briefly in Vancouver, where Cornelia was born, and for some years in Moose Jaw, Saskatchewan, the place of birth of her brother, Andre, they settled in Stratford, Ontario. Cornelia spoke German with her parents; to some extent, as I did, she straddled two countries and two cultures.

Raised as a Roman Catholic, Cornelia had converted to Anglicanism but did not feel a need to convert me. Our politics were very similar: slightly left of centre. In 1983 we holidayed together in England and Scotland during a heat wave, which confirmed our belief that we could get along together even under occasionally trying circumstances, such as driving, nervously at first, on the left side of the road, staying in hotels that had never heard of air-conditioning, and using a laundromat, in Chester, where Cornelia burned her hand on a dryer. It was reassuring that she had a good income as a lawyer at Queen's Park. This quieted my long-standing fear of marriage as likely to lead to the strained finances that had been my parents' lot. My salary alone, more than adequate for my needs, would not do for those of a middle-class family in a city like Toronto.

In the summer of 1984 we bought a house together in the Bloor-

Bathurst area, and that December we were married in St Thomas's Church, where Cornelia was a parishioner. Coincidentally, it was the first Toronto church I had ever entered, twenty-one years earlier almost to the day. Another coincidence was that the clergyman who married us, Canon Roy Hoult, had assisted at Victoria's Christ Church Cathedral in the 1960s and knew my old friend John Lancaster.

When I told Father that I was going to marry, he was sceptical. 'Op jouw leeftijd?' (At your age?) he asked, raising his eyebrows. Then he wanted to know where Cornelia had been born: the way she spelled her name seemed German. 'Vancouver,' I replied, adding just a bit maliciously: 'Maar haar ouders zijn allebei uit Duitsland' (But her parents are both from Germany). 'Godverdomme,' he said softly, then brightened: 'Tenminste is zij daar niet geboren, dus zal het wel okay zijn' (At least she wasn't born there, so it should be okay). Almost forty years after the war he had not yet forgiven the Germans, but to Cornelia he was always pleasant. (Our son Daniel, having heard about the Second World War, speculated recently that any quarrels his parents had were due to his mother being German and his father Dutch!)

I was still unsure about children. In the summer of 1986, near the end of a holiday largely spent in Westphalia and Belgium, we visited friends in Breda, Peter van Wiechen and his wife, Monique Bartels. After Cornelia went to bed, I had a late-evening cognac with Peter and Monique. The latter wanted to know whether we were planning to have children (they have two sons). It was under discussion, I answered. Peter laughed, saying he knew *that* kind of discussion. He mentioned a colleague at the hospital where he was a radiologist, a divorced man who had remarried. Having children by his first marriage, he didn't want more, but his much younger wife was of a different view. 'Door scherp onderhandelen heeft hij haar tot één kind weten te houden' (Through sharp negotiating he has been able to keep her to one child), Peter said. He laughed again and added: 'Tenminste tot nu toe' (At least until now).

Our son Daniel André was born on 7 May 1988; Patrick Benjamin followed on 21 January 1992. No experience is more gratifying than cuddling an infant or toddler one is responsible for, and raising young children has given me many enjoyable hours, as well as an increased measure of optimism for the future of humanity. Not long before writing this I found myself in a playground on a gorgeous summer afternoon, pushing the swing for Patrick while listening to the conclusion of Mahler's Eighth Symphony. It was a perfect half-hour: the green of the trees, the sun above, my son swinging contentedly back and forth, Goethe's stirring lines set to Mahler's glorious music, both culminating in the overpowering finale: 'Alles Vergängliche / Ist nur ein Gleichnis; / Das Unzulängliche, / Hier wird's Ereignis; / Das Unbeschreibliche, / Hier ist's getan; / Das Ewig-Weibliche / Zieht uns hinan.'* It made me believe, at least for a while, that there may be a heaven after all.

There is another side. Trying to raise children has given me greater sympathy for my own parents, for delightful as small children can be, they complicate life to an extent and in ways unimaginable until one *is* a parent. As Marni Jackson wrote some time ago in an article in *Toronto Life*, having children is like visiting Albania: no one who has been there can tell you what it's really like. They can be enormously irritating, and sometimes they just seem too much work.

And yet: I have come to the view that men, at any rate, are not fully human until they have children. Recently, I saw a performance of *Macbeth*, the first in ten years or so. Never before had the murder of Macduff's family hit me so hard, or did I feel so keenly Macduff's anguish upon hearing of it: 'Did heaven look on / And would not take their part?'

Talking about this with Cornelia afterwards, I remembered something Jack had said fourteen or fifteen years ago, when he was leafing through a volume of Louis de Jong's magnificent history of the Netherlands during the Second World War that I was reading. One photo depicts a tank and, between it and a damaged building, a man half-lifting a girl and dragging a boy; the caption states merely that the centre of Den Bosch is under artillery fire

---

* 'All that is transitory / is but a symbol; / all inadequacy / here is fulfilled; / the Indescribable / here is done; / the eternal feminine / leads us aloft.' The translation of these last eight lines of *Faust, part II*, is by Lionel Salter.

(the year was 1944).* Where the man was taking the children and why is not explained, but Jack observed that only a parent could fully understand the panic he must have felt. I had to take my brother's word for it then; I know now he was right.

For years, uninterrupted nights of sleep have been the exception rather than the rule, and while Daniel and Patrick are awake they demand attention. I used to do a lot of work at home in the evenings and on weekends, but since Daniel's birth that has very largely ended. Neither he nor Patrick seems to need much sleep, so that weekday evenings are of little use for anything other than clearing away dishes, settling down children, and making the next day's lunches. (It will all end soon enough, I suppose: too soon?)

My job has become a 'nine-to-five' one, which it never was before. Anyone who takes raising children seriously cannot put in the long hours on which success rests, in academe as in business, the liberal professions, and the public service, a damning comment on the demands that careers make on those who pursue them. Fortunately, my career was well established by the time I became a parent: I gained the rank of full professor in 1982.

The arrival of our sons has not only slowed down my scholarly production, it has forced me to think about nationality in new ways. Daniel and Patrick are entitled to Dutch and German as well as Canadian nationality, at least until age twenty-eight. Then their claim to Dutch nationality lapses unless they choose *it* rather than Canadian citizenship (their German nationality is, I gather, indefeasible). I find this strange but comforting: if we Canadians manage to wreck this country in the next few years, Daniel and Patrick have other countries to go to. If they want to, that is. After a visit to Holland in the summer of 1992, Daniel drew a clear distinction between himself and me: 'You are from Holland, Daddy, but I am from Canada.'

Becoming a parent also prompted a minor assertion of my Dutch roots. As I began to sing nursery songs to Daniel I found that Mother Goose, which had not been part of my own childhood, did

---

* L. de Jong, *Het Koninkrijk der Nederlanden in de Tweede Wereldoorlog*, vol. 10a, eerste helft, *Het laatste jaar* I ('s-Gravenhage 1980), opp. 477.

not appeal to me. I obtained from my sister-in-law Annètje a copy of a Dutch nursery-rhyme collection called *Rijmpjes en versjes uit de oude doos* (Rhymes and Verses from the Old Box) and found that this was more like it: the ditties I had learned when *I* was a toddler. Daniel liked them, but when he got a bit older he wanted to hear them 'in Canadian.' More recently, Patrick enjoyed them with me.

That is all for nostalgia's sake, however. Neither boy is learning Dutch at present. Does this bother me? Not really. I hope they will learn French and German, and an East Asian language as well, but can't see the point of forcing Dutch on them. It's not a world language: outside Holland and Flemish-speaking Belgium it is all but useless. Their Dutch relatives all speak English in any case. My cousin Flora even teaches it at a secondary school in Amsterdam. In 1991–2 we had several visits from the daughter of my cousin Maja, Pieta Voûte, who was working in a lab at the U of T for some months. Her English was excellent.

Perhaps my attitude reflects a very limited involvement in activities that reflect my ethnic background. Now that Father is dead I normally speak Dutch only with Annètje or when I am in Holland. Every April I get an invitation to a reception at the Ontario Club, held by the Netherlands Consulate to mark the birthday of the Queen of the Netherlands, and every second year or so I go. I sip my drink, munch cocktail snacks, and look for people I recognize. I don't always find any. I simply am not plugged into whatever expatriate and emigrant community exists (however, I *have* belonged to the Canadian Association for the Advancement of Netherlandic Studies since its founding twenty-some years ago). When the moment comes I join the rest of the crowd in singing the 'Wilhelmus,' feeling just a bit strange doing so. Having Dutch nationality, I am as entitled as anyone else in the room to sing the national anthem. But it's like singing hymns: the language clashes with what I now believe.

In 1985 I was invited to address the Dutch-Canadian Luncheon Club on the subject of the Canadian Army in the Netherlands, about which I had written the text of *A Liberation Album* five years earlier. (My contribution to this book, the research for which I began in Holland in 1976 and completed in Ottawa's National Archives three years later, was a labour of love. Working on it revived stirring memories, but above all it expressed my gratitude to the Canadians who had fought to defeat Nazi Germany and who had freed much of my native country. The other two men who worked on the book, the photographer and journalist David Kaufman, and the film-maker John Muller, shared some of my feelings.) The talk, to an appreciative audience, was a lot of fun. As well, I met two people from Baarn, including the son of neighbours there, the Langelaans.

Soon afterwards I received an invitation to a cocktail party at the home of a Dutch-born investment adviser, Hendrik Hooft. The large house was filled with people who spoke Dutch, but what they chiefly had in common was an interest in business. I talked for a while with an executive from Amstel Canada who explained to me why Heineken, the company that owns Amstel, had no intention of brewing its flagship beer in North America. 'Most people drink labels, not beer,' he said: in buying Heineken they were showing that they can afford an imported and presumably superior product. Brewing it over here would undermine that snob appeal. This was the only interesting conversation I had in the course of an hour, and I remembered why I had all but stopped going to cocktail parties: simultaneously noisy and boring. I think I was the first to leave.

A week or so later I addressed a group of retired people of Dutch origin, again about the Canadian armed forces in the Netherlands. This time I spoke Dutch. It was hard work, because finding the right word was often difficult. The occasion was also a bit melancholy. These people, all of them my parents' age or a few years younger, had adapted to the Canada they had migrated to twenty, thirty, or more years earlier, but I got the distinct feeling that not a few of them might have preferred to stay in Holland.

Unlike the members of the groups I spoke to that spring, I had neither a strong emotional nor a business reason for seeking out other expatriates and emigrants. Doubtless this was a consequence of the age at which I arrived in Canada, my determination to assimilate, and the profession I chose. My friendships are based on shared interests – mostly academic and more recently children – not on ethnicity.

My brother Peter married Raquel Rodriguez; they live near Montreal and have five children, two of whom are now married, and one grandchild. Jack and Annètje live in Guelph with their daughters, Karin and Kirstin. Joe's marriage was childless; so, too, has been Steven's marriage to Meg Richeson. Joe is dead; Steven makes his home in Whitehorse, Yukon.

Only Jan D. has never married. He is also the only one of us who tried to resettle in Holland. A victim of the recession of the early 1980s, he went overseas in late 1981 to look for work and ended up continuing his studies at the university in Nijmegen. An immigrant in his country of birth, he felt increasingly ill at ease in Holland even as his health deteriorated. In 1991 he returned to Canada and now lives in Victoria.

Joe died in an automobile crash in August 1975, going off the road at perhaps double the speed limit of fifty kilometres an hour, a short distance down the road from his house near Whistler Mountain. I knew that I would miss him, and not just because of the skiing. Although I had never been as close to him as to Jack, and our lives had diverged, I had always got on well with him. His formal education had ended with grade twelve, but he read a lot and was well-informed. Some of my memories of him were particularly enjoyable, moreover.

The times spent skiing with him, at Badger Pass and Whistler, make up a cluster of good recollections. Another memory dates from the spring of 1963, when I came home from college in midafternoon to find Mother waiting for me, a grim look on her face. 'Wat is er aan de hand?' (What's the matter?), I asked. 'Met mij niets,' she replied, 'maar wel met Joop' (I'm okay, but not Joe). My heart sank: Joe worked with explosives. 'Was er een ontploffing?' (Was there an explosion?). 'Nee, niet zó iets' (No, nothing like that), she said impatiently. Then, looking at the piece of paper she had in her hand: 'Hij is corespondent in a divorce case.' 'Thank God,' I said feelingly, only to discover that I had now become the object of her wrath for taking so serious a matter so lightly. It turned out, I learned later, that the previous fall Joe had spent a week in a hotel in Zeballos with a young woman who wanted to give her abusive husband grounds for a divorce. Joe claimed that he had mainly been doing her a favour. Only two options were available to her husband: challenging Joe to a fight or seeking a divorce, and since he was smaller than Joe he chose the latter.

Joe's size and muscular build I found to be useful later that spring. He was briefly in Victoria, and had accompanied my friend Karen Leith and me to a coffee-house located in the basement of the Westholme Hotel, on a scruffy stretch of Government Street. As we emerged around midnight, a clutch of four or five young toughs moved towards us. 'Slow down a bit,' Joe said to us, moving about two steps ahead. The young men parted as though they were the Red Sea and we the approaching Israelites.

He could be irresponsible and juvenile, but mostly he was a straight shooter who knew his rights and stood up for them. At the wake held for him in Alta Lake, one that Steven and I attended, his friend Dave Green said to me: 'Joe never took shit from nobody.' It was as good an epitaph as any.

At the time of Joe's death, Mother was ailing. The preceding autumn she had suffered a depression from which she never fully recovered. Tante Phiet, who visited Mill Bay as part of a tour of Canada and the United States in 1977, told me, when she passed through Toronto, that Mother had seemed to be quite joyless. By 1981 she was also very nearly blind. A year later she entered a nursing home in the village of Shawnigan Lake. This was convenient: it was only a five minute drive from Mill Bay. It was also sad, because the tentative diagnosis of her condition was Alzheimer's disease. Well before her death in April 1985 she was no longer able to recognize even Father.

Mother had stopped going to church after her depression, allowing her membership in a nearby Baptist congregation to lapse. Father said that she would not have wanted a memorial service there, and by the time I reached Mill Bay, two days after she died, he had already made other arrangements. There was little for me to do beyond placing an obituary in the *Times-Colonist* and driving

Father into Victoria to see his solicitor (he refused to drive there himself, saying that Victoria drivers were speed-obsessed maniacs). My main function was to keep him company for a few days.

He was stoic, the nature of her illness having allowed him (and us) to get used to her death well before it occurred. When she did die, in fact, it was a relief to all of us and perhaps also to her. Father said, with only a hint of bravado, that if he thought he were going to go that way he would get a bullet for the old .303 hunting rifle Joe had once left with him, and shoot himself. I could see his point.

We did attend a funeral service that week, however. Father's friend Bas de Groot having died of cancer the day after Mother's death, we went to the small Roman Catholic church in Mill Bay to say our farewells. I made these do double duty for Mother. After the lunch that followed the service we went home, Father to take a nap, I to listen to *Parsifal* on CBC Stereo, with Jon Vickers in the title role. Had it not been for Mother's death, Cornelia and I would have been at the Metropolitan Opera that afternoon as part of a delayed honeymoon (fortunately, a friend and former student of mine who lived near New York was able to use our tickets). Instead, I heard the performance on Father's table radio.

He emerged from his room during the second act as Kundry was singing, listened for a few seconds, then said: 'Nou, Chiel, ik heb je 'n hoop geld bespaard. Als dat Parsifal is mag je 'm van me hebben' (Well, Mike, I've saved you a lot of money. If that is Parsifal you can have him). Father was no opera lover: it was his boast to have fallen asleep while Fyodor Shalyapin was singing at La Scala, back in the 1920s. Then, too, disparaging Wagner was for him part and parcel of disliking Germany. In 1987, when Cornelia and I visited him before going on to Seattle to attend the *Ring des Nibelungen* (the musical high point of my life so far), he made it clear that he thought we were demented. (We also saw the roses in Portland, Oregon, stayed with friends at Whistler Mountain, spent several days in Pacific Rim National Park, and dined one evening at the Sooke Harbour House: a holiday to remember!)

A mother's death is an event of a singular kind: the person who brought you into the world is gone from it. Joe's death had reminded me sharply of my own mortality, but he was younger than

I was. Mother's passing was to be expected. Still, a key link to my past had been broken.

We had not been close for many years. By 1959 I had lost all patience with her fundamentalism, which had created a distance between us that remained even after she withdrew from religious practice, mainly because at the same time she very largely withdrew from life. When she died my grief was not intense. As I was writing this memoir, however, I came to regret not having known her better. I would have liked talking more extensively with her about her childhood and youth, and about the decision to emigrate. When I had raised the issue with her in 1962, she had reaffirmed the wisdom of the step she and Father had taken ten years earlier and would not listen to a contrary argument. Would she have taken a different line later in life? It is hard to say. In any case, after her illness in 1974 she showed no interest in talking at length about anything.

It would be presumptuous to try to sum up her life: I have neither the wisdom nor the necessary knowledge. When I was a young child she appeared to me as a loving and lovable parent. Later I came to see her as a nuisance who pestered me about the state of my soul and insisted that I must recant my heresies. Although she was sometimes hard on her husband and sons, however, she was hardest on herself. She was not one to whom happiness or contentment came easily. May she rest in peace.

Father outlived her by five years. His health remained good into 1989. Then, in the late spring, congestive heart failure was diagnosed. His physician, Bruce Boan, told me confidentially that he did not think that Father would see his eighty-seventh birthday. I swallowed hard and began the process of acceptance and adjustment. Father, too, knew the end was drawing near but did not seem to mind. With the exception of his sister Toos, everyone he had known when he was young was dead, he said more than once: time for him to move on, too.

More distressing to him than his heart condition was a form of arthritis that made it all but impossible for him to lift his arms. By June 1989 he had to stop driving. Being grounded in an isolated house in the country was a major blow. Worse: he soon found it hard to get around the house, even to dress and undress himself. When I was in Mill Bay in October I had to help him with these tasks. It was a weird sensation to be doing for my father what I was also doing for my one-year-old son, his namesake, in Toronto.

In November he fell and injured himself. Admitted to the hospital in nearby Duncan, he was not released until we had been able to arrange for home nursing care several hours a day. (A provincially paid homemaker, the not-to-be-too-highly-praised Maureen Dunn – she became in a real sense the daughter our parents had never had – had been providing household support since the mid-1970s.) When Cornelia, Daniel, and I visited him in March 1990, he was reluctantly thinking of placing his name on the waiting list for a nursing home near Duncan. When I saw him on his eighty-seventh birthday in late April he looked better, however, and Bruce, who had come over for a celebratory drink, said to me that Father obviously came from tough stock.

A month later he suddenly died exactly where he had hoped to, in his own bed. Jack, who was visiting him at the time, said that Father had been in good form the evening before. Bas and Willy de Groot's son Jake had been there, and Father had joined the younger men in drinking a Scotch or two and talking animatedly. Early the next morning he woke up and started to get out of bed, then fell back, his heart giving out. When Jack found him he was dead. (Cornelia's mother, Elfriede, said that he had been lucky: 'Ich beneide ihn' [I envy him]. She herself was to die of stomach cancer in the spring of 1993, a nasty death compared with Father's.)

Being a co-executor of the estate along with the family solicitor, Constance Isherwood, I had to visit the West Coast several times in the summer of 1990. As I completed the melancholy task of clearing out the house – Steven helped me in July, and Cornelia shared the packing in August – I tried to assess the significance of Father's life. He had been an irascible but not unloving parent. Was he a *good* parent? I used to be critical, but now that I, too, am a father, my criticism has largely evaporated.

Was he a good architect? That is probably how he would have preferred to be known. I think he was: his designs were imaginative and he had a passion for solidity. It seems unlikely, however, that anyone besides his sons will long remember his achievements. He left Holland when he was still making a name for himself and arrived in Canada too late to make one here. And yet: his designs survive on two continents, and he *is* still remembered by a few people in Baarn, where he did much of his best work.

Baarn is also where his remains are. Jack took his ashes overseas in the summer of 1990, scattering them in the same spot where Jan D. and I had scattered Mother's remains five years earlier: in a corner of the garden at Emmalaan 11A, the owners having graciously consented. Do their ashes belong there? That is hard to say, but I do know that Mill Bay (or Victoria) would have been the wrong place. Our parents lived on southern Vancouver Island for half of their adult lives and were as happy there as circumstances permitted, but they never really belonged there. They had become Canadian citizens but they were never anything but Dutch with a thin New World veneer.

That did not mean Baarn was the only or best choice. Father said that if I wanted to scatter Mother's ashes where she had been happiest I must take them to Bandung. I told Tante Phiet of this when Cornelia and I met her in Alsace in late June of 1985. She said that he had a point, but agreed with what we had done. Perhaps she was being diplomatic, knowing that Jan D. and I had already disposed of Mother's remains, realizing that we had done so in accordance with *our* feelings about the house on the Emmalaan, and honouring this.

Father's attitude to his own ashes was one of indifference. 'Het kan me geen barst schelen, Chiel,' he once said, unsentimental as ever: 'Wanneer ik dood ben, ben ik dood' (I don't care a fig, Mike: when I'm dead I'm dead). He was not utterly devoid of sentimentality, however: at times he expressed the hope to be reunited with his Siamese cats Phummiphon and Lord Peter, also known as *de poemel*, who had died in 1974 and 1988. (The third, Minnie, survived him and went to friends in Victoria.) Lacking directions in his case as in Mother's, I thought his remains should follow hers. None of my brothers disagreed.

Tante Phiet, in writing to me to express her condolences after she heard of Father's death, recalled that, after Opa Reitsma's death in 1958, a friend had said to her: 'Nu sta jij in de eerste rij' (Now you're in the first rank). It was a sobering thought. The human links to my own past were being severed, one by one. Still, six years later Tante Phiet, in her early eighties, and Tante Toos, in her mid-nineties, survived. (Toos died in October 1996.)

There have been other deaths. The four that have touched me most nearly were those of Neil Sampson, the Cazants, and Ruth Broek.

Neil I last saw in 1977. Looking more like Albert Einstein than ever, he seemed in fine shape mentally but said that he felt very tired and frail. He was suffering from pernicious anaemia and needed regular blood transfusions; he died the following year. Evelyn carries on and a few years ago celebrated her eightieth birthday. I haven't seen her since 1984 but write to her or phone her occasionally. Far from dimming the golden glow of those months I spent as their paying guest, the passage of time has only enhanced it.

Not long after Neil, Meneer Cazant died. In 1976, when I was in Holland to do research for what became *A Liberation Album*, he was in robust health. It was otherwise when, two years later, I visited Baarn briefly at the start of my *Barockbummel*, a trip to Prague, Vienna, Munich, and places in between. This time he was in hospital, suffering from several ailments at once. Mevrouw Cazant said that his body resembled one of those solidly made old automobiles which, having served its owner faithfully for many years, suddenly falls apart, the clutch, valves, and brakes all going at the same time. He died within a year. I had not loved him as I had his wife, but he had always been good to me.

I visited Mevrouw Cazant in 1979, 1980, and 1981. Although she was as cheerful as ever, she was declining physically. In May 1982, while briefly in Holland, I spoke to her by telephone, but when I phoned in August there was no answer. From a letter I received from her at Christmas I learned that she had entered a minimum-care nursing home. This did not prepare me for the news of her death in 1983, which I got from her nephew and my sometime skating companion, Boudy van Oort.

Because it was unexpected, her passing was actually a greater shock than Mother's would be. As a child I had loved Mevrouw Cazant deeply; this had matured into warm affection and real pleasure in her company. I always enjoyed talking with her. Even when we disagreed she listened to me and respected my point of view, as I hope I did hers. I knew I would miss her: her death was a break with the past in two ways. I valued my visits with her not just because I loved her but because I liked being in my town of birth, wandering through its streets, seeing the house where I was born, the schools I had attended, the woods where I had played and walked, Father's war monument on the Stationsplein. Since 1981 I have been in Baarn only twice, most recently in 1992, when I showed Daniel our old home and he kicked a ball around in the garden where I had done the same thing more than forty years earlier.

I had not been as close to Ruth Broek as to the other three, although I had visited her in 1977 – Jan had died a few years earlier – and saw her at Tante Phiet's place in Amsterdam the following year. Our final meeting was so memorable, however, that I felt the news of her death in 1985 as a real loss.

In the summer of 1984, Cornelia and I were in northern California. One evening we dined with Ruth at her home on Southampton Avenue in Berkeley. After dinner she read to us two episodes from memoirs that she had been writing. One story, set in 1930 or 1931, told how she, a schoolteacher trying to hitchhike her way home (in Idaho, I believe), had met Jan, a graduate student from Holland who was exploring the American West in a battered car and who gave her a ride. Perhaps he was impressed with her daring; in any case he fell in love with her almost immediately and, soon afterwards, she with him.

The other story recounted her experiences in Holland when, upon marrying Jan, she went there with her new husband for the first time in 1932. People were very kind to her, she recalled, among them, surprisingly, the young woman Ruth knew to have been in love with Jan when he had left for the States a few years earlier. This woman, like Ruth in her early twenties, had introduced her to her family and friends, had taught her Dutch, and had explained to her aspects of Dutch life and culture.

As the room gradually darkened, I listened with utter fascination. The woman Ruth was describing was my mother! I remembered things about her that evening that I had too often overlooked, especially her generosity of spirit, directed in this case towards someone who had got what she herself had wanted. It was sad to think that she was dying in a nursing home, probably oblivious to what had happened in those days, half a century earlier, that Ruth was describing so simply and movingly.

'Ashes to ashes, dust to dust ...': Father and Mother had in a sense returned to the place where more than forty years ago they planned our emigration. What if they had decided back then that, on balance, it would be better to stay in Holland than to leave? The question is unproductive, but it continues to fascinate me all the same. In life, as in history, some of the most interesting if unanswerable questions begin with the words: 'What if ...' What if the Germans had won the first battle of the Marne? What if Lenin had not been enabled to return to Russia in 1917? What if Truman had decided not to use the atomic bomb? No one can know, but the questions *are* intriguing.

Let me try another question. What were the results of emigration compared with the results that were expected from it? What Father and Mother hoped for is clear. Although their reasons for wanting to leave were more complex than the justification they offered, that justification was straightforward. They expected that their sons would fare better in Canada than in Holland. They must have known that they were sacrificing income and position; they should have realized, though perhaps they did not, that they themselves would secure no great benefit from going. They decided to emigrate all the same, in the belief that they were doing it for us.

Was emigration a success from that point of view? If the answer to that question is 'yes,' might I (or any of my brothers) nevertheless have preferred to stay in Holland? What did we gain by emigrating and what did we lose?

These questions are unavoidable yet ultimately unanswerable. Not only do they require five separate answers (Joe can't offer his), but they also require knowledge of what might have happened had we *not* emigrated. And that is beyond knowing. Let me suggest, however, that we might just as well have stayed in Holland. Our parents suffered serious financial and social loss without securing compensating benefits for their sons. Father was right: from this point of view, emigration *was* a blunder.

The issue is not as clear-cut as that, of course. Two issues are relevant, one personal and one contextual. Dealing with the latter first: has Canada since 1952 been conspicuously more successful, economically, politically, and socially, than Holland? One would be hard-pressed to argue that it has. A case can be made that Holland has been the more successful economically, an indication being that its currency, valued at twenty-five cents Canadian in 1952, is currently (October 1996) quoted at eighty cents. On the other hand, international surveys of the quality of life usually rate Canada higher than Holland.

On the personal level: has any of us been successful to a degree that would have been difficult to attain in Holland? The answer to *this* question is negative. Of my four surviving brothers, one is a professor, one is a lawyer, one is for medical reasons unemployable, and one has fallen foul of a malfunctioning economy and is unemployed. We might not have done better where we came from, but would we have done worse?

Taking myself as an example, I might have become a university professor had we stayed in Holland, just as I did here. Call it a draw. Has my life here been better in ways unrelated to my work than it would have been there? That is impossible to say. How, for example, does one rate Canada's open spaces (a plus) and relatively anarchic land-use regulations (a minus) against the crowdedness of Holland and its effective controls over the use of land? The uncrowded beaches of Lake Huron, near which Cornelia's father, Otto, has a cottage, are preferable to the beaches of the Netherlands, packed with Dutch and German sun-worshippers. Holland has banned the use of personal motorized craft off the coast of the North Sea, however, while Canada (or Ontario) has not been similarly sensible.

At another level, how would one rate the climate of Toronto (nothing to write home about) against that of Holland (ditto)?

Between Victoria and Holland there is no contest: Victoria wins hands down!

Comparisons of this kind aside, emigration had costs for me (as it did also for my brothers). Leaving friends and a familiar environment behind was unsettling. So were learning a new language and getting used to another society and culture, to say nothing of living on the edge of poverty for several years. And yet: much of this has been for the better. Had we stayed in Holland, my view of the world and of society would certainly have been more limited than became the case. Our brush with poverty, for example, may have saved me from contributing to the sort of drivel about unemployment relief, public health care, and retirement savings that often passes for informed comment in the Canadian media. Purveyed by people who seem never to have had to worry about money, such comment is remarkable chiefly for its ignorance of a reality of which for a few years I was all too conscious. (Of course, my work on the Depression has also contributed to my awareness.) On balance, then, I have no significant complaints.

All the same, had I been given my druthers in 1952 I would probably have chosen to stay in Baarn. Had our parents been able to foresee how Holland and Europe would develop I would hardly be discussing this point, of course, because it is unlikely that they would have emigrated.

Our experience has led me to be sceptical about emigration undertaken solely or primarily on economic grounds, at least by middle-class people. There are good reasons for pulling up stakes and moving to another country. Ethnic, political, or religious persecution come easily to mind; the desire for adventure may be another. The hope to secure a better living, for oneself or one's children, seems to me to be less compelling, not least because it is often doomed to disappointment.

Not a few farmers and industrial workers who left Holland in the 1940s and 1950s have done better in the New World, economically and socially, than they would have in the Old. But most professional people would, I suspect, have been wiser to make the most of the opportunities available to them in their native land. Even middle-class migrants who have prospered materially in their adopted countries may have paid a psychological price that was too high for the benefits they reaped. As for their children: who knows whether they benefited and how?

My perspective is that of someone who came from western Europe, of course. Immigrants from European countries that fell under Soviet control after 1945, or from the so-called Third World, understandably have a very different point of view.

For all that, Father and Mother could not see into the future, and I did not have my druthers. We have to live not only with the results of our own decisions but with those taken by our parents, and of *their* parents, too. We left Holland, and whether this was a mistake or not, it is now hard for me to imagine living anywhere but in Canada.

Only if this country, or a remnant of it, were to join the United States would I be tempted to return to Holland or move to a third country, such as Germany (provided, of course, that Cornelia also wanted to go). Tolerant of a widening gap between rich and poor, reluctant to tap private wealth in order to serve the public good, bedevilled by the legacy of slavery and a deeply rooted racism, unable and unwilling to restrict the private use of firearms, a democracy in which more than half the voters do not bother to cast ballots and in which the agents of plutocracy seem to dominate the legislative branch, the United States today appears to me as a model only for millionaires and madmen. I have extremely pleasant memories of my time in Berkeley, and I like visiting parts of the country, but I can no longer with any conviction think of it as a possible place to live.

Barring this country's union with the United States, I will certainly live the rest of my life in Canada. I have most of my friends as well as my closest relatives here; I have studied its history and contributed to a knowledge of it; I usually (though not always) feel at home. I have become Canadian.

Yet in becoming Canadian, what did I become? The question I asked myself in 1967 remains: what is a Canadian? The simple answer is 'a resident of Canada who has Canadian citizenship.' As a legal definition this is fine, but in a country of immigrants it unavoidably strikes many people as being too simple. Does being Canadian mean conforming to a Canadian type and accepting Canadian values? And, if so, what are they?

In this, the last decade of the twentieth century, such questions are no easier to answer than they were in the year of Canada's centenary. Four decades ago, in Victoria (and not there alone), an answer was more easily come by. A Canadian was white, spoke English without a perceptible foreign accent, and sang 'O Canada' and 'God Save the Queen' with equal conviction. As I recall that time and place, the dominant Canadian values or principles included, in no particular order: patriotism, Christianity, British institutions such as parliamentary democracy and the rule of law, deference to constituted authority, reluctance to stand out, self-restraint, a sense of superiority to 'lesser breeds without the law,' family life, hard work, and an abiding respect for the value of money. Some of these were (and are) worthwhile, others less so, a few not at all.

A few years ago, while doing research in the McGill University Archives, I came across a letter that gave me pause and some amusement. In 1952, the same year we reached Canada, one Louis Kon wrote to Principal F. Cyril James: 'I am ever since my arrival seeking not a geographical but a fully rounded up definition of a Canadian, though in vain. In my early Canadian days I was told that to be a true Canadian one must have a blue serge suit, a pair of brogues and learn to sing Britannia Rules the Waves; to own a lot of ground, preferably a corner one, build on it not a home but a house to be sold quickly at a good profit, and never to forget that a white man speaks the English language.'* This was clearly inadequate. Could James supply a better definition?

James did not reply, perhaps because he had nothing to offer, more likely because he was unwilling to write to someone who was known to be a communist. But James's career validated to a considerable extent what Kon had written. Born in England, he had gone to the United States in the 1920s for his graduate studies

---

* McGill University Archives, RG 2, Principal's Office, c.149, file 5086, Louis Kon to F. Cyril James, 30 January 1952.

and had stayed there. McGill had recruited him in the spring of 1939 to teach commerce and finance. His appointment to the principalship a few months later was greatly facilitated by his English background and British citizenship.

A comment by the protagonist of John Marlyn's novel *Under the Ribs of Death* comes to mind: ' "Pa, the only people who count are the English. Their fathers get all the best jobs. They're the only ones nobody ever calls foreigners. Nobody ever makes fun of their names or calls them 'bologny-eaters,' or laughs at the way they dress or talk. Nobody," he concluded bitterly, " 'cause when you're English it's the same as bein' Canadian." ' Sandor Hunyadi later changes his name to become Alex Hunter. Cyril James, of course, had no need to change his name when he came to this country.

Marlyn's novel, set in Winnipeg in the interwar years, appeared in 1957. At that time in Victoria, being English *was* close to being Canadian. There must have been other parts of English-speaking Canada where this was also true. It was no longer so in Toronto when I arrived there, however, and today it has quite ceased to be the case. And not just in Toronto and other large cities: the ethnic background of Canada's inhabitants is now too diverse, and newcomers have changed the country in too many ways during the last fifty years, for the old Anglo-Canadian model to be relevant.

In small-town and rural Canada, less multi-ethnic than the cities, the notion that the ideal Canadian is of British or at least Caucasian stock is not yet dead. Nowhere is it any longer possible to equate the Canadian with the British and western European type, however, without revealing oneself to be racist.

The tendency to exclude from Canadianness people of eastern and southern European stock, let alone those of Asiatic or African origin (or the Aboriginals of Canada!), was and is obnoxious. As newcomers to Victoria, my brothers and I were quickly accepted in a way that the grandchildren of nineteenth-century immigrants from China were only just beginning to experience. This was a comment on the acceptability of blond hair, blue eyes, and a European middle-class background, a comment, too, on the persistence of anti-Asian sentiment in British Columbia. Of course, immigrants should not expect to be welcomed with open arms as they get off the plane (or boat), but they are entitled to expect that their children, whatever the colour of their skins, eyes, or hair, will be regarded as being Canadian, as belonging here.

We are moving in that direction, I think. The older Anglo-Canadian sense of self, focused on the North Atlantic region, attached to the Empire and Commonwealth, convinced of the superiority of the monarchy, of British institutions, and of the white 'race,' has largely vanished except among the culturally and socially backward. (French Canadians, of course, always had a rather different view of themselves.)

It is as yet unclear what is taking the place of that old identity. This development may disturb some people quite as much as changes in the ethnic mixture, perhaps even more. Anglo-Canadians know that they are no longer British in any meaningful sense, and they have avoided becoming American. Many, however, seem unsure of what Canadians *are* becoming and dislike the uncertainty.

A flood of immigration in this century, from continental Europe and the United States, more recently from Asia, Latin America, and the Caribbean region, has had as one result that Canada's identification with Britain has waned. Millions now either lack any strong connection with or knowledge of Canada's British past or live in confusion as to its relevance today. Yet their children will define themselves as Canadian. They just won't all do it in the same way. There have always been different ways of being Canadian. Today the definitions are widening, and that is probably a good thing.

It would be dangerous to assume that everyone will want to accept this change, or that racism and bigotry will end. It is naïve to suppose, moreover, that recent immigrants of whatever origin are less racist than those belonging to longer-established groups. Netherlanders have a reputation for tolerance, for example, and some of it may be deserved. But the attitude of some of them to non-white people has been and continues to be negative. I recall the taunts directed against Indonesian and Eurasian children in my school in the late 1940s, or the hostility that I have heard directed more recently against black immigrants from former Dutch colonies in the Caribbean region.

Racism can take unexpected forms. I remember a conversation in a restaurant in Florence in 1981 in the course of which a middle-aged woman startled Jack and me by telling us that many of the Italians who had emigrated to Canada were not, properly considered, Italians at all. Speaking in French, the only language we had in common, she added: 'Comme nous disons ici, les nègres commencent à Rome.' Similar prejudices exist elsewhere in Europe: the remark seems to be akin to the English slur, 'The wogs begin at Calais.'

Furthermore, although I don't know enough about non-European peoples to make an informed judgment, I would be very astonished to learn that they are free of racism. The recent inter-ethnic bloodbath in Rwanda indicates in horrifying fashion that murderous hostility may be found among peoples whom Canadians probably (and ignorantly) tend to regard as being of one kind.

Perhaps some forms of racism will persist until and unless all human beings become uniformly khaki-coloured, and ethnicity ceases to have meaning. But the day of the homogenized human being probably will never come, and is probably not to be desired in any case. Instead we must work to minimize the effects of racism.

Is the Canadian policy of multiculturalism an effective way of doing so? The Trinidad-born writer Neil Bissoondath has suggested: 'Any country that does not claim the full loyalty of its citizens old or new, any country that counts citizens old or new who treat it as they would a public washroom – that is, as merely a place to run to in an emergency – accepts for itself a severe internal weakening.'[*] The policy of multiculturalism adopted in 1971, he adds, has encouraged immigrants to treat Canada in this way because it emphasizes 'the importance of holding on to the former homeland, with its insistence that *There* is more important than *Here* ...'

A country that is fractured politically and regionally may be ill-advised to adopt a policy that divides its people from each other

---

[*] Neil Bissoondath, 'A Question of Belonging,' *Globe and Mail*, 28 January 1993. More recently he has written a book: *Selling Illusions: The Cult of Multiculturalism in Canada* (Toronto 1994).

on cultural and ethnic lines, Bissoondath argues. And although the objective of official multiculturalism, to promote tolerance, is laudable, tolerance alone may not be enough. Citing Robertson Davies, he writes that tolerance and acceptance are not synonymous: 'acceptance ... requires true understanding,' while tolerance 'requires not knowledge but willful ignorance ... it is a shrug of indifference that entails more than a hint of condescension.' The tolerance that comes easily to people in good times can in times of stress change into 'virulent defensiveness, rejecting the different, alienating the new.'

These are points worth making. One might add that nobody should expect the laws of Canada to be modified or ignored so that customs may be accommodated that are not only illegal but, to the overwhelming majority of Canadians, repugnant. The issues of polygamy and female genital mutilation come to mind. People who wish to persist in such practices, and who are unhappy because Canada will not accommodate them, may be best advised to return to their countries of origin. If, upon reflection, they decide to stay here, they should avoid unlawful behaviour.

And yet, Bissoondath seems to be too alarmist. The policy of official multiculturalism is, I think, less disruptive and more helpful than he believes it to be. Furthermore, some of its critics may harbour motives of which he (and we) ought to be suspicious. For some of them it masks hostility to immigration from Third World countries. This is not to say that Canada's current immigration policies are beyond question or discussion: legitimate doubt exists whether the country can continue to absorb, say, 250,000 immigrants a year, *whatever* their countries of origin. But I suspect that worry about the number of immigrants to Canada would decline if all of them were white, although the economic and environmental effects would be much the same.

Other critics of multiculturalism, some of them immigrants from Europe, their children, or grandchildren, may be objecting not so much to multiculturalism as to its supposed role in giving a leg up to more recent immigrants. The motivation may partake of envy and resentment: '*I* had to make it on my own and fit in: why can't these people do the same?' (I heard a variant of this from a Dutch woman in Victoria some thirty years ago: '*I* had to learn English when I came to Canada; why was an exception made for the French?') Sauce for the gander, sauce for the goose?

One truth about Canada, though only one, is that the Anglo-Canadian majority was long dismissive of French Canadians, Jews, immigrants from eastern and southern Europe, and anyone whose skin colour was not white. For that reason, assimilating into that majority was the sensible thing to do for those immigrants who were able to do so. Doing so was no evidence of intellectual or moral superiority, however. It was often the path of least resistance. It was and is not open to everyone, however, nor should anyone feel compelled to take it.

The appeal of official multiculturalism is mainly to the first generation of immigrants (though by no means to all of them), those from whom it cannot reasonably be expected that they will forget where they were born, and who will always feel the tug of old loyalties. In so far as the policy helps to ease their way into Canada it is worthwhile.

Among those who have come here as small children or are born here, the policy seems unlikely to undermine loyalty to Canada or to diminish respect for those whose ethnic background is different. Doubtless some people who were born here nurture prejudices that reflect social or political conditions in the countries from which their parents or grandparents came, and with which they identify to some degree, and this is regrettable and objectionable. However, this tendency long antedates the policy of multiculturalism – remember the Orange Order? – and can hardly be blamed on it.

The worries today about immigration and multiculturalism are part of a larger malaise. These are difficult days for Canada: beset by unemployment, economic and political insecurity, and a financial and fiscal crisis about whose cause and cure there is no broad agreement. Furthermore, we are facing global economic and environmental changes whose effects are difficult to calculate but will for many surely be unpleasant. It is not surprising that the public mood is querulous. (And yet, many other peoples would gladly exchange their problems for ours.)

In spite of these problems, I want to believe, though it is sometimes hard to do so, that Canada has a future as a multi-ethnic and humane society, one that seeks to approximate equality of opportunity and, with it, a good measure of fairness in the distribution of income and wealth; a country as strongly united as it can be, given the many varieties of the Canadian experience. I want Canada to thrive.

I have become Canadian, after my fashion. Whether I am the 'good Canadian' that passenger on the SS *Diemerdijk* hoped in 1952 I would become, that I hoped to become when we went ashore in Victoria, is not for me to judge. I do know, however, that I haven't ceased to be Dutch. Living in Holland during those childhood years that are said to be crucial in forming personality and character, I was too old when I came here to remake myself and be remade completely. Perhaps only those who change countries before they enter school are able to expunge their pasts. I could not do it, and so I have to live with a measure of ambiguity that sometimes becomes genuine confusion.

Although I find this disconcerting, I see it also as my good fortune. It may be consoling to know exactly where one fits in, but living in more than one country and sharing in more than one culture opens up creative prospects and possibilities. Among Canada's strengths is that many of its people are thus blessed. Long live diversity!

Index

This index has been alphabetized in accordance with Dutch practice, in which the letter 'ij' is equivalent to the letter 'y' and the uncapitalized words 'de,' 'du,' and 'van' are placed behind the proper names of people.